Twentieth-Century American Success Rhetoric

Twentieth-Century American Success Rhetoric:

How to Construct a Suitable Self

John Ramage

Southern Illinois University Press • *Carbondale*

Copyright © 2005 by the Board of Trustees,
Southern Illinois University
All rights reserved
Printed in the United States of America
08 07 06 05   4 3 2 1

Library of Congress Cataloging-in-Publication Data
   Ramage, John D.
   Twentieth-century American success rhetoric : how to construct
a suitable self / John Ramage.
        p. cm.
   Includes bibliographical references (p.   ) and index.
   1. Success—United States—History—20th century. 2. Rhetorical
criticism. I. Title.
   BJ1611.2.R34 2005
   158'.9'0973—dc22
   ISBN 0-8093-2616-7 (cloth : alk. paper)   2004029613

Printed on recycled paper. ♻

The paper used in this publication meets the minimum
requirements of American National Standard for Information
Sciences—Permanence of Paper for Printed Library Materials,
ANSI Z39.48-1992. ⊚

To Sally, of course

With each job description I read, I felt a tightening of what I must call my soul. I found myself growing false to myself, acting to myself, convincing myself of my rightness for whatever was being described. And this is where I suppose life ends for most people, who stiffen in the attitudes they adopt to make themselves suitable for the jobs and lives that other people have laid out for them.

—V. S. Naipaul, *A Bend in the River*

[T]he quandary tormenting men and women at the turn of the century is not so much how to obtain the identities of their choice and to have them recognized by people around—but which identity to choose and how to keep alert and vigilant so that another choice can be made in case the previously chosen identity is withdrawn from the market or stripped of its seductive powers.

—Zygmunt Bauman, *The Individualized Society*

Modern techniques of publicity and propaganda have thoroughly exploited the plasticity of human nature which makes possible the development of new needs and the disappearance or transformation of old ones. These changes confirm that only ends stated in a general and vague manner remain invariant and universal and that the end is often made clear by examination of the means.

—Chaim Perelman and L. Olbrechts-Tyteca, *The New Rhetoric*

People who imagine themselves to be self-made seldom enjoy examining the process of manufacture in detail.

—Richard Russo, *Empire Falls*

Contents

Acknowledgments

This book took shape over many years, and along the way I incurred far too many debts to acknowledge properly. Among the many people I worked with and for during the decade I spent administering writing programs, writing-across-the-curriculum programs, and academic support programs, I found models of integrity, commitment, compassion, and selflessness, the likes of which were sadly missing from the books I read for this study. Special thanks to Stuart Knapp, then vice president for academics at Montana State University, who twenty years ago provided heroic support for my longtime friend, colleague, and coauthor John Bean and me as we set out to design a WAC program for the sort of university that some said could not support such a program. And to Milton Glick, provost and senior vice president of Arizona State University, and Kathy Church, associate vice provost, many thanks for affording me a bird's-eye view on the workings of a contemporary university.

Thanks also to the folks on the WPA-Listserv, several hundred of the smartest, most able people in the academy, and their gentle tyrant, my intrepid colleague David Schwalm, who provided me some of my most enjoyable lessons about academic management. Four years ago, I had to choose between continued membership on WPA-L or writing this book. Clearly, one could not do both. I'll return to the lists soon. To the students who stuck with me through two seminars, one on writing program administration and one on success rhetoric, as I worked out much of this material, thanks for your patience and your insights. To my two anonymous reviewers, thank you for the encouragement and suggestions. To Karl Kageff at Southern Illinois University Press, who signed this book when it was twice as long and kept the faith, I owe a big debt of gratitude.

And to Carol Burns, Kristine Priddy, and Julie Bush at SIU Press, who saw it through the latter stages, many thanks. And finally to Jennifer Clary-Lemon, doctoral student extraordinaire, thanks for all the editorial help.

Abbreviations of Burke's Works

ATH   *Attitudes Toward History*

CS   *Counter-Statement*

GM   *A Grammar of Motives*

LSA   *Language as Symbolic Action*

P&C   *Permanence and Change*

PLF   *Philosophy of Literary Form*

RM   *A Rhetoric of Motives*

RR   *The Rhetoric of Religion*

Introduction

Americans in the twenty-first century are no less vexed by the notion of success than were Americans in the seventeenth, eighteenth, nineteenth, and twentieth centuries. We are, to be sure, often vexed in different ways than our forebears, but the incomprehensibility of success remains, now as then, directly proportional to its importance. And it's always been unspeakably important and impenetrably mysterious. An errand into the wilderness, a manifest destiny, a green light at the end of the dock, a shining city on the hill, a perch atop Herbert Spencer's evolutionary ladder—whatever form it takes, the American dream remains more a mode of transport than a destination. Who and what we might be when and if we arrive remains unclear. How one becomes what one must be in order to get there is the subject of the books here collected under the "success rhetoric" rubric.

As it turns out, the key to selling audiences on their means for achieving success lies largely in their suppression of questions about the ends of that process. Success rhetoricians, like the insistent voices inside, or possibly outside, J. Alfred Prufrock's head, repeatedly implore us not to "ask 'What is it?' / Let us go and make our visit." And we heeded their importuning, signed up for their seminars, and bought their books, tapes, and CDs in astonishing numbers because the increasingly abstract, specialized, and precarious nature of work in the twentieth century created an ever-stronger appetite among us for books promising to craft readymade, off-the-rack workplace identities optimally suitable for those who defined success for us—our employers.

Apart from whatever model of success that happens to be dominant at any given moment, each of us harbors private dreams, fears, and understandings of success that are inadequately expressed by those models. Indeed, in the course of writing this book, I discovered some things about my own attitudes toward success and the origins of those attitudes that surprised me. I found myself drawn thus to certain features of the nineteenth-century "yeoman's" vision of success in ways that I seldom was drawn to anything in current visions. Moreover, I kept hearing in the platitudes of the success handbooks echoes of my paternal grandfather, a fourth-generation Scots American farmer, fond of saying things like, "Something's better than nothing," and, "A man never went broke taking a profit." When he expressed these views, a Lucky Strike dangling from the corner of his mouth and a mug of coffee cupped in his hands, to the ever-present audience of neighbors, kibitzers, and loafers in Elmer's Coffee Shop in downtown Woodburn, Oregon, I, his grandson and namesake, felt, I confess, a pang of embarrassment for him. Even at age ten, I wondered at the gullibility of adults who heard such self-evident piffle as wisdom and attributed their credulity to the fact that my grandfather was, as everyone said, a most beguiling man.

Were he still around, I now realize, my grandfather could place a number in front of each homily; put them in all-caps, bold, #14 type; and cobble them together into a success formula elaborated in a series of lovingly told anecdotes that repeatedly tested and affirmed his admonitions. Then he could take to the road and tell paying customers how he, despite a sixth-grade education, pathologically bad spelling, and an assortment of character flaws unforeseen by the yeoman's ideal, made a success of it. And if his accomplishments were relatively modest—three small landholdings, an interest in an agricultural cooperative, and a place on the board of a local agency of the federal government—one must keep in mind that few of our best-known success gurus have been remarkable for anything much beyond persuading others to heed their advice about how to succeed.

To be sure, my grandfather would have had to learn how to spin his philosophy for today's audiences, since it's been mostly out of fashion for the past century. His beliefs were much closer to those that Max Weber attributes to "traditional" peasants who held that one could either eat well or sleep well but not both and so ate a bit less well in order to sleep a bit better. These are the same sort of people, Weber tells us, who, when offered the opportunity to move from a fixed, subsistence wage to piece-work (the cutting edge of capitalism), produced just enough work to earn their subsistence—then promptly stopped. Presumably to sleep. These folk, along with my grandfather, would be poor candidates for today's brand of success rhetoric largely because of their allegiance to notions of "sufficiency." Thus, when my grandfather brokered his and other farmers' strawberries, cane berries, beans, and cauliflower through the co-op to large buyers like the California Packing Company, he used his notion of sufficiency to decide when the risks of possible future losses outweighed the rewards of potentially increased profits. Once he felt sure that he could make a reasonable profit, he would stop dickering and keep his own counsel ("A man never went broke taking a profit"), waiting to see if his buyer might not be sufficiently discomfited by his silence to start bidding against himself. Grandpa was not, after all, averse to windfalls. But once he had his profit, his primary motive was to preserve it, not multiply it exponentially. Others, less risk-averse, or with a less clear sense of what "enough" might be, would gamble that weather and/or market conditions would drive prices up later and so held out, disdaining the sure but modest profit in the name of unimaginable future rewards. Out of their failures, my grandfather could have filled a book of cautionary tales supporting the wisdom of his own course—and in truth he took an untoward satisfaction in retelling his neighbors' sad stories.

So it was that when I came across the notions of "sufficiency" and "competence," discussed in the first chapter, I found myself drawn to them in ways that most members of today's audiences, besotted with notions of "excellence," "quality," and "efficiency," appear not to be. And along with my sympathy for such notions, I found myself surprisingly partial to people like Cotton Mather and even "snuff colored" Benjamin Franklin, whose writings sustained them in the American conscience for better than two centuries. Like any set of once-dominant cultural values, Franklin's and Mather's notions persist as residual values in American culture even today, albeit to an ever fainter degree. While some of us might regret their loss and wax nostalgic over the moral superiority of the old values (indeed, a number of commentators cited in this study do just that), few of us can live by them. My grandparents, thus, were the last to live out the Jeffersonian ideal of the small landholder. With my grandfather's death, the "home place" that he and my grandmother had worked for sixty years was sold. But in truth, only one uncle was still involved in farming by that time and he only in the little time he had left after working a forty-hour week in a steel foundry where his older brother was night supervisor. My father and uncles had in fact begun transforming themselves into salesmen, small business owners, and managers of the sort required by the new economy long before the farm was sold.

And my mother and aunts worked out their own wary compromises with the new realities. Intermittently, often reluctantly, they entered a workforce still largely geared to males and single income families, less to make careers for themselves than to supplement husbands' paychecks that seemed to buy a little less each year. Among the siblings and cousins of my generation, meanwhile, the transformation and the compromises continue apace as we all make our peace with economic and workplace realities that none of us pretends fully to understand. On the rare occasions we discuss success, we tend to talk about it less as a defining goal than as one of those periodic, unexpected rewards that experimental psychologists assure us are especially effective in reinforcing desirable behaviors.

As my own cursory family history suggests, the influence of the American success ethos is ubiquitous. All of us must come to terms with the measures of success that prevail during our time. And every one of us must negotiate the conflicts between our loyalties to these measures and our loyalties to personal standards (and people) scanted by those metrics. Complicating our attempts to understand and evaluate these various measures of success are the efforts of an entire industry devoted to marketing dubious visions of success and even more dubious means of achieving them. A significant share of our cultural capital comprises books, tapes, videos, consultants, coaches, seminars, infomercials, plaques, screen savers, and the like promoting systems, techniques, and algorithms promising success. The language and ideas of this industry, meanwhile, permeate our professional and personal lives, not to mention the speech and thinking of our institutional and national leaders.

Colleges, universities, and the business of academic scholarship are not, as we shall see, unaffected by this phenomenon. In fact, my attention was first drawn to the ubiquity of success rhetoric during the years I spent as a full-time academic administrator. At one point, I was flying a good deal and began to notice many fellow passengers intently reading books. Occasionally they would be reading novels, but more often than not they would be reading, and annotating, books on how to be better managers, investors, parents, and so on. About this same time, I began getting books of the same sort from the office of the provost, books on excellence and quality and reengineering; soon I found myself working on "cross-functional teams" to carry out reforms inspired by the authors of such works. I was given opportunities to attend presentations, live and videotaped, by leading gurus, notably Stephen Covey. Clearly, something important was afoot here. The potential impact of these people on the daily operation of businesses, corporations, and even universities was, it seemed to me, enormous.

While I was not, in truth, greatly impressed with the books I read or the words I heard, I did study them conscientiously, even seeking out analysis and critical discussion of these gurus' works, which is when I discovered that, beyond a clutch of dyspeptic American business professors and occasional British commentators fascinated by this latest American aberration, "the guru," few academics gave serious attention to the phenomenon. The key word in the previous sentence is "serious." Puff pieces and interviews that sound more like "advertorials" abound. To some extent, this inattention is not surprising. Academic criticism and theory tends, by and large, to build on academic criticism and theory. It's hard for scholars in any discipline to know what to make of work that, while it may well ape academic research in format, makes outlandish claims based on anecdotal evidence without referencing sources, mentioning opposing views, or citing any ongoing conversation. Indeed, the rapid turnover among success gurus and the dizzying, often unacknowledged about-faces in their philosophies render them a difficult target. And the very fact that these works are "merely" popular rules them out of play for many academics, even when the principles being expounded are increasingly employed to manage the institutions they inhabit, increasingly mark the beliefs and discourse of the public bodies that oversee and fund their activities, and increasingly marginalize values they hold dear.

To be sure, the subjects of this study have not been totally ignored by academic critics. The peculiarly American mythos of the self-made man, which is certainly one of the themes lurking in the shadows of contemporary success rhetoric, has in recent years received serious attention from people like James V. Catano, George Dillon, and David Leverenz. And between 1950 and 1980, a number of notable scholars including Rex Burns, John Cawelti, Richard Hofsteader, Richard Huber, Donald B. Meyer, Richard Weiss, and Irvin G. Wyllie gave extended critical attention to various questions bearing on many of the issues taken up here. But little critical work of late has dealt with the influential strand of success rhetoric that focuses on the workplace and the management of people in that workplace; hardly any of it—Andrzej Huczynski's *Management Gurus* being a notable exception—extends earlier conversations about people like Norman Vincent Peale to include people like Tom Peters.

The reasons for this lack of critical attention will receive more extended attention shortly. Here I will mention only one possible reason, based mostly on personal observation from three decades in higher education: the growing divide between those who manage the university and those who teach and do research there. Increasingly, upper administrators, functionally defined as those who determine how resources are allocated and how units of the institution are organized, are drawn from outside faculty ranks or plucked from those ranks very early on. The old model of the "citizen-solons," faculty who after an extended stay at the department level served as administrators for a fixed time and then returned to their departments, has proven difficult to maintain in light of the increasing complexity of university management and the increasing disparity between faculty and administrative pay. As decision-making power shifted inexorably from faculty to administrators, the once sacred tradition of "faculty governance" significantly eroded and today, beyond the department level, has a largely ceremonial function. My own faculty senate, for example, spent three years debating the efficacy of switching to a plus/minus grading system, nearly abandoning the idea in response to student concerns that it might deflate grade point averages before finally passing it by the slimmest of margins. During the same period of time, procedures such as "post-tenure review" have been mandated by the Board of Regents, and the proportion of non-tenure track faculty has continued to grow significantly with little reasoned debate (not to be confused with endless discussion) and no decisive response (not to be confused with calls for further study) from our faculty senate. For the most part, legislatures, boards of regents, overseers, upper administrators, and corporate donors tend to see the faculty governance model as an impediment to "fast, flat, and flexible" universities capable of reinventing themselves in pace with rapidly shifting marketplace imperatives—and they appear to have little difficulty circumventing or co-opting its representative bodies.

Faculty response to all this, to the extent that faculty paid much attention to it, ranges from puzzlement to mild resentment to indifference—excepting those who read and write about such matters in the course of their research. The tasks assumed by the growing corps of professional administrators were either the sort that few faculty were qualified to perform in technical, legal, or financial areas or were the sort of routine tasks that faculty had reluctantly performed in the past for little or no reward and were happy to hand over. Consequently, faculty's administrative role in most institutions is limited to the often lugubrious chores they perform in the name of "service" or to the judgments they render about hiring, retaining, promoting, and rewarding their immediate colleagues. And even department personnel decisions are lately based on ever more explicit and legalistic criteria—recently, for example, the exchange value of articles, as in "How many articles constitute the equivalent of a book?," has commanded a good deal of local attention—handed down from above. And these days, whatever decisions a department makes are more likely to be questioned or overturned. In some cases, departments are circumvented entirely as when raises are distributed by deans and provosts to "star faculty"—if one has to ask who the stars are, one is not fit to judge them—to ensure their continued fealty.

In sum, faculty are, like most American workers in the information sector of the service economy, increasingly "managed" through processes that are increasingly mysterious by people whose vocabularies and motivations are increasingly foreign to us. Our connection to a larger institutional context that lent our professional lives one measure of meaning has mostly been severed. But while most other American "knowledge workers" have been forced to make at least some sense of management discourse in order to flourish in the places where they work, we are afforded the luxury of substituting long-distance connections to our discipline for local ties to our institutions. In fact, academic success is in most cases inversely proportional to one's immersion in local matters. The upshot of all this is that we function in an environment that is no longer buffered against the same economic, political, and social forces that shape the business world, forces that the texts to be examined here serve to articulate and advertise. But those very forces that render our immediate environs more mysterious and less friendly also create an escape route for us. So long as we are "productive" by the standards set in motion by those forces, we need not worry about having to plumb the mysteries of the new institutional reality or the ideas and values that give rise to it. And the time and energy expended acquiring the knowledge and specialized talents that render one productive by that metric prevent all but the hardiest critics from focusing on, let alone acting on, issues in the academic workplace.

In some respects, thus, we are not just similar to those who constitute the primary audience for works dealt with in this study; we are their very model. And in some respects, we are not only not immune to the forces of globalization and individualization discussed in chapter 1 but rather are its cutting edge. Long before management gurus began selling American workers on the virtues of "free agency," American academics had embraced autonomy and academic freedom—most reliably secured through highly visible acts of knowledge production—as touchstones of their professional identity. And consequently, "the academic community" remains as abstract and almost as oxymoronic a notion as "the business community." Neither community promotes a strong sense of affiliation among its populace, and neither provides meaningful public spaces where individual and community interests might be articulated and negotiated or collective ends might be contemplated. Being a "good citizen" within either community is more likely to be measured by one's willingness to perform thankless tasks than by one's resolve in questioning systemic assumptions or defending those victimized by such assumptions. Much as we may wish to believe that we are too sophisticated to be taken in by the rhetoric of success critiqued here, our indifference may be less a function of our sophistication than of our acceptance, long ago, of the myths of individualization such rhetoric promotes.

Chapter 1 begins by examining the most "unmethodical" methods of Kenneth Burke, whose approach underlies the approach used in this study. The paradoxes of success and its meaning "in terms of" its traditional dialectic partner, happiness, are then examined. At the center of this examination lies Charles Taylor's magisterial *Sources of the Self: The Making of the Modern Identity* and what Taylor calls "the punctual self" of John Locke, a figure who anticipates the ideal audience member for twentieth-century success rhetoric. The rest of the chapter deals with the shift from late-eighteenth-century success rhetoric, represented by Benjamin Franklin, through the nineteenth-century success handbook tradition, to the unbuttoned twentieth-century vision of success offered up by people like George Horace Lorimer.

Chapters 2 through 4 discuss the work of Bruce Barton, Dale Carnegie, Norman Vincent Peale, Tom Peters, and Stephen Covey. The discussions focus on the ways in which these authors discovered means of persuasion available for their given situation. To the extent that one might assign a pattern to this succession of works, it is a recurrence of two alternating ideas whose significance is neatly captured in a remark by Richard Harvey Brown about the revolutionary shift in identity that arises with Protestantism: "Sincerity—the matching of the self to its social expressions—was benighted. Authenticity—the assertion of a self against social conventions—was ennobled" (34). Back and forth between the yin of sincerity and the yang of authenticity, the valence of American success rhetoric forever shifts. When one's identity is vouchsafed by its place in some overarching structure, sincere attachment to that structure is the watchword of the day. Absent such a superstructure, one's identity lies in its uniqueness, and expressions of difference from social convention are tolerated, even required.

The protagonist of Bruce Barton's *The Man Nobody Knows*, Jesus Christ, like the "code heroes" of the day, clearly embodies the values of authenticity. Barton recasts him "in terms of" the values of contemporary commerce and equates Christ's rejection of Old Testament mores and his antinomic stance toward the secular authority of the day with twentieth-century America's rejection of the yeoman's vision and its exuberant tilt to consumerism. Couched in the language of advertising, Barton's "retelling" of Christ's life serves also to legitimate the marketing profession from whence Barton emerges.

In the work of Peale and Carnegie, meanwhile, sincerity turns out to be the holy grail of success rhetoric. Both men spend inordinate amounts of time persuading their acolytes not just to embrace their "go along to get along" philosophy of impression management but to do so "sincerely." Implicit in the appeals made by both Peale and Carnegie is the assumption that "God's in his heaven and all's right with the world." The system within which their followers appear to operate is a just and ordered world, a Great Chain of Corporate Being. It is a self-contained, self-authorizing world no longer in need of the elaborate rhetorical ploys or mythic underpinning of *The Man Nobody Knows* for its legitimation. Their readers must merely match their own expressions and behaviors to the requirements of that system, "positively" and "sincerely," to be successful (that is, convincing). As evidenced in the episodic structure of their narratives, strings of "purpose built illustrations" that illuminate without ever complicating their principles, there is little conflict of the sort glimpsed in Barton's extended narrative account that might render their own story plausible. Chapter 3 ends with an extended look at Richard Nixon's unsuccessful struggle to achieve a plausible pose of either sincerity or authenticity in *Six Crises*, a work heavily indebted to the success rhetorics of Peale and Carnegie.

In Tom Peters's *In Search of Excellence*, we return to the search for authenticity—with a postmodern twist. While successful corporations are characterized as places where workers are licensed to engage in various deviant behaviors, their actions are circumscribed and carefully monitored by benign and watchful corporate "champions" far up the food chain from the aberrant minions. Upper management tolerates rebellion in the name of keeping the corporate juices flowing, allowing a bit of novelty to creep up from the "skunkworks." And in the end, the protagonist of Peters's work is not to be found among the various managers and CEOs lionized in his book; the prime movers of *In Search of Excellence* are the companies, the fictional corporate selves served by the various human agents. They are the ones who must fight to maintain their authenticity, "stay close to their knitting," and resist the dilution of core values. In Peters the author, meanwhile, one finds a sly ironist who offers much of his counsel with a wink and a disquieting sense that for all his avowed populism, the locus of power is not in people so much as it is in the machinations of markets that determine our fates.

With Stephen Covey's *7 Habits of Highly Effective People*, we return to the search for sincerity with a vengeance. While Covey is ostensibly committed to an "inside out" version of human development betokening an affinity for authenticity over sincerity, he locates the origins of identity in an act of submission to laws and principles that lie outside the human agent. While Covey never acknowledges the source of those values, it is clear that they are consistent with the Mormon theology that Covey, who holds a doctor of religious education degree from Brigham Young University, elaborates in his dissertation. One's progress along Covey's "spiral of growth" depends in turn upon one's having internalized Covey's principles to the point that they are "habits" requiring no reflection to put into action.

In chapter 5, we leave off our historical account and return to questions raised above and in chapters 1 and 4 concerning the relative ineffectuality of academics in critiquing success rhetoric or in offering the general public alternative visions of success. The chapter begins with a discussion of Deborah Tannen's not wholly unsuccessful attempt to bring academic or "expert" wisdom to the marketplace. What remains unclear after examining *You Just Don't Understand* and *Argument Culture* is the extent to which her success depends on her seemingly impoverished assumptions about identity and disciplinarity.

To some extent, Tannen's attempt to cross the border from academe to the marketplace confirms the strictures of Stanley Fish against academic border crossing examined in the remainder of the chapter. But however justified Fish's critique may be in the case of Tannen, his oft-repeated claim that practitioners cannot speak to "politically emancipatory" (*Professional Correctness* 44) or socially significant ends without distorting and trivializing their disciplinary practices and without violating the professional decorums that give them status is rejected. Having established the theoretical viability of border crossing, the book concludes with a brief discussion of some practical impediments to entering the popular marketplace and some ways around them via some new routes and relays unacknowledged by Fish.

1 Kenneth Burke and the Paradoxes of American Success

In this chapter, I examine the problematic and paradoxical nature of success throughout our country's history. Much of that examination is organized around the precursors to modern success rhetoricians, people like Cotton Mather and Benjamin Franklin and countless nineteenth-century success manual authors, who, like their modern-day counterparts, both construct and reflect popular understandings of the term. But first I consider the primary means by which that examination will be conducted, Kenneth Burke's rhetoric.

The Burkean Way

The choice of Burke to guide us through the demimonde of success rhetoric is open to question on a couple of grounds. A number of critics, Frank Lentricchia points out, have argued that Burke is uniquely difficult, if not impossible, "to take in small bearable doses" ("Reading History" 119), forcing us to swallow him whole somehow. A more common criticism of Burke suggests, often tacitly, that his work is dated. This criticism is related to the first insofar as those who hint at his diminished relevance seem to be most offended by the pure scope of his theory and its superficial resemblances to what Richard Rorty refers to, not altogether kindly, as "systematic" philosophies (*Mirror* 367). These philosophic dinosaurs are unfavorably compared by Rorty to far more nimble, scrupulously non-metaphysical, "edifying" philosophies. The fact that Rorty explicitly links Burke to John Dewey, an exemplary edifying philosopher, appears to have done little to dispel suspicions about Burke's grand design (*Achieving* 142). In the discussion that follows, thus, the decidedly unsystematic elements of Burke's approach will be emphasized. In this regard, it is useful to recall that Burke characterized his approach as judiciously skeptical, lying "halfway between the extremes of hagiography and iconoclasm" (*ATH* 337), and as "the Lord" admonishes "Satan" at the conclusion of Burke's *Rhetoric of Religion*, "terminology is suspect to the extent that it does not allow for the progressive criticism of itself" (303). This relentlessly self-questioning attitude means that to the extent Burke has a method, it can never be reduced to a replicable series of steps one might apply uniformly under all circumstances to any material no matter what its composition in pursuit of foreseeable results.

To understand Burke's method, it is useful to remember that the Greek root of the word is *hodos*, or "the Way." It was eventually stuffed inside the word "method" or "way after" (*P&C* 234). As such, it was shorn of teleological implications and placed off-limits to eccentric pilgrims pursuing less premeditated paths. Burke's "way," as opposed to modernist notions of method, is more open-ended, less objective, less likely to result in greater certainty than in greater perplexity. In the words of Timothy Crusius: "Burke is not concerned with method as logic, with evaluating propositions, nor with issues of experimental design, control, replication, and so forth. As the Cartesian tradition understands method, it is not method at all. But it is also not *anti*-methodical in the sense of Feyerabend's *Against Method*. It is only *non*-methodical" (214). Or as Burke himself sums it up in *Rhetoric of Motives*:

> So we must keep trying anything and everything, improvising, borrowing from others, developing from others, dialectically using one text as comment upon another, schematizing; using the incentive to new wanderings, returning from these excursions to schematize again, being oversubtle where the straining seems to promise some further glimpse, and making amends by reduction to very simple anecdotes. (265)

That said, one must still confront the undeniable reality that Burke's most influential works were written over half a century ago, and in those works he does draw a worrisome number of insights from out-of-season systematizers like Spinoza, Kant, and Bentham. Based on that evidence, anyone taking a progressivist view of theorizing, anyone assuming that new theories supplant older theories by falsifying their assumptions and disproving their conclusions, could be excused for declaring Burke passé. But hardly anyone today holds that theories progress in this fashion— even if our emphasis on novelty as a theoretical virtue occasionally hints at a powerful but unspoken progressivist bias. A more representative view of historical succession in the realm of theory is articulated by Barry Brummett, who likens rhetorical theories to fishing lures that "are discarded only if they *never* seem useful," with usefulness measured by their heuristic and pedagogical power:

> [R]hetorical theory and criticism's ultimate goal and justification is pedagogical: *to teach people how to experience their rhetorical environments more richly.* . . . The more rhetorical theories one is familiar with, the more one can consciously and richly see, understand, and appreciate rhetoric no matter what the circumstances. (658)

Brummett's argument here is very much in tune with Burke (cited frequently in Brummett's essay), who rejects the notion that different "orientations," "terminologies," or theories are capable of overthrowing or "debunking" each other and advises the critic instead to adopt a comedic attitude toward her subject—comedy being "our attitude of attitudes"—and to understand "human antics" as an admixture of good and evil, noble and base, "ever on the verge of the most disastrous tragedy" (*ATH*, "Introduction" n. pag.). The job of the critic is to "cajole" opposing views and to understand her own views "in terms of" opposing theories. In this spirit, two of Burke's most influential advocates in the social sciences, Hugh Dalziel Duncan and Joseph Gusfield, remind us that Burke "demands that we become masters of *many* perspectives in order that we may understand *one* perspective" (Duncan, "Introduction" xv) and that he continually exhorts us "to see the limited nature of any one cognitive framework" (44). In other words, Burke himself casts doubt on progressivist views of theorizing of the very sort that might slight his own work. In lieu of a linear model for the history of theory, Burke offers the dialectical or conversational model, very much like the one Rorty valorizes in *Philosophy and the Mirror of Nature* (389–94). In Burke's version, as exemplified in the figure of the "Burkean parlor," theories enter, leave, and reenter the conversation, never toppled, though sometimes slighted, never triumphant, forever gaining and losing adherents, forever modifying one another.

But that is not to suggest that Burke's model, in the act of denouncing debunking, debunks progressivist history. Belief in progress is one of those hardy perennials in the human situation that Burke's realism acknowledges; the job of criticism and literature is not to do away with such phenomena but to provide us with "equipment for living" by modeling appropriate responses to their inevitable recurrences. As a process, progress is associated in Burke with that "process of processes," the "bureaucratization of the imaginative," the name Burke gives to "the vexing things that happen when men try to translate some pure aim or vision into terms of its corresponding material embodiment, thus necessarily involving elements alien to the original, 'spiritual' ('imaginative') motive" (*ATH*, "Introduction" n. pag.). Bureaucratization is not in itself an ignoble act; turning visions into laws, goods, and institutions can be a most noble activity. But, inevitably, "vexing things" attend these attempts, and all sorts of "unintended byproducts" ensue. Thus, for example, writing in the midst of the Depression, Burke meditates on the mixed blessings of technological progress:

> How many people today are rotting in either useless toil or in dismal worklessness because of certain technological successes? We do not here aim to discredit the accomplishments of science, which are mainly converted into menaces by the inadequacies of present political institutions. We desire simply to indicate that *the region where testing is of vital importance*, where the tests of success are in turn to be tested, is the region of *weltanschauung*, of cultural, moral political emphases, of ambition, concepts of the good life, notions of ultimate human purpose. (*P&C* 101–2)

The problem with progress, with all processes, is that in order to realize the vision that initiates it, one must ignore the multiple possibilities of that vision: "Call the possibilities 'imaginative.' And call the carrying-out of *one* possibility the *bureaucratization* of the imaginative" (*ATH* 225). It is futile to renounce this move as reductive because visions can be realized only one possibility at a time. It can, however, be "cajoled" and questioned by invoking whatever "concept of the good life, notions of ultimate human purpose," launched it and testing one's "tests of success" against this ultimate standard. Working against this comedic critical stance is the other side of ultimacy in Burke—and there are always two sides to everything in Burke—which is the tragic tendency to push every possibility to its singular perfection. The closer bureaucratization comes to its limit—"rotten with perfection"—the more likely it is that those who inhabit its "social texture" will suffer outbreaks of cognitive disorders that Burke refers to alternately as "cults" or "psychoses," as in "the cult of questionnaires" (*RM* 15), the "uncritical cult of facts" (28), or "'hierarchical psychosis'" (*P&C* 279), obsessions that blind us to the limited nature of our cognitive framework and to alternative possibilities available in a given situation. The nearer we get to the "end of the line," the full realization of our vision, the more pronounced our obsessive behavior and the harder it is to heed our comedic hecklers' admonishments and to avert tragic reversal, the ultimate "unintended byproduct" that our increasingly myopic "successes" lead us into.

Up until now, we have been using Burke's ideas to heckle progressivist views of theory-making that would have us reject Burke as an anachronism. This manner of proceeding anticipates our use of Burke throughout the rest of this study and, I would argue, calls into further question the claim that he must be used whole or not at all. Indeed, it is hard to imagine just what the "whole" might be of an approach whose "main ideal" is, as it turns out, "to use all that is there to use. . . . [And] if there is any slogan that should reign among critical precepts, it is that 'circumstances alter cases'" (*PLF* 21). If Burke asks us to believe that there is no such thing as a wholly adequate "cognitive framework," that "circumstances alter cases," that "a way of seeing is also a way of not seeing" (*P&C* 49), that every reflection requires selection which in turn requires deflection, that in designating what something *is* we must say what it *is not*, and so on, it is hard to see how he might dupe us into embracing—assuming we could even get our arms around it—this great, shaggy beast that is his "system." And the figurative nature of his own terminology is forever being foregrounded by his use of nomenclature, so homemade, at times so downright off-putting, as to render the most credulous readers wary. And clearly this is intentional. Hence his fondness for the term "bureaucratization": "an unwieldy word, perhaps even an onomatopoeia, since it sounds as bungling as the situation it would characterize" (*ATH* 225).

In so much of what he writes, Burke anticipates criticisms that might be used against him. Instead of debunking those charges, he acknowledges their partial truthfulness and attempts to "round out" the criticism by understanding it "in terms of" an opposing truth. The human commitment to progress, thus, is part of a larger process, bureaucratization, which up to a certain point is a boon and past that point is a bane to those who engage in it. Where that point may lie is the job of criticism generally and rhetoric specifically to determine. But in arriving at that determination, critics and rhetoricians must accept their own inevitable complicity in the very processes they would admonish. Their theories ("imaginative possibilities") and their methodologies (the realization of those possibilities in the form of insights) are as prone to the logic of bureaucratization as technology, socialism, or capitalism. Thus, when Burke considers his own "'perspectives by incongruity'" as a "'methodology of invention'" that "'bureaucratizes' the mass production of perspectives," he acknowledges both the boon and the bane of his transformation of theory into method.

> Must there follow the usual deterioration in quality? Unquestionably. But deterioration from one standpoint is "improvement" from another standpoint. The deterioration that would go with the democratization of planned incongruity should be matched, we hold, by a corresponding improvement in the quality of popular sophistication, since it would liquidate belief in the absolute truth of concepts by reminding us that the mixed dead metaphors of abstract thought are metaphors nonetheless. (*ATH* 229)

One of the major reasons, thus, that the specter of using Burke "whole" need not exercise one overmuch is that he is constantly forcing us to "liquidate belief in the absolute truth of concepts," including his own, and to recognize that our most sacred concepts always turn out on closer inspection to be metaphors.

But beyond all the internal safeguards Burke provides to prevent lapses into what he himself might term a "Burkean psychosis," the characteristic way that theory and method function in rhetoric militates against monomania. While theorizing and applying a methodology derived from that theory are typically quite different matters in the sciences and social sciences, in rhetoric "a method is [usually] the exercise of an insight engendered by the theory itself" (Brummett 653) rather than a different, and "lower," order of strategic propositions operating independently of the theory. The methods used to affirm the big bang theory, for example, will be pretty much the same as the methods used by advocates of another theory to disconfirm it. Scientific methods, in the eyes of many who apply them anyway, comprise a neutral ground untainted by the aims and prejudices of any particular theory, a realm where theories may be extended and tested without the aid of conscious reflection. Some have, to be sure, attempted to employ Burke in precisely this manner, even though one would be hard-pressed to find places where Burke himself follows a similarly "methodical" procedure. Thus, a number of attempts have been made over the years to routinize his pentad—act, agent, agency, scene, and purpose—and render it so "cheap and easy" (*ATH* 228) that one could apply it absent any knowledge of the theory that gave rise to the procedure. Unfortunately, such attempts appear much more apt to result in "unintended byproducts" in the form of unconnected glimpses of a subject than to realize the imaginative possibilities of a coherent theory.

The more fruitful uses of Burke appear to follow a pattern sketched out by Brummett whereby "the major points of his theories are . . . treated as categories of critical analysis" (654). For the most part, this is the way in which Burke is used in this study. To illustrate this process, I look ahead to how one major point of his theory, occupational psychosis, will be used as a category of critical analysis in chapter 2. Like most of the foibles and human failings that Burke inventories in his work, occupational psychosis results from overdoing an otherwise benign, indeed unavoidable, tendency. Thus, Burke is careful to remind us that John Dewey, from whom he borrows the term, "does not use the word 'psychosis' in the psychiatric sense; it applies simply to a *pronounced character* of the mind" (*P&C* 40). Those activities that "occupy" our time and attention will necessarily, for good and for ill, affect our perceptions of the world. Like all orientations, they represent ways of seeing that are simultaneously ways of not seeing, "*modes of thinking . . . that are by the same token 'trained incapacities'*" (4). Mark Twain the steamboat pilot thus "reads" a river quite differently from the way that, say, Norman Maclean the fisherman reads a river. According to Burke, Dewey's thesis suggests "that a society's patterns of thought are shaped by the patterns of livelihood, that 'spiritual' values get their authority because they reinforce the ways of thinking and feeling by which man equips himself to accomplish the tasks indigenous to his environment" (*PLF* 272).

Occupational psychosis fills a role in Burke's theory of human understanding and symbolic action quite distinct from the role filled by his pentad. And while the pentad appears to offer a neutral method of generating perspectives, occupational psychosis is by definition always "interested." And as it turns out, one can never neatly separate the two. In his *Grammar of Motives,* thus, Burke categorizes seven major "casuistries" or philosophical schools according to their focus on one of his five terms and suggests that "in developing a vocabulary designed to allow this one term full expression," the adherents of that term inevitably slight the other terms or place them "in the perspective of the featured term" (127). In other words, as "specialists" in act, agent, scene, agency, or purpose, each of the philosophic schools is vulnerable to the "trained incapacities" of an occupational psychosis. By the same token, in applying Burke to the subject of this study, occupational psychosis functions as a "category of critical analysis" that helps explain not only why success rhetoricians' understanding of workplace identity may be reductive but also why critics have in recent years failed to give significant critical attention to this phenomenon. If "methodology" in the modernist sense insulates us from this second concern, Burke's demand that any terminology "allow for the progressive criticism of itself" (*RR* 303) goads us to confront it.

Representative Anecdotes and History

One element of Burke's approach employed here that would appear to be methodological in the more traditional sense is the representative anecdote. It is a key concept for Burke and underlies the historical approach taken in this study. The "gist" (to use a Burkean term) of representative anecdote goes something like this: It is to Burke's dramatistic approach what a historical event is to history. It is "itself so dramatistic a conception that we might call it the dramatistic approach to dramatism" (*GM* 60). It is a part that best represents the whole without ever being completely absorbed by that whole.

In his fullest discussion of the representative anecdote in *Grammar of Motives*, thus, Burke settles on the "making of the Constitution" as the anecdote that best represents his grammar. He chooses the Constitution after considering and rejecting the railway terminal. While the latter trope reflects one dimension of a grammar—its use of a stable set of elements to limit and direct meaning—it is finally reductive, incapable of explaining the ways in which language is a human act both motivating and motivated. For Burke, the trope of the terminal is a case of metonymic reduction, while the Constitution is a case of synecdochic equivalence:

> We might say that representation (synecdoche) stresses a *relationship* or *connectedness* between two sides of an equation, a connectedness that, like a road, extends in either direction, from quantity to quality or from quality to quantity; but reduction follows along this road in only *one* direction, from quality to quantity. (*GM* 509)

This equivalence relationship is exemplified by the agent/act relationship:

> The agent is an author of his acts, which are descended from him, being good progeny if he is good, or bad progeny if he is bad. . . . And, conversely, his acts can make him or remake him in accordance with their nature. They would be his product and/or he would be theirs. (*GM* 16)

Likewise, the Constitution is a product of human action and a specific set of circumstances that in turn motivates human acts. It is born out of a "dialectical opposition to feudal authorities" (*GM* 363) but contains within itself mechanisms that allow future subjects to alter its entailments and directives in response to changing conditions unforeseen by its originators. Thus, as feudalism eventually fades, rights secured by the Constitution are increasingly understood "in terms of" their opposition not to some foreign despot but "to the authority of the people's government itself" (363). Moreover, the Constitution, as act, creates a sovereign nation and stands as guarantor of that sovereignty. As such, it expresses our nation's "intrinsic" identity. But insofar as the Constitution allows for a change in identity through amendment and leaves room for reinterpretation of itself as "circumstances alter cases," it acknowledges the "extrinsic" dimension of that identity. Those human agents whose act the Constitution is are remade by their own act into "citizens" of a sovereign nation who possess, by virtue of that act, the power to redefine the nature of citizenship. Quite literally, we produce and are produced by our Constitution.

The making and remaking of our Constitution is a representative anecdote about the ongoing drama of American identity as well as an exemplification of Burke's dramatist approach and the act of creation underlying that approach. It is not in either case, however, *the* representative anecdote, because no such ideal anecdote exists. Each anecdote offers only one perspective on the world, and Burke requires us to "become masters of many perspectives in order that we may understand one," which is one reason why they are "anecdotes" rather than myths, axioms, or master narratives. That is not to say there is not some sort of hierarchy of anecdotes—hierarchies being as inevitable in Burke as bureaucracies—and rational grounds for preferring one over another. Specifically, they must "'have a form sufficiently clear to be contemplated, yet sufficiently complex to defy simplist description'" (*GM* 324). The railway terminal fails the test of sufficient complexity, as do anecdotes put forth by Burke's bête noire the behaviorists, whose animal experiments are "notably *informative* . . . [but] not *representative*, since one cannot find a representative case of human motivation in animals" (59).

In the above spirit, the texts that serve as subjects of this study may be viewed as a series of representative anecdotes about American workplace identity in the twentieth century. Their relationship with their subject is indeed synecdochic insofar as both reflect and construct the reality they represent. But they are more "informative" than "representative" insofar as they lack the scope and circumference of fully rounded anecdotes.

They are informative about the changing requirements of the American workplace as those requirements are determined by employers and corporations responding to shifts from industrial to consumer to global capitalism. Moreover, while their formal choices tell us which forms of representation are privileged within a given epoch, their thematic choices inform us about the dominant myths, fears, and desires of that epoch. They are unrepresentative and reductive insofar as they treat workplace identities as if they were autonomous and ignore a more comprehensive notion of identity, the identity of "*man in general*," which, according to Burke, will be "'over-socialized' or 'over-biologized' or 'over-psychologized' or 'over-physicized' or 'over-poeticized' or so on, depending on which specialized terministic screen was being stretched to cover not just its own special field but a more comprehensive area" (*LSA* 51–52). Like the behaviorists, they offer a version of identity that cannot be represented insofar as it does not exist in its pure form in the world we inhabit. And it falls to rhetoric, according to Burke, to sort out the conflicting demands of all the various forms of "identification," chosen or ascribed, that comprise our full identity.

> The human agent, *qua* human agent, is not motivated solely by the principles of a specialized activity, however strongly this specialized power, in its suggestive role as imagery, may affect his character. Any specialized activity participates in a larger unit of action. "Identification" is a word for the autonomous activity's place in this wider context, a place with which the agent may be unconcerned. The shepherd, *qua* shepherd, acts for the good of the sheep, to protect them from discomfiture and harm. But he may be "identified" with a project that is raising the sheep for market. (*RM* 27)

The task of rhetoric and role of this study in relation to the texts that it treats is not to protect an autonomous, central self from the blandishments of heteronomous forces that would rob it of authenticity. No such self exists in rhetoric or in Burke where individual identity is conceived of as "a unique combination of experiences, a unique set of situations, a unique aggregate of mutually re-enforcing and conflicting 'corporate we's'" (*ATH* 289). For Burke, we can only be "substantially" autonomous, which means, according to the logic of his paradox of substance (*GM* 21–23), that we are never fully autonomous any more than a statement that is "substantially true" is wholly true. We remain "a unique locus of motives" that is "consubstantial with" (*RM* 21) other people, other interests, the contingencies of our time and place, and all the roles and categories to which we might be assigned. It is here, in this ambiguous space where "identification and division [are put] ambiguously together, so that you cannot know for certain just where one ends and the other begins, [that] you have the characteristic invitation to rhetoric" (25). The task of rhetoric, in turn, is not to refute something that is untrue so much as to enrich something that is impoverished. In the present study, this rhetorical imperative translates into an effort to show how the texts in question employ the available resources to promote a given identity, to suggest alternative means of persuasion not employed, and to enumerate alternative ends, other notions of "the good life," and identity implied by those alternative means, thereby rounding out rather than refuting their claims.

It is because of the above assumptions about the relationship between rhetoric and identity that the literature of self-help, a genre often associated with success rhetoric, is for the most part ignored here. To be sure, the distinction between the two categories blurs in several instances, notably in the cases of Peale and Carnegie, and to a lesser extent Covey. But it remains a distinction worth maintaining. If the goal of the texts featured in this study remains success—however elusive that concept may prove to be—in the domain of business, the goal of texts in the self-help field feature recovery, usually of an identity lost to outside forces or addictive inner demons, in the domestic sphere. The tension between the public and the private, that sphere where "identification and division [are put] ambiguously together" that Burke deems the native ground of rhetoric, is thus largely absent from self-help literature and all its New Age cousins. Consequently, such literature, along with a certain "therapeutic" strain of success rhetoric that is almost purely exhortative and inspirational (for example, the work of Tony Robbins), offers less grist for the rhetorician's mill than do the works treated here. Likewise, recent bestsellers like *Who Moved My Cheese?*—an Orwellian panegyric, in the form of a child's fable, to the obsequious, low-maintenance roboworker—defies parody, leaving one little to do but debunk.

But—and here one must pause to acknowledge one's discomfort in offering up what looks uncannily like a pseudo-confession of the sort beloved of self-help gurus—one must also take one's personal limitations into account in deciding what subjects to pursue. It is difficult enough at times to offer criticism in the spirit of "comic corrective" and "cajolery" to some notions promoted by the works studied here. Trying to maintain that decorum throughout the study of works by people like

M. Scott Peck, M.D., or Deepak Chopra, M.D., simply requires a more magnanimous spirit than the one possessed by your current guide.

These, then, are my reasons for looking at these particular works as representative anecdotes. There remains the question of how these works can be understood in relation to each other and to assumptions about historical succession entailed by my treatment of them as representative anecdotes. Burke offers little explicit direction in this regard. His representative anecdote may itself be a historic sequence, as in the case of the making of the Constitution, or it may be a particular act or even "thing" (for example, a railway terminal) viewed as a "paradigm" (*GM* 61) that sums up a sequence. And while we are offered grounds for preferring one anecdote over another, we are offered little in the way of specifics about how to connect one anecdote to another or how we might create some sort of synthesis from multiple anecdotes. At a very general level, Burke does call for a shift from a "dialectic" to an "ultimate" order or hierarchy that would transform the "out and out antithetical vocabulary" (*RM* 192) of the dialectical order into a harmonious whole. But he never discusses this move with the representative anecdote specifically in view. And given what he says about the nature of representative anecdotes, the move from the divisions of dialectic to the harmonies of hierarchy would be especially daunting. Fortunately, other theorists for whom the anecdote functions as a central element of historical method have discussed the logic of its employment extensively and suggestively. By way of clarifying the role of representative anecdotes in this study, thus, I will briefly consider the analogous role of anecdotes in new historicist accounts according to Catherine Gallagher and Stephen Greenblatt.

In their description of the role of anecdotes in historical accounts, Gallagher and Greenblatt focus on a tension between "focus" and "scale" analogous to Burke's concern with the relationship between "clarity" and "simplification" in representative anecdotes (*GM* 324). In the case of "thick description," the anthropological forerunner to the new historian's anecdote, this tension is likened to the phenomenon of "foveation" in optics, which involves

> the ability to keep an object (here a tiny textualized piece of social behavior) within the high-resolution area of perception. Foveation in cultural interpretation is rather difficult because of problems of both scale and focus. The interpreter must be able to select or to fashion, out of the confused continuum of social existence, units of social action small enough to hold within the fairly narrow boundaries

of full analytical attention, and this attention must be unusually intense, nuanced, and sustained. (Gallagher and Greenblatt 26)

Unlike the philosopher's "purpose built illustration" that obediently explicates a general principle with a specific case, anecdotes or thick descriptions are "more resistant to simple appropriation and hence more nearly autonomous" (25), causing Clifford Geertz to liken thick description to a "note in a bottle" (qtd. in Gallagher and Greenblatt 22). In the case of historical anecdotes, this resistance is powerful enough to constitute a form of "counterhistory" that reveals "fault lines" (17) in any historical *grand recit* into which it may be inserted, reminding us of the contingency, the resistant singularity of material we would subsume under some principle of succession. Elsewhere, Greenblatt argues that the "historical anecdote functions less as explanatory illustration than as disturbance, that which requires explanation, contextualization, interpretation" (*Learning* 5). The singularity of Greenblatt's anecdote is not, it should be emphasized, of the purely nominalist variety; in the end, the anomalous part can be explained, contextualized, and interpreted "in terms of" some larger whole. But it requires a visible act of intervention by the interpreter to make the anecdote fit, thereby undermining any illusion of inevitability the interpreter might wish to sustain for his audience.

This resistance to assimilation by Greenblatt's anecdotes, a trait Burke sometimes refers to as "recalcitrance," is the strongest point of resemblance to Burke's representative anecdotes. Representative anecdotes are, as their would name suggest, incapable of being fully commensurate with that which they represent. They are, after all, merely anecdotes about their subjects, capable of providing "glimpses and inklings" but never the full story. Thus, Burke's introduction to his discussion of the term:

Men seek for vocabularies that will be faithful *reflections* of reality. To this end, they must develop vocabularies that are *selections* of reality. And any selection of reality, must, in certain circumstances, function as a *deflection* of reality. Insofar as the vocabulary meets the needs of reflection, we can say it has the necessary scope. In its selectivity, it is a reduction. Its scope and reduction become a deflection when the given terminology, or calculus, is not suited to the subject matter which it is designed to calculate. (*GM* 59)

To see a larger piece of reality in terms of some smaller part of that reality is necessarily to purchase focus at the expense of scale, and because no terminology is perfectly suited in all circumstances "to the subject matter which it is designed to calculate," there will always be a certain amount of deflection associated with that move. And the harder one strains to make one's anecdotes fit seamlessly into a line of succession or to illustrate some synthetic principle, the more likely one is to increase the ratio of deflection to reflection. Consequently, the texts dealt with in this study are treated less as members of a particular category or genre than as members of a somewhat heterogeneous family, each of which is singularly interesting on its own, capable of rewarding our "full analytical attention."

The representative anecdote, viewed as a tool of historical analysis, is ill-suited to historical narratives fashioned as progress, decline, or an illusion masking stasis. It is best-suited to historical narratives stressing the tension between events and patterns assigned those events. In Burke's case, this tension is manifest in his notion of history as recurrence, an ineluctable blend of "permanence and change," reminding us how "our stupidities are ever born anew" (*ATH* 259) and how we may "discern the naming of the one situation" (*PLF* 260) beneath the many names we give it. Burke's clearest articulation of a critical program entailed by his belief in history as recurrence occurs in *The Philosophy of Literary Form*, in particular in the essay "Literature as Equipment for Living." Insofar as that essay anticipates this study in several particulars, it is worth reviewing.

Burke's goal in "Literature as Equipment for Living" is to establish a "sociological criticism of literature" (*PLF* 253), treating literature as a form of proverbial wisdom that "name[s] typical, recurrent situations" (253) and "impl[ies] a command (what to expect, what to look out for)" (254). In categorizing the various situations and the sorts of strategic responses appropriate to such situations, Burke's concern is not taxonomic—"to find categories that 'place' the proverbs once and for all" (255)—but rhetorical. The critic's task is to "assemble and codify this lore" (260) according to the strategies employed, even if it leads her "to outrage good taste" (260) by mingling canonical literature with popular literature, dirty jokes, and sermons. In order to carry out this task, the critic must also free herself from the "categories of modern specialization" (262) that prevent literary critics from examining "non-literary" texts or sociologists from looking at literature. "The new alignment will outrage in particular those persons who take the division of faculties in our universities to be an exact replica of the way in which God himself divided up the universe" (262).

When literature, so conceived, offers inadequate strategies and direction, that failure typically follows from its inability or unwillingness to "size things up properly" to "chart" the situation accurately. Conceived of as a representative anecdote, such literature maintains an unacceptable ratio of deflection to reflection—which brings us, so far as I can tell, to Burke's lone mention of success rhetoric. Books collected under the heading "inspirational literature," including "our current output of books on 'How to Buy Friends and Bamboozle Oneself and Other People,'" are rebuked for offering "a strategy for easy consolation" plausible only because it "plays down" the realistic obstacles to achieving success and because "in an era of confusion like our own the need [for consolation] is especially keen" (*PLF* 258). As far as it goes, it is an astute diagnosis of success rhetoric's central flaw and of the cultural dynamic that fosters it. Unfortunately, Burke's dismissal of the phenomenon is uncharacteristically curt, insufficiently extensive to qualify as debunking but considerably more iconoclastic than hagiographic. Whatever satisfaction these books offer is said to be vicarious—"It is *while they read* that these readers are 'succeeding'" (258)—and that is Burke's final word on the subject.

What Burke fails to anticipate in this early Depression-era essay is that the "era of confusion" he finds himself in will not end with economic recovery, and the need for "easy consolation" will grow apace for the rest of the century. He does, however, recognize that the need for consolation satisfied on the cheap by success rhetoricians is not itself trivial. It is as fundamental as the needs for "vengeance, for admonition or exhortation, for foretelling" (*PLF* 253) met by literature as equipment for living. However inaccurate the "charts" by which they navigate or the strategies they employ, the office filled by works of inspirational literature or success rhetoric is a worthy one deserving of better-rounded texts. But so long as criticism is bound by the pieties of "modern specialization" and so long as academic disciplines perceive their boundaries to be preordained, success rhetoric will go unattended and meet no resistance when it offers faulty nostrums and bad strategies for dealing with recurrent situations. The modest goal of this study is to at least make these works a subject of conversation.

The Mystery of Neglect (Continued)

There are, thus, two representative anecdotes at work in the present account. The first sets out to understand how and why a peculiarly twentieth-century rhetorical genre managed to persuade so many members of a new "professional-managerial class" to adopt identities so ill-suited to their own interests and so well-suited to the interests of corporate America; the second sets out to understand how and why American academics have failed to offer an effective critique of, or alternative to, so influential and pernicious a phenomenon. Both anecdotes, it will be recognized, shed light on related twentieth-century phenomena involving the manufacture of desires in the commercial sphere and the secession of academics from the public sphere. We begin with the second anecdote.

In the case of rhetoricians, this neglect of success rhetoric is particularly difficult to understand, given that we attend primarily to the impact of arguments and the means by which that impact is achieved rather than to their truthfulness or elegance. Perhaps part of the problem lies in the fact that the success ethos touted by gurus, for all its self-evidently spurious advice and corrupt values, occasionally bears an uncanny resemblance to our own professional ethos. While we may reject the way gurus define success, the methods they prescribe for achieving it, and the prose they use to express it, academics' belief in meritocracy—typically couched these days in the language of "excellence"—possesses virtual hegemonic status within our community. Moreover, rhetoricians—for all our ancient heritage—are disciplinary arriviste in today's American university, typically harbored as a "subdiscipline" within English or speech communication departments, and like any marginalized group, our loyalties to dominant group beliefs can be particularly ferocious.

In coming to terms with our motives for neglecting success rhetoric, our possible consanguinity with the tribes of success, and our shared reverence for their idols, we take our cue from Kenneth Burke's notion of identity. We are all, Burke reminds us, "consubstantial" with all sorts of things that, like embarrassing relatives, we may not wish to acknowledge.[1] In this regard, it may be blindingly obvious to us that people who husband Rolodexes with thousands of names, reviewing and freshening them constantly to maintain a proper "network"—what *The Great Gatsby*'s Meyer Wolfsheim might call "gonnections"—are probably deranged, afflicted with a particularly virulent strain of Burke's "occupational psychosis." But what may well remain unclear to us are the links between this behavior and some of our own stratagems for professional advancement. We might of course argue in our defense that whatever we do in the name of getting noticed and moving up to a higher tier department or a more elite institution ultimately serves the interests of producing and disseminating knowledge, noble goals that none or few Keepers of the Rolodex might claim. But to the extent that "excellence" has become for universities the same end in itself that it appears to have become for corporations, the comparison is less reductive than it might at first seem. Indeed, without benefit of the sorts of clear measures of material profit and loss to which corporations have access, universities' potential to let "excellence" be all and to lose sight of other goals, noble or otherwise, is arguably greater.

The last point will be recognized by some as belonging to the late Bill Readings's argument in *The University in Ruins* that we have lately been assimilated into what he termed the "university of excellence," an institution that pursues success as heartily as any of the transnational corporations whose behaviors we increasingly ape. And while the rationale for that pursuit could once be tied to noble goals such as self-enlightenment and the preservation of a national culture, the withering of nation-states in a global marketplace undermines the need for cultural guardianship or national self-awareness and renders the telos of excellence alarmingly circular: "'Excellence' is like the cash-nexus in that it has no *content*; it is hence neither true nor false, neither ignorant nor self-conscious" (13). It is an adjective masquerading as a noun, a place on a scale meaningful only in relation to other places on the scale. Thus, when a university committee declares scholarly "excellence" to be the major criterion for selection to a summer fellowship program, Readings retorts that

> excellence is not a fixed standard of judgment but a qualifier whose meaning is fixed in relation to something else. An excellent boat is not excellent by the same *criteria* as an excellent plane. So to say that excellence is a criterion is to say absolutely nothing other than that the committee will not reveal the criteria used to judge applications. (24)

Readings's references to universities' growing fascination with and mostly unexamined use of "excellence" as a god term will resonate especially well with those who have been involved in universities for twenty years or more. Those who have watched various local departments and offices and sundry sleepy institutes magically morph into "Centers of Excellence" or "Center for Excellence in [Fill in the Blank]" throughout the 1980s and 1990s know well whereof he speaks.

Indeed, as Readings notes, the circular and sometimes pathetically self-aggrandizing notion of "excellence" that prevails in contemporary universities—he cites one case in which a university transit service was declared a model of excellence because of its aggressive collection of parking fines—has a longer history in America than elsewhere. The excellence ethos has played a prominent role in higher education here because American colleges and universities have always competed in a crowded marketplace for customers and, of late, for "brand recognition" like any other purveyor of consumer goods. This need to compete for resources and students has undermined our capacity to claim the quasi-religious status of cultural guardianship that European universities could take for granted. And even to the extent that American universities did manage to invest themselves with an ecclesiastical aura, that investment could not yield the cultural capital that it did for European universities. Having "quasi-religious" status in America, where religious denominations must also compete in a crowded marketplace for souls to save, has less cachet than in Europe, where state-sanctioned faiths were traditionally spared the indignities of self-promotion, let alone the unspeakable embarrassments of televangelism.

The stunning success in recent years of "for profit" or proprietary colleges represents a logical next step in the development of our entrepreneurial higher ed market, just as the various news magazine ratings of colleges as "best buys" represents the logical next step in consumer response to that market. As public universities went from "state-supported" to "state-assisted" institutions in the "every tub on its own bottom" political environment of the 1980s and 1990s, they were forced to market themselves ever more relentlessly to their "clients"—students, parents, alumni, and corporate donors—to replace the dwindling stream of federal and state dollars.

As Readings also suggests, America has never celebrated its cultural heritage in the way Europe has, mostly because we have no single ethnic heritage to commemorate. In lieu of a common ethnic heritage, our connections to one another tend to be legal rather than organic. The university's cultural role, as T. H. Huxley recognized a century ago in a commencement address that Readings summarizes, "is not to bring to light the content of its culture, to realize a national meaning; it is rather to deliver on a national *promise*, a contract" (34, Readings's emphasis), which returns us to the vexed notion of success discussed earlier. American academics are no more sure about the "promises" we have contracted for than we are about the dreams all of us are supposed to be pursuing.

Certainly many academics, especially in the humanities, have protested this shift toward a "university of excellence," however slender their grasp of its workings or import. Unfortunately, those most strongly opposed to the creeping instrumentalism of American higher education have tended to oppose these encroachments on traditional grounds that themselves sound suspiciously elitist. The traditionalists have not thus rejected the notion of a success ethos so much as they have opposed a technocratic success ethos with an aristocratic one. And the "excellencies" promoted by the counterinsurgents appear to be, if anything, even murkier than the "excellencies" promoted by the insurgents.

The origins of this older success ideology derive from an earlier moment in the history of capitalism and the initial shift to a market economy in the early nineteenth century. It was in that moment, Magali Sarfatti Larson suggests, that professions arose in order to control and regulate the sale of new kinds of "'fictitious commodities'" (210), like professional expertise to a clientele not yet aware that it needed the expertise in a marketplace that had heretofore dealt primarily in straightforward matters such as land, labor, and material goods. Through a number of mechanisms, especially academic credentialing, professions limited the number of practitioners and lent their expertise a tangible form measured by years of study, examinations, degrees, and certificates, thereby justifying the relatively high cost of the fictitious commodity they were selling. Over time, academe became even more thoroughly integrated with the professional project by producing producers of knowledge (that is, graduate students) as well as practitioners (that is, undergraduates) and by itself becoming a primary site of knowledge production. Particularly in America, these functions loomed considerably larger than the maintenance of a cultural heritage in establishing the legitimacy of higher education both in the minds of the populace and of most academics.

Because universities are at one remove from the crudest workings of markets that mete out ordinary people's material fates, they may freely ignore their crucial role in what Larson calls "the meritocratic legitimation of social inequality" (51). In America, higher education is where aspirants to various occupational roles and status are sorted out, where Ivy League students are segregated from state college students; where the pre-med, pre-law, and engineering students are separated from the education and social work students; and general business students are culled from among the MBA-bound. Depending on how students perform in their academic majors, they are in turn channeled into the appropriate professional schools, school districts, and consulting firms. Describing the process as "a brutal (and continuing) selection among potential recruits" (55), Larson argues that thanks to the screening function we perform, all professions, including our own, may subsequently "emphasize inclusion and operate *in the mode* of a community" (55).

Whatever notional assent we give to academe's egalitarian claims or its "service" ethos, a success ethos still clearly prevails. We are in fact as relentless in tracking and ranking each other as we are in tracking our students. We expend increasing amounts of time—thanks in part to the demand for constant assessment initiated by several of the most prominent recent works of success rhetoric—selecting, evaluating, promoting, tenuring, and, increasingly, post-tenure reviewing ourselves, and we expend greater and more baffling amounts of time ranking each other every year for ever more minuscule merit pay increases.

While some of these behaviors might be justified as the sort of scrupulous self-policing that is the essence of professionalism, other of our fascinations with status are less easily accounted for by our professional canons. Consider, for example, the distressing tendency for many academics to mistake their vitae for, well, their lives, a tendency exacerbated by all the aforementioned rites of self-scrutiny that we compulsively reenact. Too many of us are possessed of too much or too little self-esteem based on the length of our résumé. And by the same token, we are increasingly fascinated with the doings of academic luminaries whose moves from one elite institution to the next are followed as avidly by some as the movement of baseball superstars between teams. Will Stanley Fish, we wonder, be able to turn around the fortunes of the *other* Chicago university— the one that's "in" Chicago as opposed to being "of" Chicago—which brought him onboard as dean for many of the same reasons that K-Mart once brought Martha Stewart onboard as public spokesperson? The fact that Fish makes slightly less than the major league minimum salary and a fraction of Stewart's fee in no way changes the nature of the transaction or lessens our fascination with it. It is the aura of success surrounding these tales that fixates us. And it is the assurance that we will be mesmerized by this move that causes those who hired Fish to make the transaction in the first place. In a world where, as Bill Readings argues, all measures of success boil down to a matter of institutional reputation (26), hiring "names" is the most direct route to excellence. Or, to put the matter in the vernacular of advertising that seeps into success rhetoric through every pore: "Hiring academic superstars strengthens brand identity in the minds of the target demographic."

Like every other American success ethos, there is at the heart of our traditional ethos a paradox that we tend to resolve, in time-honored

American fashion, by ignoring one side. Larson describes this contradiction in the following way:

> [A]t the core of the professional project, we find the fusion of antithetical ideological structures and a potential for permanent tension between "civilizing function" and market-orientation, between the "protection of society" and the securing of a market, between intrinsic and extrinsic values of work. (63)

Even as we celebrate the "intrinsic" value of our work, in some cases fetishizing its ennobling "uselessness," we do so from what amounts to a monopoly position in relation to the market we disdain. Within the protective walls of that monopoly, we are free then to play what amounts to intramural versions of the varsity blood sports played outside in the larger marketplace. Individually and collectively, our professional fortunes have in the past risen and fallen, not according to the social utility of our contributions or the extent to which we serve our "clients," but according to a scorekeeping system that can be as circular as the one being imposed on us within the newly emergent "university of excellence." For the most part, academic success hinges on an ability plausibly "to claim esoteric and identifiable skills" (Larson 180), whose value is better measured by scarcity than by utility. In many important respects, then, the more traditional and currently more widely acknowledged success ethos ascribed to by humanists shares the same affiliation with the "cash-nexus" and processes of "dereferentialization" (Readings 17) that we find in Readings's university of excellence. Or as Larson notes of the traditionally conceived professional project: "From a broader analytical perspective, the professional project is part of a basic structural transformation—namely, the extension of exchange relations under capitalism to all areas of human activity" (209).

So, whichever success ethos one sees at the heart of the academic enterprise, one tends to end up in the same place, faced with many of the same disquieting similarities between that ethos and the ideology of mainstream success texts, forced thus to implicate one's own practices in any critique one offers of that ethos, to which a critic like Burke would say, "Well, of course. Any act of critique, even debunking, implicates the critic." For Burke, we are all subject to whatever standards we may set for our subject, and any attempt to stand outside or above our subject is doomed (*GM* 100). But few of us possess Burke's critical double-jointedness, his uncanny ability to examine himself in the process of examining others and to recognize his own foibles in the failings of others. Moreover, the application of one's esoteric and identifiable skills to such matters as bestselling success texts diminishes the value of that contribution in the eyes of those who measure success by the traditional metric. Indeed, by straying beyond disciplinary bounds and the particular job of work that one's discipline is enfranchised to perform, one threatens to blur the very distinctiveness that ensures one's disciplinary niche and the monopoly privileges that go with that niche. This tension between one's desire to act consequentially in the world and the desire to act autonomously within one's profession is, like the paradox of success explored in the rest of this chapter, one that cannot be resolved, only returned to. And return to it we will, particularly in the last chapter.

Success v. Happiness

Before going any further, I need to clarify my usage here of the term "success." Potentially, of course, success, like excellence, can be applied to any endeavor. In theory, one can be a "successful" parent as readily as one can be a successful investment banker. But in daily discourse, the first usage sounds less natural, more in need of quote marks than the second. By the same token, one could treat the works of Peter Drucker as success books. And while Drucker appears to promote some of success rhetoric's favorite notions and to wear the "guru" laurels happily, his own works possess a sort of gravity and intellectual acuity seldom found among works treated here. Intuitively, one does not wish to lump his work—at least most of it—with that of, say, Stephen Covey. So, how does one construct an understanding of success that does not do too much violence to ordinary usage or stretch the notion of family resemblance too far?

Let us begin in sound Aristotelian fashion by suggesting what success is *not*. And the most salient of the many things success is not—in America, at least—is happiness. In America, happiness stands in the same relation to success as the "householder's" ethos stands in relation to the "warrior's" ethos in Charles Taylor's account of modern philosophy (26)—which is to say, happiness is a "pusillanimous second best" reserved for those who, instead of struggling manfully for success, tend to natter on about such matters as a "web of relationships which give fulness and meaning to human life" (46). From the perspective of latter-day warrior/careerists, the happy householder is a timid soul unwilling to strive or to seek, eager to yield. While success is sometimes mistakenly viewed as a means to happiness—never the reverse—it neither functions as a necessary condition for happiness nor stands in a relationship of reciprocity with happiness. Indeed, most popular literature—including, ironically enough, Horatio Alger novels—and reams of proverbial wisdom attest to the fact that one can be happy without being successful and one can be successful without being happy. Happy poor people and unhappy rich people, wisecracking minions and humorless, scheming bosses, are staples of popular entertainment.

But having said that, it is also true that we are much more likely to be entertained by the misery of successful people than we are by the contentment of unsuccessful ones. However much lip service happiness gets in our culture, including the sacred right of each of us to pursue it, our daily investment in success and its pursuit is much greater. And like every binary, the terms of this one are unequal. Success is a male term, privileged and unmarked, while happiness is a female term, cherished but little esteemed, and marked. Success is a public prize achieved in the workplace, while happiness is a private blessing enjoyed in the home. To be sure, because success rhetoric has infiltrated every area of our lives via therapeutic culture, one may hear today of "successful" or "failed" marriages—but, as of yet anyway, never of living "successfully ever after." And the reigning deity of the American success myth is the "self-made *man*," whose First Law is Emerson's Law of Compensation ("Nothing is got for nothing") and whose proper demeanor is stoic, an expression of Puritanic "worldly asceticism." Thanks to the utilitarians, meanwhile, happiness has been largely stripped of its ancient, spiritual connotations and is today often confounded with mere pleasure of the fleshly, feminine sort.

To be sure, one important reason why success has been so decisively privileged over happiness has to do with our tendency to view success as boundless and as such endowed with a spurious spirituality. Burke finds a version of this logic in Goethe's *Faust*, whose "official moral" is "that endless striving is a kind of divine discontent and should end in heaven" (*LSA* 180). The "cult of endless *streben*" (169), however, can never plausibly answer the questions "Striving for what? Towards what?" (169). Striving becomes an end in itself and is thereby "ethicized." Faust's heroism, thus, lies in his willingness to sacrifice everything for the ends he seeks, however unworthy, however trivial they turn out to be. And there appear to be a growing numbers of Faustian heroes about these days, spending legendary amounts of time making legendary amounts of money performing feats that add little to the common store or to progress toward any responsible notion of a good life. But anyone impertinent to question the ends to which so much striving is currently being put will get short shrift from contemporary economists like Stanley Lebergott who repeatedly admonish us never to substitute human judgment—"moral or aesthetic criteria that some thinkers excogitate" (7)—for the providential workings of the market. "Does Western engineering declare that some expenditures are unfunctional? Or Western morality? Even if they did, Western economics cannot" (6). In Lebergott's world, no murky notions of justice should impede progress. According to his analysis, each of us ought to be immensely grateful to our forebears for their transformation of former luxuries like refrigeration and speedy transportation into staples and should derive therefrom a moral obligation to continue their conversion of felt desires into met needs. In the process, thankful figures of our fancied posterity nudge aside the shadowy others presently occupying our third worlds and our park benches in our moral imaginations.

If striving licenses one not to be self-aware, not to engage in "progressive criticism" of one's means of understanding, happiness requires some level of self-knowledge. One can no more be happy without realizing it than one can be amused or saddened without realizing it. Not realizing that one is happy is grounds for being declared unhappy. And no one else need perceive or celebrate our happiness to make it real to us or to ensure its continued existence. Conversely, not realizing that you are successful is considered by many a necessary condition for continued success. As countless contemporary management gurus remind us, whenever one stops to contemplate one's successes, one's momentary inattention to the rapidly changing landscape can be fatal. Being "nimble" is to contemporary managers what being contemplative was to medieval saints. While managers are universally encouraged to "celebrate success," these brief, carnivalesque moments of time-out are mostly intended to reaffirm the status quo for the minions.

The fact that happiness requires no external validation may be problematic from the perspective of both a traditional success ethos and traditional ethics. Specifically, happiness so understood can be purchased on the cheap in the form of ignorance or smugness. Happiness that calls upon us only to "be" happy while ignoring others' misery, that does not oblige us to define and justify our definition of happiness or to create happiness for others, may produce a Donald Trump or some other student of hedonic calculus as readily as a Thoreau. One who has developed a high threshold of tolerance for social injustice and the suffering of others may possess "happiness" of a sort that many of us would find hard to admire or aspire to.

This last point underlies the complaints of Alasdair MacIntyre in *After Virtue* about the decline of civil society, particularly in America, over the past two centuries. Specifically, MacIntyre decries the lack of objective moral criteria that force moral judgments beyond the expression of personal feelings and the desire for others to share those feelings to a common sense of obligation transcending the interests of all parties. In lieu of such criteria, "[o]thers are always means, never ends" (24) to the realization of each moral agent's moral agenda. Moreover, when moral agents speak "unconstrained by the externalities of divine law, natural teleology or hierarchical authority" (68), it is not clear why anyone else might listen to them. MacIntyre calls this phenomenon "emotivism" (11–12) and deems it the most prevalent and most misguided mode of ethical thought of the twentieth century.

Emotivism is, for MacIntyre, a postlapsarian phenomenon originating in the very act of splitting success off from happiness. And in his account of the fall, the philosopher's traditional scapegoat, the sophist, looms large. "So the sophist of whom Plato's Thrasymachus is the type makes success the only goal of action and makes the acquisition of power to do and to get whatever one wants the entire content of success. A virtue is then naturally enough defined as a quality which will ensure success" (139), with "success" defined willy-nilly by the moral agent. This view, MacIntyre notes, contrasts sharply with Aristotle's view that rests upon a notion of human nature toward which all humans are moved by the forces of entelechy. The fullest realization of our human nature is "*eudaimonia*," which is associated with "blessedness, happiness, prosperity" or the "state of being well and doing well in being well" (148). Virtues, in this scheme, "are precisely those qualities the possession of which will enable an individual to achieve *eudaimonia* and the lack of which will frustrate his movement toward that *telos*" (148). A society where success is wholly subordinated to happiness is what MacIntyre calls a "heroic society" in which social role and individual identity, "morality and social structure are in fact one and the same" (123).

While there is much in MacIntyre's view of the relationship between happiness and success that supports the argument being developed here, it shares some limitations common to nostalgic, straight-line accounts of historical decline from organic unity to inorganic disarray. In particular, it assumes, in the words of Barbara Herrnstein Smith,

> that a community prospers . . . in proportion to the extent that its members have achieved consensus or that it prospers more as

communal norms become more uniform, coherent, and stable. But the well-being of any community is also a function of other and indeed opposed conditions, including the extent of the *diversity* of the beliefs and practices of its members and thus their communal resourcefulness, and the flexibility of its norms and patterns and thus their responsiveness to changing and emerging circumstances. (93)

In sum, MacIntyre's ideal deserves to be questioned on two grounds: in order for local and universal values to be synonymous, ideal "conditions of usage" (B. Smith 90) that are clearly unrecoverable, if in fact they ever existed, must prevail; and assuming one could achieve a perfect fact-value synonymity, that achievement would come at the cost of diversity and adaptability that would eventually be fatal to any society that managed it. As such, MacIntyre's view represents a potent tool for debunking but not for reforming twentieth-century success rhetoric. His heroic vision precludes a world of "creative dissensus" where competing views of happiness may coexist in continual dialogue.[2]

Charles Taylor, a philosopher whom Smith claims shares MacIntyre's "reactionary nostalgia . . . [for a] (lost) sense of 'community'" (172) is deserving of more extended consideration. His *Sources of the Self: The Making of the Modern Identity* (published after Smith's rebuke) offers an invaluable account of how a concept of self of the sort required by the success ethos came to be developed.[3] In particular, Taylor's book reminds us that the notion of identity underlying American success rhetoric—a pliant, open-ended self shaped by its attentiveness to external stimuli—is a social construct that Western philosophy spent several hundred years legitimating. According to Taylor's account, there was no fatal fall, à la MacIntyre, just a long and gradual descent down the slippery slope of post-Enlightenment thought. And in the end, if Taylor calls for "frameworks" (16) and "hypergoods" (63) that would, like MacIntyre's "externalities," chasten overly subjectivist or hypertechnical thinking about moral matters, he also envisions a less monolithic, more pluralist, and more corrigible set of standards than MacIntyre's:

Our forebears were generally unruffled in their belief, because the sources they could envisage made unbelief incredible. The big thing that has happened since is the opening of other possible sources [than God]. In a predicament where these are plural, a lot of things look problematic that didn't before—and not just the existence of God, but also such "unquestionable" ethical principles as that reason ought to govern the passions. Who knows whether further transformations in the available moral sources may not alter all these issues again out of all recognition? I want to argue that our present predicament represents an epistemic gain, because I think that the alternative moral sources which have opened for us in the past two centuries represent real and important human potentialities. (312–13)

Taylor is, in sum, more sanguine than MacIntyre about the changes that initiated this shift and more balanced in his views about the effects of those changes then and now. Modernist thought does not, Taylor counters, rule notions of the good life out of play; neither does it simply reverse the polarities of higher life and ordinary life. Rather, modernism "displaces the locus of the good life from some special range of higher activities and places it within 'life itself'" (213). And along with this valorization of ordinary life, says Taylor, comes a number of benefits, including the displacement of monarchy by democracy and of theology by philosophy and science; the latter shift in turn motivates knowledge seekers to, in Bacon's words, "'relieve and benefit the condition of man'" (qtd. in Taylor 213). Finally, it made ordinary work, providing it was performed with right intentions, a noble act—which is to say, in Taylor's account, success and *eudaimonia* are not mutually exclusive. Something like a state of "blessedness" was now open to all who would be serviceable to others within the realm of "production and reproduction, that is, labour, the making of things needed for life, and our life as sexual beings, including marriage and the family" (211). Aristotle's good life, which Taylor describes as restricted to deliberations about moral excellence, contemplation of the order of things, and determinations of the common good by an intelligentsia (211–12), was opened up to ordinary people engaged in productive labor. Under the Puritans, scrupulous self-examination became an obligation, not just for "a small elite of spiritual athletes, but for all Christians" (184).

For a time at least, the good life and ordinary life along with the concomitant notions of happiness and success were effectively, albeit uneasily, integrated according to Taylor. While one eschewed "the presumption of superhuman spiritual aspirations" (175), one also eschewed the mindless pursuit of personal desire and pelf. So long as we viewed "the things of creation merely as instruments [of service to God] and not as ends valuable in themselves" (232), one's worldly labors were spiritually meaningful: "This means that the instrumental stance towards the world has been given a new and important spiritual meaning" (232). The devolution of instrumentalism into a devil term parallels the gradual separation, to their mutual detriment, of worldly success in ordinary life and human happiness. What was lost, in Taylor's terms, was a "framework" within which these notions could be properly understood and evaluated.

Originally, the framework that held things together was a cosmic order, such as the Great Chain of Being, with its attendant "theory of ontic logos" (190). Within this framework, the identity of any particular is defined and ennobled by its place in the order. Enlightenment and post-Enlightenment thinkers, by moving the reality principle inside and making it accessible only to disengaged reason, cut the subject off from its objects and localized the meaning and valuation of objects in the mind of the perceiver. What is lost in the process is the sense "within a theory of ontic logos" that our understandings and valuations "straddle what we think of as the gap between subject and object" (187). The things we make and use are thus "disenchanted," to borrow Weber's term, and the spirituality of "instrumental" use dissipates rapidly thereafter.

Which signals that point in the narrative when one is obliged to round up the usual suspect: Descartes. And to be sure, Taylor offers a deft critique of Descartes's contribution to the emergent notion of the atomistic, autonomous self to which America's own "self-made man" owes so much. But in the context of this account of the gradual recession of happiness and the good life from the sphere of success, a far more crucial figure is Taylor's John Locke, in particular Locke's "punctual self" (160).

A punctual self, says Taylor, is an offshoot of Descartes's disengaged self; it also bears a strong resemblance to the "disciplined" self of Foucault and to Greenblatt's self-fashioners. It is part of many related changes occurring throughout the Enlightenment and exemplifies

> the growing ideal of a human agent who is able to remake himself by methodical and disciplined action. What this calls for is the ability to take an instrumental stance to one's given properties, desires, inclinations, tendencies, habits of thought and feeling, so that they can be *worked on*, doing away with some and strengthening others until one meets the desired specifications. (159–60)

Whereas instrumentalism formerly called upon us to treat the things of the world and our labors as instruments for serving and honoring God, our labors and products now serve a more proximate master—our selves. In the process, the self becomes a godlike agent capable of transcending his situatedness, his interests and appetites, and all the conditioned elements of his personality in the name of re-making himself, not in conformity with an immutable cosmic order or divine law, but with the more immediate, more mutable "externalities" of social and workplace demands. "I" in effect becomes an instrument of "me," which is always an extension of a given institution. The suitable self of this study is, in short, a direct descendant of the punctual self.

Taylor dubs Locke's self "punctual" in the geometrical sense: "[T]he real self is 'extensionless'; it is nowhere but in this power to fix things as objects" (172). It is pure consciousness, "radical reflexivity," the most immediate but least tangible element of human existence, like point of view in a novel, at once ubiquitous and invisible. Ironically, thus, at the moment when ordinary people were licensed and encouraged to engage in strenuous self-reflection, the self to be reflected upon and the vantage point to which the self might repair in order to carry on those reflections recede from view.[4]

In the nineteenth century, the figure best representing the punctual self and "our inescapable contemporary sense of inwardness" (Taylor 160) is the flaneur, the boulevardier who eschews human connection in favor of motion and the power to fix things as objects. In the twentieth century, meanwhile, one could argue that the figure most representative of the punctual self is the bureaucrat or corporate manager—not coincidentally the primary audience for success rhetoric. In fact, Richard Sennett's *Fall of Public Man* makes just such an argument. While Sennett's immediate focus is on corporate technical workers, it is easy to see today how his analysis applies more broadly to all middle managers. Corporate workers, says Sennett, form a "*classes moyeness*" who are

> subject to institutional definitions of their work which are to a large extent also an institutional definition of their personalities. Against this institutional process, they have few countervailing traditions or artisanal standards; instead these arrivals to a new class accept the institutional definitions of themselves as valid and seek to work out patterns of defense and meaning within a situation in which class circumstances and personality are so closely allied. (328)

To the extent that the "boundaries between self and world . . . are erased" (328) for these workers, Sennett calls them "narcissistic" and argues that narcissism is "the Protestant ethic of modern times" (333). They are pure "potential" (328) to be made and remade in response to rapidly changing corporate exigencies and various "just in time" management philosophies that articulate those exigencies. That workers internalize this "erasure of distance between self and position" (331) is evident in their patterns of speech, particularly when they refer to themselves.

> Thus, in an American study of such workers, one hears them describe a promotion as something an abstract "they" gave to "me" and seldom hears workers speak as follows: "I did X or Y" and so "earned" a promotion. When workers in these middle-rank jobs use the "I" forms in their speech about work it is directed toward fraternal relations or feelings about other workers. (331)

In the argot of contemporary management, such workers are "free agents" unfettered by loyalty longevity or binding contractual ties. Their history, experience, and personal idiosyncrasies, everything palpable, particular, and cumulative about them, is devalued. They are "suits," and the fashion system that deems them in or out of season follows the logic of the corporation. Punctuality is all.

Or at least that's the worst-case scenario. Here, and throughout this study, one needs to remember that resistance to such designs is plentiful and that many of those targeted by success rhetoric and the institutional processes justified by that rhetoric are keenly aware of the game being played and savvy about how to play it. There are plentiful examples of people, often those directly targeted by success rhetoric, spoofing the pretensions of the genre in novels, cartoon strips, *Saturday Night Live* skits, and parodies of guru books. But because my focus will be on how the most successful of these works persuade substantial numbers of people to buy into their message, I may seem at times to credit them with magical powers they do not in fact possess. To say that success rhetoricians have managed to deceive large numbers of people for the shelf life of their message is not to say they have successfully created anything like a false consciousness in everyone exposed to that message. Thus, for example, those I spoke with during my administrative years about the books we were reading were far more likely to report experiencing boredom, skepticism, or outright hostility than enthusiasm, enchantment, or a commitment to becoming the sort of self called for by the author. While those who appear to consume these books so credulously are a worry, a greater worry is the lack of alternatives available to those who read them more critically.

Literature and the Problematics of Success

In his treatment of the emergent modern identity, Charles Taylor turns frequently to literary texts on the grounds that they serve an "epiphanic" function once served by a "publicly accessible cosmic order" (512). Such works simultaneously articulate frameworks for understanding and evaluating our moral sources and endow those sources with the "personal resonances" required—in the wake of modernist "disenchantment"—to motivate our action.

> The great epiphanic work actually can put us in contact with the sources it taps. It can *realize* the contact. . . . [W]e delude ourselves if we think that philosophical or critical language for these matters is somehow more hard-edged and more free from personal index than that of poets or novelists. The subject doesn't permit language which escapes personal resonance. (512)

Following Taylor's example, I will in the coming pages frequently use literary texts to gloss certain key issues. But the thrust of these literary interludes is perhaps closer in spirit to Kenneth Burke's critical view than to Taylor's. Burke, operating at a considerably lower pitch than Taylor, claims merely that literature is a kind of "equipment for living," less epiphanic than useful, a tool for solving problems in the manner of proverbs that model responses to recurrent situations. In the key more of Burke than of Taylor, thus, we take up *Don Quixote*, one of the earliest critiques of success rhetoric. Not coincidentally, the text also represents an early break with allegorical and iconographic traditions of narrative reliant on a cosmic order for "resonance".

The "reality problem" arises for Quixote thanks to his immersion in chivalric romances, books that prescribe behavior necessary to a successful quest and a persona suitable for the station that comes of successful questing—which is to say, books that served a function in medieval Spain like the one books in this study served in twentieth-century America. These books inspire in Quixote impossible dreams and in their wake all the moral ambiguities that attend such dreams. To the extent that Quixote acts on his dreams, we rightly consider him heroic; to the extent that he substitutes those dreams for a shared reality, we rightly consider him delusional.

Don Quixote is at once a reenactment of a chivalric romance, a genre for which Cervantes was known to have a particular fondness, and a critique of the genre. Cervantes doesn't merely "debunk" romance through negation and unmasking; rather, he applies a "comic corrective" to the genre. In Burke's terms, Cervantes lets a good deal of "physicality" into the rarefied world of the romance and allows us to see the romance "in terms of" a newly emergent notion of realism. Cervantes maintains this double perspective throughout the work, allowing us to see the world through both Quixote's and Sancho's eyes. What results is what Burke called "true" or "humble" irony, which, unlike either/or irony,

> is based upon a fundamental sense of kinship with the enemy, as one *needs* him, is *indebted* to him, is not merely outside him as an observer but contains him *within*, being consubstantial with him. This is the irony of Flaubert, when he recognizes that Madame Bovary is himself. (*GM* 514)

In part 2 of *Quixote*, meanwhile, Cervantes enlarges this sense of irony through extensive allusions to the text of part 1, published eight years earlier, and the effects of that awareness on both his characters and his readers. And 350 years later, Jorge Luis Borges further exploits readers' self-conscious awareness that they are reading fiction and even the characters' sense that they have been invaded by fiction in "Pierre Menard, Author of Quixote," an eight-page, "infinite" version of Cervantes' work. Whereas *Quixote* functions always at two levels, "Menard" functions more like an Escher print where any notion of "levels," or stable irony, makes little sense. Unlike an optical illusion that offers the viewer a standard figure-ground switch, Escher and Borges render multiple alternatives continuously across an extended narrative space, making it impossible to say precisely when a switch in meaning occurs.

On the face of it, the premise of Borges's story is absurd. Menard, we are told, has "written," through "endless" late-night drafts, an exact duplicate of *Don Quixote*, which he ensured would disappear upon his death, but which the narrator now claims is Menard's greatest, albeit invisible, work. "His admirable ambition was to produce a number of pages which coincided—word for word and line for line—with those of Miguel de Cervantes" (91). The narrator even quotes a sentence from Cervantes, then repeats the sentence word for word with the second version attributed to Menard. He pronounces the difference in import "staggering" and the contrast in styles "striking" (94), then dismisses Cervantes' version as conventional. Sorting all this out is complicated by the anonymous narrator's flagrant unreliability. He hints throughout at his ambition to replace a clearly unsavory Menard in the affections of his wealthy and singularly gullible patrons, who are clearly the primary targets of his self-serving tale.

Borges's eight-page story, like Menard's, is infinite insofar as it resolutely resists closure. But in the final paragraph, there is a moral of sorts, one that directs readers' attention away from the machinations of Menard and the narrator and reminds us of our own role in the fiction. Perhaps, the narrator suggests not implausibly, Menard's experiment represents a genuine contribution to "the slow and rudimentary art of reading" (95). If indeed the point of the experiment is to rescue *Quixote* from the curse of respectful reading accorded canonical works ("Fame is a form—perhaps the worst form—of incomprehension" [94]), who better to perform that service than an egregious lickspittle like Menard who gives fresh meaning to the phrase "the hermeneutics of suspicion"? To read *Quixote* under the sign of Menard is to allow all the contingency that fame excludes to creep back into the work, forcing each of us to question and reconstruct the text, reminding those who perform it how much we are implicated in its creation.

Which brings us back to the beginning of this brief literary excursion and what it tells us about our subject. If Cervantes persistently and Borges obsessively address us as "readers" and meaning makers, the works encountered in this study relentlessly address us as consumers. They address us as managers, workers, investors, and so on but never as wary and reflective readers who must negotiate among our many roles, making sense of the world less in the manner of Locke's "punctual self" than in the manner of Burke's "parliamentary" self. And they address us not in the present but, in the manner of advertisements, in the future, as we shall be after we have consumed the text and been transformed by its wisdom. The almost complete absence of humor, irony, uncertainty, paradox, precedent, countertexts, well-marked exaggerations, blatantly unreliable narrators, or any other rhetorical device that might heighten our critical awareness of text and the moment of reading renders the text invisible and keeps us pointed toward the promise of transformation. Conversely, in reading the difficult texts of Cervantes and Borges, replete with all these devices, we learn what Quixote learns from difficulties encountered within the texts: "[T]he suffered is the learned" (*GM* 39).

In MacIntyre's language, the rewards of the quest in Borges and Cervantes are "intrinsic." In contrast to extrinsic rewards, which accrue to winners in zero-sum games, intrinsic rewards accrue to all who commit themselves to the mastery of a given practice. If the National Book Award is an extrinsic good that goes to an outstanding writer, all serious writers who struggle to improve their craft realize the internal good of that craft. By the same token, those who attempt to learn without suffering, to realize success vicariously by reading about those who achieve it magically, have at the end of their painless quest no greater capacity for success and hence no intrinsic goods. The experience of reading such texts is captured perfectly in advice given by a *Harper's* editor to Michael Berube on how to render his academic prose palatable for popular audiences: "[I]deally, she said, you should be done reading [it] before you realize you've begun" (*Employment* 219).

It was not always so in the realm of success rhetoric. Without demanding the extreme reflexivity required to read a Cervantes or a Borges, success texts once demanded considerably more of their readers, both in terms of the behaviors toward which they pointed them and the attention required to "perform" the text.

Franklin's "New Man"

According to Sacvan Bercovitch, the Puritans were the first in a long line of Americans to negotiate that delicate balance between "piety and prosperity" (33), in particular between their hunger to own and profit from America's bounty and their belief that America is God's garden, a sacred place. In order to reconcile these two seemingly irreconcilable ends, the Puritans recast their emigration to America as an errand into the wilderness, the acting out of a script already written by a divine hand. Their America was simultaneously an enormous piece of real estate west of Europe and "a New Canaan" (3) ordained as theirs before they ever arrived. So though "they were as eager as any other group of emigrants for land and gain . . . they managed more effectively to explain away their greed. Other peoples, they explained, had their land by 'common providence'; they had it by prophecy and promise" (32). They were not self-interested individuals but "representative" (33) selves following a cosmic script.

Variants of this rhetorical strategy will show up in American success literature for the next several centuries as ever-resourceful American go-getters cobble together sundry metaphysical magical solutions—manifest destinies, invisible hands, enlightened self-interests, laws of natural selection, trickle-down theologies, and free markets—that transform their secular causes into holy obligations. Doing whatever is to be done in the go-getter's interests—privatizing public resources, deregulating energy prices, creating more regressive tax structures, tolerating monopolies, firing thousands of workers—turns out, inevitably, to be the one thing that maximally benefits the rest of us. Originated by the Puritans in the seventeenth and eighteenth centuries, refined by the robber barons in the nineteenth century, perfected by transnational corporations in the twentieth century, the "ethicizing" gambit is a rhetorical staple of American success apologists. (Burke deals most shrewdly and directly with the phenomenon in *Rhetoric of Motives* during a discussion of Pascal's "Directing the intention" [154–58].) While it is tempting today simply to debunk all such claims of spiritual ends for material schemes, some seem to have been invoked more sincerely and justly than others. All our ambivalence toward the practice is manifest in our contradictory responses to Benjamin Franklin.

Benjamin Franklin is the primary inheritor of all the Puritan contradictions, which is why one will find him likened to such disparate figures as Cotton Mather, whose *Bonifacius: An Essay to Do Good*, is arguably America's first piece of success rhetoric and one Franklin cites as a major influence, to John D. Rockefeller, who turns Mather on his head, using the doctrine of election to justify unsavory practices of monopoly capitalists. At the hinge point in American history between theological and secular eras, Franklin is one of our great representative figures. Thus, in Richard Ruland and Malcolm Bradbury's history of American literature, *From Puritanism to Postmodernism*, Franklin is introduced as the "supreme example" of "self-created American type," the incarnation of de Crèvecoeur's "'new man'" (41). His *Autobiography* is meanwhile treated as what one of his contemporaries called an "'efficacious advertisement' of the nation's character: 'All that has happened to you is also connected to the detail of the manners and situation of a rising people'" (qtd. in Ruland and Bradbury 43). Franklin is a secular version of the Puritans' "representative self" whose life self-consciously traces the shift in eighteenth-century America from Enlightenment to post-Enlightenment values. His *Autobiography* is freighted thus with all the contradictions and casuistry that inevitably accompany revolutionary change.

Given all this, it is not surprising to discover that at about the same time Franklin was enjoying his greatest national celebrity, thanks to George Horace Lorimer, who lent badly needed cachet to his *Saturday Evening Post* by claiming Franklin as its "founder" (he wasn't) and liberally slapping his avuncular image all over the best-selling magazine in America, D. H. Lawrence was writing perhaps the most scathing—certainly the most frequently cited—indictment of Franklin's legacy. The best-known line from Lawrence's critique is his response to Franklin's "virtue number twelve": "Rarely use venery but for health or offspring—never to dullness, weakness or to the injury of your own or another's peace or reputation." "Never," Lawrence comments tartly from the margins of history, "*use* venery at all" (18). It's an irresistible sentence, a one-liner that reduces Franklin not just to a prude but to the worst sort of utilitarian bean counter unable to imagine any activity, even sex, except as a means to a useful end.

Which is almost precisely how another emigre from the United Kingdom, Alasdair MacIntyre, sees Franklin fifty years after Lawrence. MacIntyre faults Franklin for being among the first to treat acquisitiveness, which the Greeks called *pleonexia* and considered a vice (183), as a virtue. While acknowledging that Franklin's account of virtue, like Aristotle's, "is teleological" (185), MacIntyre sharply contrasts the ends-means relationships in the two accounts:

> [A]lthough Aristotle treats the acquisition and exercise of the virtues as means to an end, the relationship of means to end is internal and not external. I call a means internal to a given end when the end cannot be adequately characterized independently of a characterization of the means. So it is with the virtues and the *telos* which is the good life for man on Aristotle's account. The exercise of the virtues is itself a crucial component of the good life for man. (184)

In Franklin, meanwhile, MacIntyre sees the means-end relationship as "external" insofar as "[t]he road to success in Philadelphia and the road to heaven may not coincide after all" (198). Of Franklin, MacIntyre complains, a show of virtue may do the job of actual virtue insofar as either serves equally well the utilitarian ends to which Franklin is said to subordinate virtue. If your neighbors *believe* you to be virtuous, one will have gotten all that is to be gained from *actual* virtuous behavior without assuming the handicap that honesty, fairness, truthfulness, and the like imposes on one in the competition for external gain.

Clearly, Franklin belongs to the "postlapsarian" phase of MacIntyre's history of moral decline. Moreover, Franklin's "liberal individualism" (195) can be seen in the very design of American form of government, which substitutes contractual (external) for organic (internal) connections of the sort MacIntyre commends in the medieval kingdom and the ancient Greek polis: "Both are conceived as communities in which men in company pursue *the* human good and not merely as—what the modern liberal state takes itself to be—providing the arena in which each individual seeks his or her own private good" (172). The American Constitution with its checks and balances and its tone of wary hopefulness and dark suspicion, a document that reads in places like a political version of a prenuptial agreement between survivors of particularly rocky unions, is the apotheosis of that vision—and Franklin's fingerprints are all over it.

In defending Franklin against MacIntyre's charges, it is useful to recall earlier stated reservations about MacIntyre's assumptions, particularly his assumption that "ideal conditions of usage" must prevail for right action to occur. Franklin's virtues, which are mainly designed to help people make their way in a fallen world, are shown off to least advantage in the context of ideal conditions. He is, in the long tradition of American pragmatism celebrated by Burke, a "meliorist" (*ATH* 12), eschewing superlatives for comparatives and best for better, content to seek the "purest means available" in given circumstances.

If one judges Franklin by MacIntyre's imperative to choose the one true means prescribed by a given order, he might well sound suspiciously emotivist. But if one views Franklin from a Burkean perspective, the sins attributed to him by MacIntyre may look at worst to be errors and at best virtues. Consider thus the matter of *pleonexia*, that ancient vice made respectable by Franklin, according to MacIntyre (183). Burke is considerably more tolerant of *pleonexia*, which he in turn interprets more broadly. Because Burke assumes at the outset a world in which difference, division, and hierarchy prevail, the seeking of "'advantage' (*pleonexia*)" (*RM* 60) is seen as a "reasonable and ethical enough" end for human beings to pursue.

> Surely all doctrines can at least begin by agreeing that human effort aims at "advantage" of one sort or another, though there is room for later disputes as to whether advantage in general, or particular advantages are to be conceived idealistically, materialistically, or even cynically. (*RM* 61)

Clearly in Burke and arguably in Franklin, the end of advantage-seeking cannot be disentangled from the pursuit of all other goals anymore than private and public interests can ever be neatly sorted. One may, after all, seek advantage in the name of world peace as readily as one may seek it in the name of "purely individualist cunning or aggrandizement" (*RM* 61).

Franklin's version of advantage-seeking is usually treated under the heading of that most eighteenth-century virtue, "enlightened self-interest." While enlightened self-interest has come for many to be synonymous with "individualist cunning or aggrandizement," it too can be recuperated by treating it rhetorically as a matter of "how much or how little" enlightened one's self-interests are. It is, for example, in one's self-interest that the planet not be rendered uninhabitable or that the value of human life, including one's own, not be unduly cheapened. As a rhetorical device, the appeal to enlightened self-interest may be the most effective way to increase adherence to altruistic notions. In this regard, many of Franklin's most controversial arguments are, Rex Burns reminds us, his most rhetorically marked writing. "Way to Wealth," thus, was written after more straightforward appeals to virtue—for its own sake—failed and was fashioned as

> an appeal to the unenlightened which led them unknowingly and relatively painlessly to virtue via the lesser pursuit of wealth. . . . [It] demonstrates his use of the persona to assume a voice that speaks the audience's vocabulary and logic. Although Franklin's means were material, his purpose was to lead his readers to enlightened self-interest, and the promised material success is in reality only the first step in the attainment of a greater goal. (10)

John Cawelti extends Burns's argument by claiming that Franklin did not "confuse . . . economic success and moral merit . . . [and] viewed the pursuit of wealth as a purely pragmatic matter. In order to achieve higher human ends, the individual had to free himself from the bondage of economic necessity" (53). Cawelti's gloss on means-end relations in Franklin here echoes Franklin's avowed model Cotton Mather, who encouraged thrift and industry in the name of accumulating "wealth somewhat beyond one's basic needs" (Burns 1) so that one could then contribute one's surplus to socially useful ends.

> All property that is necessary to a man, for the conservation of the individual and the propagation of the species is his natural right, which none can justly deprive him of; but all property superfluous to such purpose is the property of the public, who, by their laws, have created it, and who may therefore by others dispose of it. (qtd. in Carey 207)

For Franklin, wealth is justifiable as a necessary condition for public virtue, just as the adoption of a persona may be justified as a necessary condition for public acceptance. These may be "impure" means, to be sure, but they are arguably the purest available in the given circumstances. Franklin's argument offers no guarantee that one's ultimate ends will be beneficent rather than simply self-serving. But it does underscore the necessity of material means, however grubby, to spiritual ends, however lofty.

Mather and Franklin for the Masses:
The Nineteenth-Century Success Handbooks

Early in the nineteenth century, success books began exploiting Americans' growing fascination with a new sort of secular success, simultaneously fueling Americans' longing for prosperity and reassuring them that the only path to bounty was the high road of piety. The creation of a mass audience for such works coincides with a "key moment" in the creation of modernity—the movement of production outside the home.

> As, and to the extent that, work moves outside the household and is put to the service of impersonal capital, the realm of work tends to become separated from everything but the service of biological survival and the reproduction of the labor force, on the one hand, and that of institutionalized acquisitiveness, on the other. (MacIntyre 227)

While MacIntyre's version of this argument is more hyperbolic than most, his conclusions are consistent with others'. These drastic changes in the economy required new codes of behavior and new ways of measuring success. But success writers of the day ignored the new realities and protested the new accounting measures—even as they exploited widespread insecurities to which the changes gave rise.

The eighteenth-century tensions between piety and profit, individual self-interest and communal good, grew ever more difficult to harmonize. The "yeoman's dream," a dominant eighteenth-century vision of the good life, featuring rural holdings large enough to sustain a "competence" but small enough to require the interdependence of land holders, looked ever more vestigial. But the dream maintained (and maintains) a tenacious hold on the American imagination, and in the face of industrialization, mechanization, and urbanization, success authors reaffirmed the dream, however remote from most Americans' everyday lives, rather than charted new realities.

> To judge from the rather great discrepancy between the recommendations of the most popular self-help books and the behavior of Americans as described in the testimony of observers, the primary function of the self-improvement handbook was not so much to guide behavior as to explain the dynamic changes of American life in terms of badly shaken traditional verities. (Cawelti 47)

This focus on traditional values is partly explained, Judy Hilkey suggests, by the background of success authors, most of whom were clergymen who naturally stressed character, exhorting their readers to "internalize authority and self-control as a means to both individual success and social stability" (67). Moreover, stressing character served also to divert readers from possibly noticing how little the clergy had to say about worldly matters they knew so slenderly. Which is why, according to Irvin G. Wyllie, one finds in

> these self-help handbooks [so] little practical advice on advertising methods, accounting systems, investment procedures, production techniques and other such mundane matters. Technical considerations are quite remote from their main discussion which revolves around private character and morality. (34)

Throughout the century, as the brute facts of history reduced the status of the yeoman's dream from a dominant cultural ideal to a residual utopian notion, as entrepreneurship, mental and moral agility, and calculative intelligence displaced pluck, punctuality, reliability, and loyalty as keys to success in the actual America, success writers clung to their eighteenth-century norms partly out of concern for their readers' souls and partly because their education, experience, and place in the world left them innocent of workplace realities. The only succor they could realistically offer their audiences was a reaffirmation of faith in the traditional pieties.

This may explain why, by the time of the Gilded Age, the primary audience for the success manual was not the urban go-getter but "a rural and small town population of native-born Protestants, people of modest means and modest educations, yet people of some aspiration, not the destitute or the dispossessed" (Hilkey 22). Farm families bought the manuals for their sons, gratefully paying the equivalent of "one-quarter to one-half the weekly earnings of the average wage earner" (25) in hopes of demystifying, if not mastering, the new realities.

After 1880, the accelerating pace of agricultural mechanization initiated a precipitous decline in farm labor, foretelling the virtual disappearance of family farms by the end of the twentieth century. In conjunction with a devastating two-decade-long depression, one can readily understand why so many rural Americans felt a powerful need to succeed and an equally powerful desire to proclaim the primacy of values that had previously sheltered them from such catastrophes. While still "predominantly a rural nation," late-nineteenth-century America was moving rapidly away from its rural origins and in the process marginalizing "a very large ma-jority of the American population, a fact that no doubt heightened the sense of crisis in the hinterland" (Hilkey 105).

But despite all the disturbances set in motion by these shifts—there were "close to 37,000 [strikes], involving 7 million workers on record between 1881 and 1905" (Trachtenberg 80), and between 1875 and 1910 "state troops were called out nearly 500 times to subdue labor unrest" (Hilkey 123)—one would be hard-pressed to find any evidence of social protest or any signs of labor-management tension in nineteenth-century success manuals. While metaphors of competition predominate in the success literature of the period, the major competitors are not the usual antagonists in the economic struggle: "[T]he two great classes were not capital and labor, but rather the successful and the failures, the industri-ous and the lazy, the honest and the spendthrift" (Hilkey 88).[5]

In turn, the image of the good worker that emerges in the handbooks is exemplified by the good servant in the success authors' favorite bibli-cal parable, the parable of the talents from the Gospel of Matthew. The good servant, it will be recalled, reinvests and doubles the number of talents left him by his master, while the bad servant buries his in the ground out of fear. The good servant is celebrated by his master for his industry, while the bad servant is pronounced "wicked and slothful." Success authors took this parable as

> a prescription for the "good worker" idealized from the point of view of the employer: an employee whose honesty, industry, and initiative multiplied the employer's wealth. The ambiguity of the image of the "good and faithful servant" captures a paradox that pervades the success manual genre. (Hilkey 98)

The paradox alluded to here is that of the totally self-reliant, but absolutely subservient, worker. Success authors resolved tensions between these seem-ingly contradictory traits by sedulously dissociating self-reliance from a capacity for independent thought, equating it instead with the alacrity that one displayed in doing management's bidding before management thought to ask. (Today such a worker would doubtless be celebrated as a "low main-tenance" employee.) Questioning one's work conditions or the charac-ter of one's employer, meanwhile, was considered weak and effeminate behavior in a genre that prized manliness above all virtues.

Loyal, manly workers were stoic, adept at turning unfortunate circum-stance to personal gain, strengthening their character by adversity and emerging from every crisis a stronger, better person. Every *culpa* imagined by the success book author turns out to be *felix*. To be sure, not all individual success seekers recover from their falls, but their demise turns out to be better for the rest of us, since only those not fated to succeed fall short. In the words of Orison Swett Marden, always among the more muscular of the Christian success apologists, "In all my acquaintance I have never known a man to be drowned who was worth saving" (*Pushing* 139). Failure, in that curious mixture of Darwinist brio and Protestant apology that marks the prose of nineteenth-century success writers, is God's way of cleaning up the gene pool.

The Mass Market Magazine and the Death of Success Handbooks

As the century wore on, success writers' attempts to mask the manifest contradictions between their ideologies and the realities facing their audiences grew successively less compelling. Early in the century, thus, when relatively few among their audience faced failure, axioms like Emerson's Law of Compensation made sound sense; later, when a majority of their rural audience faced failure, those same principles seemed to mock them. Finally, in the last decade of the nineteenth century, a defining moment occurred that signaled the beginning of the end for the success handbook.

Richard Ohmann marks that moment, with becoming reticence, by claiming that "1893 was indeed a year when something happened" (25) in American culture. While lacking the dramatic impact of Virginia Woolf's pronouncement that the world changed in 1910, Ohmann's pronouncement may hold up better on closer inspection. For while Woolf is responding to a specific event, the 1910 post-impressionist exhibit at the Grafton Gallery, whose immediate impact is limited to a small and elite group, Ohmann is responding to a phenomenon, a change in the marketing practices of American magazines, whose impact is immediate and enormous among a much broader population. Specifically, 1893 is the year that publishers, led by McClure, began to sell their publications at or below cost and to derive their profit from the sale of advertising, the rates for which were determined by circulation. With this change in marketing strategy, publishers' emphasis shifted from selling magazines to readers to selling readers to advertisers. The causes of this shift are too numerous to detail here. But the consequences of the shift for the formation of consumer culture generally and for success rhetoric specifically are enormous.

First, one needs to understand that the new mass market magazines found their audience not among the disappearing rural population but among the emergent urban "professional managerial class," the rapidly growing army of "service sector" workers hungry for a new, progressive vision of the world with values closer to the professional codes by which they conducted business everyday and expressed in prose closer to their workplace vernacular. Enter George Horace Lorimer, editor of the *Saturday Evening Post* and author of *Letters from a Self-Made Merchant to His Son*, his best-selling collection of *Post* columns. No one catches the spirit of the age or exemplifies the new mode of success rhetoric better than Lorimer, whose popularity is reflected in the eightfold growth of the *Post* from 250,000 subscribers at the turn of the century to nearly 2 million subscribers by 1914 (Greene 174). His *Letters* deserves closer attention insofar as the volume exemplifies this shift and anticipates much that is to come.

The putative author of Lorimer's letters is meatpacker John "Old Gorgon" Graham, and the recipient is his son, Pierrepont, initially a Harvard freshman and ultimately a member of Graham Senior's firm. The style and sentiment of the wisdom that Graham Senior passes along to Graham Junior is captured in passages like the following:

> [Y]ou've got to add dynamite and ginger and jounce to your equipment if you want to get the other half that's coming to you. You've got to believe that the Lord made the first hog with the Graham brand burned in the skin. . . . You've got to feel the same personal solicitude over a bill of goods that strays off to a competitor as a parson over a backslider, and hold special services to bring it back into the fold. . . . You've got to eat hog, think hog, dream hog—in short, go the whole hog if you're going to win out in the pork-packing business. (142–43)

For all his bluster, Lorimer clearly intended "Old Gorgon" to be a sympathetic character giving voice to views his audience doubtless found sagacious and commonsensical even as they were titillated by their irreverence. Any residual Puritan concern to maintain harmony, to mitigate the corrosive effects of competition on the social compact, is long gone.

If there were any doubts about the residual status of the yeoman's dream by the century's end, a brief sampling of "Old Gorgon" Graham's assorted sallies will erase them. Thus, for example, he enthusiastically recommends going along to get along ("You'll meet a good many people on the road that you won't like, but the house needs their business" [132–33], and, "There isn't any such thing as being your own boss in this world unless you're a tramp, and then there's the constable" [82]), using appearances to best advantage ("There's nothing helps convince some men that a thing has merit like a little gold on the label" [95] [the punch line to a tale of fobbing off surplus corned beef by changing the label and raising the price], and, "Appearances are deceitful, I know, but so long as they are, there's nothing like having them deceive for us instead of against us" [178]), and marrying a pretty woman ("Beauty is only skin deep, but that's deep enough to satisfy any reasonable man" [116]).

Apropos of this last declaration, Graham offers a parenthetical insight—"(I want to say right here that to get any sense out of a proverb I usually find that I have to turn it inside out)" (116)—applicable to all his proverbs. Old Gorgon is an inside-out version of Mather's "Good Gentleman," and his explanation of success makes clear how thoroughly the secular has displaced the religious: "There are two unpardonable sins in this world—success and failure. Those who succeed can't forgive a fellow for being a failure, and those who fail can't forgive him for being a success. If you do succeed, though, you will be too busy to bother very much about what the failures think" (182–83). Or as he more starkly puts it: "Poverty [like money] talks . . . but nobody wants to hear what it has to say" (59). So much for the denizens of the yeoman's dream, those simple, steadfast souls with the gift for seeing past deceptive appearances to the heart of things. Lorimer's Graham has learned from hard experience about the cupidity and vanity of human nature—and the best ways to take full advantage of human foibles.

The success handbook did not, of course, disappear overnight. The aforementioned Orison Swett Marden published *Rising in the World: Or, Architects of Fate* in 1897, and it sold well. But even a cursory reading of the book suggests why the genre would not outlive its dwindling audience of farm families and why it was so readily displaced by the sort of wisdom Lorimer and the *Post* were dispensing to less credulous urban readers. According to the frontispiece, the book is "[d]esigned to inspire youth to character building, self-culture and noble achievement." While published only a few years before Lorimer's *Letters*, it seems to come from a long bygone century. Every chapter is copiously illustrated with legendary and historical incidents and stirring accounts of success achieved against great odds through acts of uncompromising virtue. In fact, the illustrations and anecdotes overwhelm the scattered bits of decidedly impractical proverbial advice (and Marden *never* turns a proverb inside out) that the author uses to glue his anecdotes together. But whatever the differences in sentiment and method, the most important differences between Marden and Lorimer lie at the level of voice and prose style.

The most striking of these differences is in their mode of address. Lorimer's epistolary address allows him to speak directly to his reader, through young Graham, as "you." Marden, meanwhile, to the extent that agency is ever visible in his work, is relentlessly third person, the voice of history, not a single individual. Marden weaves his way back and forth between accounts of good deeds done by the archetypal aspiring "young man," magnificent deeds accomplished by legendary "great men," misdeeds committed by lackluster anonyms—weak-charactered "they's" who mostly lurk in the shadows—and, most importantly, triumphs achieved in the subjunctive imperative by "the man" who would heed Marden's advice. Hence, in the matter of decisiveness, referred to by Old Gorgon in the passage above as "getting the other half that's coming to you," Marden has this to say:

> The man who would forge to the front in this competitive age must be a man of prompt and determined decision; like Caesar, he must burn his ships behind him, and make retreat forever impossible. When he draws his sword he must throw his scabbard away, lest in a moment of discouragement and irresolution he be tempted to sheathe it. He must nail his colors to the mast as Nelson did in battle, determined to sink with his ship if he cannot conquer. Prompt decision and sublime audacity have carried many a successful man over perilous crises where deliberation would have been ruin. (369)

Beyond the figurative nuances that distinguish burning one's ships, unsheathing one's sword, or nailing one's colors to the mast from "going whole hog," much separates the two passages. The language of Lorimer is colloquial, oral, and direct. The author's persona looms immediately before us as he delivers rapid-fire imperatives through the singular "you" that is Pierrepont directly to the plural "you" that is us, his readers. The language of Marden, meanwhile, is measured, abstract, allusive, and distant, more in the register of the schoolmaster than the bigger-than-life, semi-mythic "Gorgon" Graham. The audience imagined and shaped by these two forms of discourse is as different as the urban and rural environs where their readerships reside. And it was already clear which of the two readerships would flourish in the coming century.

While Americans will continue to give notional assent to the major elements of the yeoman's dream—the importance of independence and frugality, of hard work and direct contact with nature—these homely virtues increasingly assume the ceremonial status of family memorabilia that Americans keep locked up in sideboards or boxed up in attics, pieces of dishware or postcards from long-dead ancestors not known personally to their inheritors, who hang on to them out of nostalgia, or respect for the past, or a possible flutter in the commemorative plate market, rather than for any use value these keepsakes might possess. With the waning of the populist movement in the 1890s, the last nationally organized political expression of the yeoman's dream faded from the scene. Those who displaced Marden and his ilk were in turn products of a "recessive gene" in the nineteenth-century success genre, represented by a succession of hyperbolic, fraudulent, unabashedly acquisitive folk-heroes-cum-con-artists who may have represented us more acutely to ourselves than we care to admit.

The Nineteenth-Century Success Hucksters

While the clergy-authors of success handbooks struggled to shore up the yeoman's dream and a quasi-religious vision of success, there existed in America an undercurrent, a success rhetoric demimonde, of those who reveled in the new unbuttoned materialism of the day. The latter group consisted of legendary and semi-mythical characters like Davy Crockett, P. T. Barnum, Brother Jonathan, Sam Slick, and Simon Suggs. In them we begin to get closer to the actual spirit of the times, not to mention to twentieth-century success gurus.

Perhaps the keynote of that spirit is best captured by Simon Suggs's famous motto, "IT IS GOOD TO BE SHIFTY IN A NEW COUNTRY," a sentiment echoed in Robert Coover's *The Public Burning* by Sam Slick, an "American Autolycus," with "cunning powers of conjuration, mutation and magical consumption" (8). Daniel Hoffman, meanwhile, calls Sam a "masquerader" whose "image . . . exists on a psychological plane comparable to that of adolescent or pre-adolescent fantasy" (79). These nineteenth-century tricksters are mostly confidence men with a tendency to celebrate rather than disguise their predatory designs on us. But for all that, we usually forgive them, like so many "bad boys," in the name of their high spirits and humor, their capacity for acting on forbidden impulses and for making us laugh. As in the case of the century's master huckster, P. T. Barnum, "audiences expected humbug and admired his skill at it. There was a kind of inside joke between the humbug and the suckers" (Fox and Lears 8). Such characters show up in our fiction, our history, and, of late, our airwaves, selling elixers, magazine subscriptions, lightning rods, Bibles, success handbooks, ab-tightening devices, and Jesus with a wink and a pitch. And for many of us, they hold a fascination that the more sober, less ironic success rhetoricians with their pieties, solemnities, and homilies can never quite evoke.

Throughout the nineteenth century, certainly, a growing element of the population found orthodox success rhetoric more cloying than reassuring, more unctuous than inspirational, and took heart from those who undermined the genre, including, in addition to the hucksters, our foremost humorist, Mark Twain, whose "The Story of a Good Little Boy" is a scathing send-up of traditional success rhetoric from the perspective of an author who always found more to love in scalawags than seraphs. The story's hero, Jacob Blivens, "always obeyed his parents, no matter how absurd and unreasonable their demands," observed every rule and convention imaginable, and "read all the Sunday school books" (67) to learn how to act. His major goal in life, in fact, is to one day be the subject of such a book. Despite following the formulas laid out in his books to the letter, Jacob experiences one disappointment after another: "[N]othing ever turned out with him the way it turned out with the good little boys in the books. They always had a good time, and the bad boys had the broken legs; but in his case there was a screw loose somewhere, and it all happened just the other way" (68). In the end, Jacob gets blown up in the act of seeking out some bad boys to admonish, admonishment being one of the obligatory acts expected of all budding success pilgrims. Tongue firmly in cheek, Twain concludes: "[T]hus perished the good little boy who did the best he could, but didn't come out according to the book. Every boy who ever did as he did prospered except him. His case is truly remarkable. It will probably never be accounted for" (70).

Jacob, like so many adherents of the handbook tradition, from Don Quixote to Jay Gatz, lacked the "creative self-awareness" to read reflexively and imaginatively. And in following the book's prescriptions literally, he does himself in. In many ways, Twain's critique of success books is as applicable today as it was then. Indeed, one measure of its continued salience is its similarity to contemporary critiques of the success ethos, including Joseph Heller's *Catch-22*.

Catch-22: In Praise of Minimalist Dreams

Ostensibly a book about war, *Catch-22* is in fact a book about the *business* of war and, according to Heller, "'an encyclopedia of the current mental atmosphere'" (qtd. in Bradbury vii), which includes the sixteen years of postwar prosperity preceding the publication of his novel, seven of which Heller spent working in corporate America. It offers a microcosm of midcentury American culture with a particular emphasis on the impact of market values and corporate ethos on that culture. First published in 1961, it would sell 7 million copies in the next ten years as the life of the Vietnam War and the lives of David Halberstam's "best and brightest," recruited from corporate America to conduct that war, relentlessly imitated Heller's art. Thus, for example, when a military spokesman claimed during the Tet offensive that an American unit had been compelled to destroy a Vietnamese village in order to save the village, a generation of readers brought up on *Catch-22*, remembering the defenseless Italian village that General Peckem ordered wiped out because it afforded the perfect opportunity for a "neat bombing pattern," smiled ruefully and nodded in unison. Some of us, to be sure, may silently have added that "*Only* villages in need of saving are to be destroyed," thereby converting the observation to a rule with a catch, like the dozens of rules with catches boilerplated from catch-22, "the best [catch] there is" (47).

The logic of catch-22 goes to the heart of the workings of modernist institutions reliant less on coercion than on their denizens' capacity for self-management to get things done. The logic of the rule, the logic of modernist workplaces, is to simultaneously offer and restrict choice. The soldiers in Heller's novel must freely choose to do what the increasingly elusive authorities wish done. While coercive force looms ominously behind the various memos, directives, and policy changes that move the novel along, the authors of these dicta go to elaborate lengths to hide their identities and disguise their intentions. Prosecuting and winning the war is little more than an afterthought for those atop the hierarchy, whose self-serving schemes and scams absorb them entirely. Absent any visible source of human authority, the various rules take on a life of their own. Catch-22, the essence of this peculiarly modernist mode of control, spawns dozens of similar rules. Thus, for example, the rule governing the asking of questions during military briefings: "[T]he only people permitted to ask questions were those who never did" (36). The logic is always the same. Start with a prohibition—you must never quit flying more missions, you must never ask questions—then work backwards to a rule that appears to legitimate the prohibited behavior, but adds a requirement that is either impossible to meet or cancels the effect of the behavior licensed by the rule. Those who fall under the jurisdiction of the proscription are de jure free to do the de facto impossible. Sure, you can ask questions, so long as "you" are a person who never asks questions; sure, you should save villages, as long as you destroy them; sure, you can quit flying missions, if you are insane—keeping in mind that by seeking permission to quit, you vouchsafe your sanity. Ontic logos is no more, and only the law of contradiction remains to enforce a perfect, if absurd, consistency.

All these elaborate manipulations raise an obvious question. Why not simply use force, which clearly lies with the rule-makers? This is exactly the question that Yossarian puts to his arch-capitalist antagonist, Milo Minderbinder, after Milo has cheated an Italian thief out of a bedsheet by pretending to trade him some dates.

> "Why didn't you just hit him over the head and take the bedsheet away from him?" Yossarian asked.
>
> Pressing his lips together with dignity, Milo shook has head. "That would have been most unjust," he scolded firmly. "Force is wrong, and two wrongs never make a right. It was much better my way. When I held the dates out to him and reached for the bedsheet, he probably thought I was offering to trade."
>
> "What were you doing?"
>
> "Actually, I *was* offering to trade, but since he doesn't understand English, I can always deny it."
>
> "Suppose he gets angry and wants the dates?"
>
> "Why, we'll just hit him over the head and take them away from him," Milo answered without hesitation. (68)

What Milo offers here is a lesson in the subtle differences between tyranny and hegemony. In its nuanced distinctions, Heller's fictional exchange recalls an earlier, actual exchange between the "father" of modern management, Frederick Taylor, and a congressional committee before which Taylor testified in 1912.

> [I]t is the duty of those who are in management to use all the arts of persuasion first to get the workman to conform to the rules, and after that has been done, *then to gradually increase the severity of the language* until practically, before you are thru, *the powers of the English language have been exhausted in an effort to make the man do what he ought to do.* And if that fails, then in the interest of the workman, some more severe type of discipline should be resorted to. (qtd. in Banta, *Taylored* 133, her emphasis)

Taylor's logic here follows the logic of his model for modern organization. The routinization and deskilling of labor meant that one could widen the "spans of control" between numberless interchangeable (probably foreign-born) workers and a few rational (surely native-born) managers. Avoiding labor unrest and bloody conflict—conditions that gave rise to Taylorism in the first place—entailed manipulating workers, whose numbers and physical strength were now overwhelmingly superior, through managerial cunning rather than coercion. In this context, success rhetoric will play an increasingly critical role among the "arts of persuasion" in getting workers "voluntarily" to conform with management's designs.

These distinctly twentieth-century management strategies are evident throughout *Catch-22*, most vividly in the workings of its dominant institution—not the U.S. Air Force, but M&M Enterprises. The M&M stands for Milo Minderbinder, the master manipulator of the novel, Heller's own version of the "American Autoclytus" whose goal is not to win the war but merely to "put it on a businesslike basis" (262). M&M Enterprises is the ultimate "win-win" organization, a "mart" in which "every man will have a share" (68)—though one is never sure how to go about redeeming one's share or assessing its worth at any given moment. How, for example, might Yossarian peg the value of his share in M&M Enterprises when his friend Snowden is dying of shock and he opens the first-aid kit to find a "cleanly lettered note that said: 'What's good for M&M Enterprises is good for the country'" (446) instead of twelve Syrettes of morphine?

Collective nouns like "the country" in the above note, along with personal pronouns like "we" and "you," play a treacherous role throughout *Catch-22*. "We" is rarely everyone, and "you" is rarely anyone in particular. Thus, Colonel Cathcart, who is as keen to secure himself a place in the *Saturday Evening Post* as Twain's "good little boy" is to get himself enshrined in a Sunday school book, endorses a scheme dreamed up by Sergeant, née Corporal, Whitcomb (bad guys are distinguishable from good guys in *Catch-22* by the tendency of the former to get promoted and of the latter to get killed) that entails sending out a letter of condolence that begins: "Dear Mrs., Mr., Miss, or Mr. and Mrs.: Words cannot express the deep personal grief I experienced when your husband, son, father, or brother was killed, wounded or reported missing in action" (289).

Cathcart's condolences are formally equivalent to the condolences offered up by recorded phone messages one receives when put on hold by one of America's numerous "customer-centered" enterprises: "Your call is very important to us," we are assured. "Please stay on the line until the next available personal service representative becomes available." What the message reminds us of, and the longer we stay on the line the more strongly we are reminded, is the difference exploited in Cathcart's note between the singular "you" who is a customer and the generic "you" who is a consumer. The former, Raymond Williams reminds us, has "some degree of regular and continuing relationship to a supplier," while the latter is a "more abstract figure in a more abstract market" (*Keywords* 79). Consumers are the demand side's version of the supply side's "punctual self," apparitions who exist only as "needs and wants and particular ways of satisfying them" (*Keywords* 79).

The power to transform individual "you's" and particular "we's" into generic instruments of one's own advancement is the exclusive possession of malign forces of *Catch-22*. Only proper names betray the guilty and protect the innocent. Hence, Scheisskopf (who dreams of wiring his men together to create the perfect parade) and Peckem (who is indeed full of evil), Major Major and Minderbinder—all live out their names with a vengeance (or in the case of Korn and Dreedle, with utter banality). The good characters in the novel, meanwhile, possess names that are not so much positive as mysterious, uncategorizable, like Yossarian, that most acrobatically elusive and least heroic airman with his indelibly un-American name.

Nowhere is this principle more clearly at work than in the case of "Orr," who, more than Yossarian, is the hero of the novel. Orr's name first of all invokes the homonym "oar," an anticipation of the Dixie cup spoon he will use to paddle, perhaps, to Sweden. Unlike Popinjay, whose Kafkaesque trial exemplifies the arbitrariness of both language and authority in the novel, Orr will never be "up shit creek . . . without a paddle" (81). He *is* the paddle. Orr is also "Or," the none-of-the-above alternative to all the impossible conundrums and catch-22s that ensnare and ultimately kill so many of the other characters. He is a trickster who loves playing with language in imaginative ways. Thus his game of putting crab apples into his cheeks: "'Why?'" Yossarian wants to know. "Orr tittered triumphantly. 'Because they're better than horse chestnuts,' he answered" (23). While formally similar to the sorts of absurd language games practiced by the malignant characters in the novel, Orr's language games are self-consciously playful, designed to "fool" the other person in a game whose end is laughter, mutual acknowledgment of the absurdity, not manipulation.

And Orr is, not incidentally, the most "Franklinian" character in the novel. In a world dominated by exchange relations and evil masked as reason, Orr is about meliorism and survival. In the spirit of Franklin, Orr creates a gasoline stove, one of many small "utilitarian pleasures" he creates, to warm his and Yossarian's tent. And like Franklin, Orr is an experimenter, endlessly taking apart and putting back together the faucet to his gasoline stove, endlessly practicing crash landings, and endlessly adapting whatever is at hand to his larger purposes, like his Dixie cup spoon. But unlike Milo, the ultimate shape-shifter in whom dwells the adolescent spirit of Sam Slick, there is a fixed purpose to the roles and disguises Orr assumes.

Homely, dwarfish, the master of minor schemes, little comforts, and playful jests, Orr triumphs by plugging doggedly away at the possible. And even the one time he apparently violates his code and bashes Appleby, his action serves an important symbolic function. Appleby, it would appear, is Orr's doppleganger, his dark twin easily confused with our "apple cheeked" hero. He is what D. H. Lawrence fears Franklin to be, the bloodless instrumentalist, humorless perfectionist, American as apple pie. Appleby never loses at Ping-Pong or billiards and never misses on the firing range. He's "rotten with perfection" in Kenneth Burke's memorable phrase, and unctuously so. But his perfections serve no purpose other than to turn play into the zero-sum game of work in which only the outcome matters, and that outcome is always foretold. It's this life-denying spirit of Appleby's that Orr must exorcise to make way for his own decidedly impure and limited notions of success.

In a the midst of a Kafkaesque dystopia of "excellence" and inversion, where, says Yossarian, "'When I look up, I see people cashing in. I don't see heaven or saints or angels. I see people cashing in on every decent impulse and every human tragedy'" (455), Orr teaches us to keep our gaze resolutely fixed on the tasks at hand, tasks that are useful to others as well as to ourselves, and to perform those tasks competently without worrying about the rewards extrinsic to their doing or the inevitable corruption that ultimately attends them. Orr leaves it to the Cathcarts and the Peckems to "aspire" and endlessly strive for ranks as meaningless as Milo's shares, choosing instead to become one of those "good grey preterite souls whose only achievement is that they are demonstrably 'human'" (Banta, *Failure* 242). It is a vision of success almost entirely absent from the most popular versions of success rhetoric in twentieth-century America.

2 | Bruce Barton, Advertising Man: The Man Nobody Knows

The chapter title is something of a play on words. Bruce Barton was indeed an "advertising man," a founding partner of Batten, Barton, Durstine & Osborn, one of the early giants of the American advertising industry, a frequent spokesperson for his profession in popular magazines of the day, and a shrewd practitioner of the arts of consumer and political persuasion.[1] He's also Advertising Man, *homo advertisus*, the very embodiment of a species, the incarnation of a *weltanschauung*, almost, like his alter ego Jesus Christ, a superhero of American business. And, alas, he's also, like the Christ he imagines, often cited but seldom discussed. Advertising was Barton's defining activity and in turn the defining activity of his age, and *The Man Nobody Knows* (1925), his popular retelling of the Gospels, is a book that expresses the logic and the values of that belief system as lucidly—and unselfconsciously—as any book of its time.

The rise of advertising is one of a series of cultural, economic, and social changes, including incorporation, consumerism, and the movement toward national media that redefined success, not only in terms of the career and personal possibilities opened up and foreclosed by these shifts, but in the myths, symbols, and icons used to embody the desired ends of success and the approved means of its achievement. The logic, language, and values of advertising saturate Barton's text; by century's end, advertising would be the lingua franca of success texts.

Bruce Barton: Man of His Time

A November 1, 1930, *New Yorker* profile of Barton, then forty-four years old and at the height of his advertising success, noted:

> One senses that underneath his apparently perfectly self-controlled
> exterior there is much nervous energy. He always seems to be at
> odds with himself—a hail-fellow-well-met who enjoys a burlesque
> show and a drink but who writes piously about churches and mor-
> als and believes in what he writes. (qtd. in Fox 110–11)

Tall, handsome, and stylish, Barton wrote warmly and often about the joys of family life; he also had a very public and messy affair with an employee that ended with her conviction (the first in New York state history) on a charge of extortion after she demanded $50,000 from Barton to suppress a novel she had written about a thinly disguised version of their affair. He was a vocal apostle of boosterism and the breezy, attaboy Babbitry of the day who also read Spengler and Ortega y Gassett and once checked himself into a mental institution for an extended stay. He was advertising's point man in its vast public campaign to reform its dubious image, even as he privately expressed misgivings about the value of his profession. He was a one-time author of Horatio Alger–style fiction who ultimately did as much as anyone to popularize a decidedly more Nietzschean view of success in America.

Perhaps Barton's most basic paradox, the one on which *The Man Nobody Knows* is grounded, involves his penchant for inverting business and religion so that religion becomes a vehicle for understanding business, while the lives of contemporary businessmen become models for the life of Christ. This may account for the legendary Maxwell Perkins's rejection of the book, for which he foresaw healthy sales, as irreverent. Because Barton was, like a disproportionate number of American advertising pioneers, the offspring of a minister, his seeming inversion of secular and religious values may seem odd. In fact, Barton's religious views comport well with those of his father and with the temper of his times, from whence arose New Thought and various other strains of theology that persist today under the name New Age. Barton's father, William E. Barton, was a liberal Protestant clergyman and prolific author of more than fifty books. He was, moreover, a therapeutic religionist who had, Barton *fils* assures us, "'less interest in calling [his parishioners] to repentance, and more interest in cheering them up'" (qtd. in Fox 102). He was not alone. According to Jackson Lears, American churches of the time were undergoing a profound shift from "a Protestant ethos of salvation through self-denial toward a therapeutic ethos stressing self realization in this world" (Fox and Lears 4).

The ties between religion and advertising, then as now, are strong, as evidenced by James Twitchell's list of nine "early apostles of advertising" (not including Barton) with "deep evangelical roots" (33). Twitchell in fact apologizes for the triteness of a "hoary comparison of advertising with religion. . . . I am hardly the first to recognize that advertising is the gospel of redemption in the fallen world of capitalism" (30). Beyond their common promise to transform audiences, in the case of advertising through consumption and in the case of religion through reverence, the links between the two are extensive. Especially in Barton's day, advertisers' attempts to foreground those links can be seen as a legitimation strategy of the sort that arriviste professions traditionally employ to justify claims on privileged social space. In the case of advertisers, several factors lent a certain measure of credibility to their claims. In their new and mysterious role as the primary instrument of "distribution" in the economy, advertisers were a crucial, if largely intangible, element of American capitalism. Many observers, not just advertisers, shared the view that advertising was essential to the prevention of under- or overproduction and the economic spasms that attended such miscalculations. Advertisers were foremost among that host of intermediaries within the American economic system that at the turn of the century "took up positions in previously simpler market relations, and added complexity or mystery to certain exchanges of meaning" (Ohmann 104).

In sum, their powers were impressive (or at least they were quite skillful at persuading the world of their magical abilities), they operated according to largely mysterious "scientific laws" unknown to the uninitiated, and they were themselves almost totally invisible. And they were sometimes paid salaries of deific proportions. Claude Hopkins's 1908 salary of $185,000 dwarfed the earnings of the day's sports stars—it would be twenty years before Babe Ruth became the first sports legend to earn an $80,000 salary, which even then was the cause of considerable controversy.[2] Given all these factors, it is not hard to see how advertisers of the day could begin to believe in their own myth and sacralize their function.

However singular Barton may appear today, thus, he is a creature of his age. His tendency to conflate religion, business, and advertising was anticipated by numerous predecessors and echoed by many contemporaries. Indeed, relative to some of these other figures, Barton's claims look rather modest. Consider, for example, one of Barton's best-known predecessors in the business-religion line, the redoubtable Henry Ward Beecher, a prominent Brooklyn clergyman who extolled the virtues of trusses in magazines and, in a particularly slippery bit of reasoning, touted Pear's Soap as a form of religious salvation while simultaneously rationalizing his commercial endorsement in a six-term analogy executed in one astonishing sentence: "If cleanliness is next to godliness, soap must be considered as a means of Grace, and a clergyman who recommends moral things should be willing to recommend soap" (qtd. in Bledstein 52). He ultimately wrote a book on the life of Christ from which he "both anticipated enormous profits" and a boost in "public morality" (Bledstein 53).

One of Barton's contemporaries is worthy of more extended notice: G. Stanley Hall, a psychologist, wartime propagandist, and college president, who, after rejecting conventional morality and religious dogma in the name of "morale," also wrote a version of Christ's life, preparing the way for Barton's peculiar blend of business and liberal Christian theology. Hall remains an important figure in the history of psychology's emergence as a field and was a respected voice in his day. His 1920 book, *Morale: The Supreme Standard of Life and Conduct*, meanwhile, can be read either as the apotheosis of nineteenth-century "muscular Christianity" or its secular successor. Either way, its affinities to *The Man Nobody Knows* (*TMNK*) are unmistakable, particularly in Hall's decidedly Nietzschean hero figure who is obsessed with authenticity and personal growth and defies convention. *Morale* exemplifies Jackson Lears's contention that in the early twentieth century,

> [s]elf-help advisers, social scientists, popular literati, and the avant-garde all began to elevate becoming over being, the process of experience over its goal or result. Some employed fashionable evolutionary analogies. . . . [A] dread of stasis affected many among the educated. (Fox and Lears 15)

Indeed, morale, which Hall calls the "chief end of man," turns out not to be much of an "end" at all. It names no moral virtues after which "man" is to strive but rather names a process. The goal of morale

> is simply this—to keep ourselves, body and soul, and our environment, physical, social, industrial, etc., always at the very tip-top of condition. This super-hygiene . . . implies the maximum of vitality, life abounding, getting and keeping in the very center of the current of creative evolution; and minimizing, destroying, or avoiding all checks, arrests, and inhibitions to it. (1)

Morale is a state of ever-readiness to do whatever ought to be done, which will at once be recognized and done instinctively at the proper moment by those with high morale. The almost perfectly hermetic circularity of morale obviates the need to debate moral ends or to formulate complicated and tiresome codes of ethics, which at best second what morale commands and at worst impair one's moral reflexes.

Morale thus comprises "instinctive impulsions to virtue" (Hall 2), a quick-twitch moral response system whose enemies are "self-consciousness" and the divided self it creates, which is why conscience is for Hall a liability. In an interesting twist on Christian doctrine, Hall argues that

> [t]o be conscious of conscience means that evil has found entrance and that if we now do right, we do only with a majority of our faculties and not unanimously with them all. Very much good is done in this way, to be sure, but it is not virtue of the purest order but of a secondary quality. Virginal purity never debates or parleys, for to deliberate is too often to be lost. (5)

For Hall, conscience is a product of the Fall, and ethics is mostly a matter of willing ourselves back to the prelapsarian state of "virginal purity" by participating in a cult of condition and following a regimen of "superhygiene." Once grace is recovered, one does not anguish over moral choices; one simply performs moral acts, thereby giving one a decided advantage over those impaired by conscience. Hence the importance of unfettered competition to the triumph of morale:

> [A]ny political, social, or industrial organization that prevents superior men from attaining superior rewards is doomed to failure. The history of this country . . . is a triumphant vindication of the principle that the freer men are the less equal they become. . . . Interference with [the instinct of competition] will always bring not even mediocrity but inferiority and stagnation. (Hall 150)

Not surprisingly, given Hall's elevation of competition above cooperation, his representative anecdote is war. Whatever specific misgivings he may have had about World War I, which he sees as a conflict among various outmoded codes of conscience, Hall venerates war. Conscientious objectors, thus, are viewed as dupes of conscience, while soldiers are viewed as gods of morale: "Morale is the very soul of the soldier," ever ready to say at every opportunity not just "I can" but "I will" (18). To be sure, some of this glorification of warriors stems from Hall's anxiety about the feminization of modern culture. "War is, in a sense, the acme of what some now call the manly protest. In peace women have invaded nearly all of the occupations of man, but in war male virtues come to the fore, for women cannot go 'over the top'" (102).

In his discussions of contemporary business, Hall makes the usual pacific gestures of solidarity with labor. Echoing the standard wisdom of the age—which followed several decades of bloody strikes—he assures his readers that "labor is no longer a commodity but a partner and must be accepted sympathetically as an intelligent cooperator" (201). But everything in his philosophy, including the condescension implicit in the preceding quote, suggests that the lambs of labor are a lesser species than the lions of morale and that his concern is at best an expression of a none-too-enlightened self-interest. Thus, for example, he recommends giving workers a share of ownership in business mostly to assuage their feelings of frustration and desperation, "the most dangerous and inflammable explosive of all psychic states" (207). And Hall's obligatory paean to "service," in opposition to the "hyperindividuation and greed which has destroyed every great state in the past" and "rampant selfishness" that he sees taking over postwar society "to an almost mad and orgiastic degree" (367), is as hollow as his calls for inclusion. "Service" functions within Hall's system the way "character" functioned within nineteenth-century success philosophy. It ethicizes attitudes and behaviors that benefited employers far more than the employees to whom they were touted.

In sum, Hall's work emphasizes the highly masculinized single individual who, by virtue of his oneness with himself, is possessed of quasi-divine powers unknown to the conflicted masses. Traditional dogmas are renounced in the name of a progressive or evolutionary view of humanity, according to which we are compelled toward a numinous, if murky, destiny by natural law rather than by moral codes, in much the way that economic markets are infallibly guided by invisible hands. Social institutions are consigned to the role of bystanders who watch while those of abundant morale emerge from the masses. The line between the somatic and the spiritual is blurry at best, and it is unclear at various points which of the two is in service to the other, all of which prepares us for Bruce Barton's Jesus Christ, ad executive.

The Man Bruce Barton Knew

In his brief, unpaginated preface to *TMNK*, "How It Came to Be Written," Barton says his purpose in writing the book was to recuperate the image of Jesus, the effeminate "'lamb of God,'" the "physical weakling!," the "kill-joy," or the "failure" he learned of in Sunday school. Barton's Christ would be "the founder of modern business" whose story would inspire "every businessman," moving him to "send it to his partners and his salesmen" so they could learn how Christ "forged ... an organization that conquered the world" using "twelve men from the bottom ranks of business." His will be a "simple" story, Barton promises, the product not of some symbol-mongering churchman's overactive fancy but of the virginally pure imagination of the little boy, young Bruce Barton, who first conceived of writing the "real" story of Jesus. Like the child of fable who points out that the king is naked, the child who originates Barton's text sees all *wie es eigentlich ist*, in the same surefooted, untutored way that his subject, Jesus Christ, will see things.

Barton's preface deserves scrutiny on at least two grounds. First, given his father's theology and the regnant muscular Christianity of his youth, his claimed encounters with a "sissified" Christ seem implausible. But more importantly, Barton's putative motives appear questionable. He clearly intends to do more than simply refashion Christ so as to inspire modern businessmen. His book is in fact part of a much larger project carried out by advertisers of the era to reform their lackluster image. And what more stunning way to elevate the prestige of the advertising business than to claim Jesus Christ as its originator? If Horace Lorimer could dramatically rachet up the prestige of the faltering *Saturday Evening Post* by bringing Benjamin Franklin posthumously onboard as a founder, what might Jesus Christ do for the advertising profession? In "Human Appeals in Copy," an essay Barton earlier contributed to *Masters of Advertising Copy*, one of many books published by advertisers of the day in their campaign to sanitize their image, he in fact lays out the rationale for just such a book as *TMNK*.

In his first bit of copywriting, recalls Barton, he attempted to boost the flagging sales of a book club by adding human interest to the copy. He thus featured an illustration of Marie Antoinette being towed in a tumbrel to her execution and wrote copy promising to put readers in touch with the great tragedies of history through books in "Dr. Eliot's" club. He put a human face on the business, or, in advertising argot, "gave it a soul." Shared experiences such as these, promised Barton, "make the whole world kin" (66) and connect "the little age in which we live [which] is merely a drop in the great river of eternity, and ... extend our contacts ... [to] the great spirits that have lived in other times" (67). If one thinks of *TMNK* as an "advertisement" for the advertising profession, it follows a similar sort of logic. Christ's untold story serves as testimonial for the product, with Christ serving as celebrity spokesperson who gives advertising a soul and connects that soul to "eternity." So understood, it constitutes one of the first truly modern success books that, while putatively showing audiences how to succeed, "advertise" their authors and legitimate their authors' dubious profession. But the use of a figure from "eternity" to pitch a product is not without risks. Equating the divine and the secular, even metaphorically, may devalue the spiritual term as readily as it ennobles the secular term.

Chaim Perelman and L. Olbrechts-Tyteca pose the rhetorical dilemma Barton faces here succinctly: "[T]he popularization of the model robs him of the value arising from his distinctness" (366). And the more legitimate the model's claim to public attention by virtue of outsized deeds or important offices, the more likely the strategy is to backfire. While actors and athletes whose luster is based on physical performance for glamorous sums of money are little tarnished by product testimonials, political and professional figures who perform tasks much like the ones all of us perform for less glamorous sums risk being labeled corporate "shills" if they endorse products. (Witness Bob Dole's highly paid post-election "appearances" for Viagra. These were not, we were solemnly told, "testimonials" but rather public service statements on behalf of those suffering from "erectile dysfunction.") All of which underscores the enormous rhetorical challenge Barton faces here. In what follows, we will review several major strategies Barton employs to meet that challenge.

Bruce Barton's Tabloid Bible

The first thing Barton does in *TMNK* by way of refashioning a Christ who can endorse secular values without diluting his divine authority is to stress the "news value in the copy" and treat his subject in the manner of a journalist—which is, Barton assures us, exactly what Christ did by way of advertising his new approach to theology. Thus, we are told, Christ was "never trite or commonplace; he had no routine. . . . Reporters would have followed him every single hour, for it was impossible to predict what he would say or do; every action and word were news," which also demonstrates Christ's marketing savvy, his recognition "that all good advertising is news" (126). Indeed, Barton at one point recounts the sequence of events in Christ's life as a series of boldfaced headlines ("PALSIED MAN HEALED/JESUS OF NAZARETH CLAIMS RIGHT TO FORGIVE SINS" [129]) as though were a "breaking" news story. Barton's Jesus, who "hated prosy dullness"

(148) and used language that was "marvelously simple" (149) was a journalist in savior's robes.

Barton's Christ is both subject and model, newsmaker and news reporter, thus personifying the basic ambiguity of the term "news," which, like its sister term "history," can be at once both the event and the report of the event. This ambiguity in turn reflects the privileged role of news and history. They are presumed to be more transparent, closer to the events they depict than other accounts, and as such more plausible. Jesus the newsmaker and Jesus the newsman, it is easy to forget in all this, are both products of Bruce Barton's text, which is neither journalism nor history so much as the product of Bruce Barton's fertile imagination.

The use of journalistic narrative to enhance the plausibility of a fictional text is a technique Barton, a frustrated novelist, derives not just from advertising practice but also from Hemingway, Dos Passos, and countless other novelists of the time, many of them former journalists, who were in the process of creating a new "objective" realism. While Phyllis Frus has argued that "this kind of realism did not grow out of journalism" (xvii) so much as it did imagism, there are connections and tensions between the two practices that, after reading a passage from Barton, we will look at in more detail.

The opening scene of *TMNK* offers a fine example of Barton's style of reportage and the surreptitiously persuasive nature of that style. It opens in medias res with the declaration that "[i]t was very late in the afternoon" (1). The time is past, the world we are entering is given but unspecified, and the voice that transports us there is anonymous. The next passage, meanwhile, shifts to the present tense and the second person vatic voice: "If you would like to learn the measure of a man, that is the time of day to watch him" (1). We are very much "addressed" or, in Althusser's phrase, "interpellated" in this passage. If the opening one-sentence paragraph places us in a scene, the first sentence of the second paragraph imposes a universal rule upon us that is to be used in interpreting the scene; "late in the afternoon" denotes a test of character for distinguishing "the little man," who loses his grip, from "the big man [who] takes a firmer hold" (1). The voice of the second paragraph is the "tutelary" voice of advertising, the voiceover for the TV commercial, speaking only of the self-evident, never importuning, merely relating what everyone already knows. It is a voice that addresses, engages, and infantilizes us.

After a long, hot day on the road, Jesus and his disciples have spied a village. Christ deputes two of the disciples to seek accommodations there.

When they are rebuffed, the other disciples clamor for Jesus to "'call down fire from Heaven and consume [the villagers]'" (3), thereby marking themselves as the sort of "little men" who wilt and grow peevish late in the day. At this point, Barton once again "pulls us aside," and in the present-tense, tutelary mode tells us what to make of things. "There are times," he confides, "when nothing a man can say is nearly so powerful as saying nothing" (3), which is of course exactly what Christ does. With the "instinctive" understanding possessed by "[e]very executive" (3)—not to mention every redeemer whose "morale" is tip-top and every Hemingway code hero who stoically does "what a man's gotta do"—Christ simply heads down the road trailed by his chastened, if still baffled, disciples who "had failed again to measure up" (4) to a standard that requires no articulation.

In its immediacy, in its presumptions about the role and values of readers, and in its seamless melding of Barton's prose and point of view with the Bible's, this scene is typical. It is also, like Barton's Christ, impossible to argue with. The "givenness" of the scene derives in part from Barton's use of emergent, increasingly "positivistic" journalism practices of the day based on a "spectator theory of knowledge" (Frus 108) first articulated for journalists by Walter Lippmann. Such practices naturalized the world as given and objectified human beings, reducing them to their roles. It was, Frus argues, a most mischievous way to represent reality (77).

While all of these tendencies can be found in Barton's work, other more prominent tendencies link his writing to a much later fusion of journalism and fiction, New Journalism, which Frus finds at least as mischievous as its modernist predecessor. Certainly Barton's highly self-conscious, "participant observer" point of view, so intimate, according to Richard Huber, that he "might qualify as the thirteenth apostle" (204), anticipates Tom Wolfe's "chameleon" point of view. And in his scene-by-scene narrative construction, emphasizing a series of dramatic moments resulting in a "portrait" as opposed to a series of causally linked events resulting in a climax and a denouement, Barton anticipates Wolfe as well. Whereas the modernist practitioners of journalistic narrative hid their subjectivity and their moral judgments behind a pose of objectivity, new journalists, according to Frus, tend to hide conservative, mainstream views behind exuberantly subjective, apparently unconventional "bad boy" narrators like Wolfe and Hunter S. Thompson. In her critique of Wolfe's fast and loose historiography in *The Right Stuff*, Frus pinpoints why it is so difficult to take issue with Wolfe; her argument here goes to the heart of *TMNK* as well.

> Wolfe offers to readers only his view of what happened, only this position from which to critique. Arguing over which parts a writer "got right" in terms of accuracy is a hopeless exercise, because we have no primary or original text to compare later versions to, and these narratives are paramount in determining the history we have of events in the past; in fact, they are all we have, for we cannot retrieve the past except from texts, including our memory as a text. (229)

While one can of course compare Barton's account to the Gospels themselves, the sometimes contradictory, often bare-boned accounts of the Gospel writers seldom offer a "baseline" that one could confidently use to measure the accuracy of Barton's fanciful reconstructions.

The willingness of many to forgive Barton and his new journalistic heirs for playing fast and loose with history can perhaps best be explained by the fact that their imaginative refashionings so often make for compelling reading. (In comparison to most success rhetoricians to follow, Barton is a Flaubert of the genre.) And as Barton makes clear in several comments about the book, he set out to engage audiences by returning a sense of immediacy to Christ's life. Barton does so, he says, because theology has taken the "thrill of [Christ's] life by assuming that he knew everything from the beginning. . . . What interest would there be in such a life? What inspiration?" (*TMNK* 8). He wants to rescue "Christ the man" from myth, put creed aside—not to mention memory—and have us "gradually feeling his powers expanding" (8) and experience his unforeseen triumphs and reversals simultaneously with him. This is what Tom Wolfe sets out to do in *The Electric Kool-Aid Acid Test* where in his prose he tries to embody the Merry Pranksters' attempts "to overcome the lags—sensory, social, historical, psychological—which prevent us from living in the present moment and which make our lives in effect secondary, based on received perceptions" (Frus 125) and to banish "belatedness" from the writing.

Barton's Christ, like the later subjects of new journalists, not to mention the "new and improved" products in Barton's ads, springs to life in defiance of traditions, assumptions, and expectations. And for Barton's original audience, beguiled by dominant progressivist myths of the day, the novelty of Barton's Christ was doubtless a selling point. But the price Barton pays for the immediacy of this rendering is not inconsiderable.

In rescuing his hero from dogma, Barton must be careful not to weaken the Christian mythos that gives him his aura. And the authority of religious myth rests largely on its venerability. Myths are supposed to deal with origins and "first things" that those closer to the source know directly, leaving those who follow to interpret what they experienced. And novelty is not a value in myth; it is an illusion. Myth celebrates eternal return and "what happens" again and again, not the newness of "what happened" once in time. That Barton is sensitive to this problem is evident in his careful handling of the materials on which his retelling is based.

Newsworthy Truths v. Textual Dogmas

So long as Christ is engaged in activities that comport with Barton's secular ideology, his use of the journalistic account and the heightened sense of immediacy such an account gives his story works well. But whenever Barton needs to deviate from or put a new spin on primary materials, he foregrounds the secondariness of his textual sources and stresses the fallible nature of their authors. And once again Barton justifies his selective deviations from myth and his antinomian attitudes to textual sources by citing his subject, Christ, whose prophetic role is to invite "frail bewildered humanity to stand upright and look at God face to face!" (96). This eyebal-to-eyeball encounter with God is for Barton "the basis of all revolt, all democracy" (96) in the face of which "authorities trembled" (97).

> No wonder that succeeding generations of authorities have embroidered his Idea and corrupted it, so that the simplest faith in the world has become a complex thing of form and ritual, of enforced observances and "thou shall nots." It was too dangerous a Power to be allowed to wander the world, unleashed and uncontrolled. (97)

Barton's Christ, like the heroes of Hall, has more than a little of the *beau savage* about him. His virtue is less a product of learned conscience than a natural outgrowth of his "virginal purity." Repeatedly thus, Barton reminds us that his Christ is no friend to "dogma" or "creed" or "formalism." In stark contrast to those "long, involved arguments backed up by many citations from the law," beloved by the scribes and Pharisees, Christ "quoted nobody; his own word was offered as sufficient" (22). "Jesus seldom argued," we are told on more than one occasion. The crowds accept his contentions at face value because "[s]incerity glistened like sunshine through every sentence he uttered" (151) and, Barton assures us, the public's sixth sense for insincerity is—all evidence to the contrary notwithstanding—unerring.

We get a fine example of Christ's (qua Barton's) nominalist style of debate when he is questioned by an emissary from John the Baptist about his failure to be properly self-denying. Here Barton slides imperceptibly, via ellipses, from Christ's biblical response (Luke 7.22–23 and Matthew 11.4) into his own response attributed to Christ: "It is true that I do not fast nor forego the every-day pleasures of life. John did his work and it was fine; but I can not work in his way. I must be myself . . . and these results which you have seen . . . these are my evidence" (68). And those who questioned the sincerity of Christ's motives then or truthfulness of Barton's version of things now are said to have had their sensibilities warped by tradition and "the numbing grip of ancient creeds" (181) that reduce Christ's story to "[a] hollow bit of stage-play" (180).

The responsibility for the perennially gloomy "graven image" of Christ lays with the "early theologians," who, says Barton, were men living "in sad days; they were men of introspection, to whom every simple thing was symbolic of some hidden mystery; and life, itself, a tangle of philosophic formulae" (59)—perfect foils, in short, for Barton's manly, instinctive, single-pointed Christ. Whenever Barton depicts scribes, Pharisees, or theologians, they are pasty-faced, flabby products of too much time spent indoors. They are the direct descendants of those dreary Old Testament prophets whose portraits hang on the wall of the Boston Public Library. "You are moved by their moral grandeur, but rather glad to get away. They are not the kind of men whom you would choose as companions on a fishing trip" (66).

Whenever Barton deals with supernatural events in Christian myth, particularly when such events undercut his focus on commerce, he is again careful to foreground the fallibility of texts and authors that report them. Thus, the Gospels' unhealthy (in Barton's view) fascination with the Crucifixion is attributed to the callow sensibilities of their authors. They were "men of simple minds, and naturally gave greatest emphasis to the events which impressed them most" (60). And what impressed them most would of course be sensational events like nailing people to crosses and rising from the dead, hardly the sort of thing Barton was eager to emphasize in a book dedicated to the religious uplift of consumers and salesmen and originally published by *The Woman's Home Companion*. Barton did not, after all, wish his readers to follow Christ's example to the bitter end. Mortification and self-denial (except in the sanitized form of "service" to a commercial project) will do little to encourage some to buy and others to sell consumer goods.

Barton's final chapter does acknowledge the Crucifixion, but he devotes relatively little discussion to the event itself, skipping lightly over matters of anguish and suffering and stressing Christ's ability to "bear disappointment" (193) in yet another test of his executive prowess. Barton's steadfast aversion to the darker themes inherent in his material finally puts one in mind of a more recent "retelling" of the Gospels, Monty Python's *Life of Brian*, where the crucifixion scene culminates in a sunny tune entitled "I Always Look on the Bright Side of Life" sung by the Christ figure "Brian" and a motley assemblage of thieves and onlookers who sing and whistle along.

Barton's Disneyesque version of the Crucifixion is of a piece with his upbeat account of Christ's temptation and his forty days in the wilderness. Mythically, this episode functions as a night sea journey, featuring mortification of flesh, death of ego, and spiritual rebirth, hardly the sort of thing consumers will wish to linger over. So, Barton recasts the episode as something akin to a New Thought conversion experience climaxing in an "awakening of the inner consciousness of power" (11). In a characteristic inversion of tenor and vehicle, Barton understands Christ's suffering "in terms of" Lincoln's (15), characterizing it finally as a victory for "mysticism," which turns out to be "the very soul of leadership" (17) in all life's arenas, from theology to monopoly capitalism, and almost certainly beyond the ken of those callow souls who wrote the Gospels.

Yet another element of Christ's temptation that Barton must sanitize is the nettlesome presence of Satan, a pioneer in the promotion of consumption. On the one hand, to acknowledge Satan's reality is to acknowledge the reality of evil and, along with it, the limits of human potential and the dangers of consumption. On the other hand, to ignore Satan is to stray dramatically from the source that lends his account credibility. So Satan stays in but as little more than a dramatic device: "In our simple story we need not spend much time with the description of Satan. We do not know whether he is to be regarded as a personality or as an impersonalization of an inner experience" (14–15). In his references to Satan, Barton underscores his textual origins: "*The narrative describes them* as a threefold temptation and introduces Satan *to add to the dramatic quality of the event*" (14); "Satan, *says the narrative*, tempted him . . ."; "Satan comes in again, *according to the narrative* . . ." (16, emphasis added). As Barton suggests wistfully at one point, "The temptation is more real without him, more akin to our own trials and doubts" (15).

Parabolic Persuasion

In his attempt to stay within the framework of Christian myth while re-working and inverting many particulars of that myth to accommodate it to his own secularized version of Christ, Barton also turns to another of advertisers' favorite tools, the parable. Modern advertisers' reliance on parables was anticipated by nineteenth-century preachers for whom "[t]he sermon, with its detailed discussion of the virtues, was replaced by the inspirational parable with its dramatic story of success or failure" (Cawelti 175) and by turn-of-the-century success rhetoricians like Russell Conwell and Elbert Hubbard who performed their "Acres of Diamonds" and "Message to Garcia" parables respectively before packed houses for decades.

The particular usefulness of parables to preachers, advertisers, and success writers lies in the nature of the values they were used to promote. While the sermonic "detailed discussion" of values works well when audiences already share the values under discussion, it is less effective at selling an audience on novel values. In particular, unfamiliar values benefit from the indirection of parables, which rely on exemplification, figuration, and delayed annunciation rather than straightforward exposition. Thus, for example, the materialism implicit in Conwell's "Acres" was rendered more palatable to largely Christian audiences by offering it in the form of a conclusion drawn from a particular experience rather than as an explicit rule of behavior prefacing an illustration. Conwell's tale, with its darkly ironic twist—his farmer protagonist travels the world in search of a treasure that was under his feet the whole time—does more, after all, than illustrate an accepted moral principle; it promotes a principle that in fact inverts a traditional value. Were the farmer a sturdy yeoman, his foolishness would lie in his restless striving after material gain. Within the framework of Conwell's version, however, the farmer's foolishness lay in his failure to hear opportunity knocking on his very own door.

Barton's use of parables follows the example set by Conwell and Lorimer's "Gorgon" Graham—"I want to say right here that to get any sense out of a proverb I usually find that I have to turn it inside out"—which is to say, he revises the particulars of a traditional story so as to predispose the audience toward an untraditional interpretation and an unconventional if not blasphemous injunction that is "discovered" at the end of the tale. Barton gambles that his audience will see enough similarities between his version of the story and the original to grant his version the same status that makes the original an attractive vehicle for persuasion.

In this light, consider Barton's retelling of the parable of the prodigal son. While the original version stresses the prodigal's miraculous rebirth, Barton stresses the father's condemnation of the older brother, the "obedient son" described by Barton as "sullen and self-pitying" (74), the comedic butt to the prodigal's comedic hero. When the older son complains about all that his father does to celebrate the return of his wayward brother, his father "*rebuked*" him, making none of the conciliatory gestures featured in the biblical version. The implication of the story to Barton is only "too plain" (74). The sins of the two sons are "equally wrong." But in fact, by the end of Barton's version, the older son's uncharitable response seems far worse than the prodigal's excesses, especially in a work where evil is exemplified by life-denying, humorless scribes and Pharisees. The moral Barton draws from the tale makes these Christ/prodigal, obedient son/Pharisee equations explicit:

> God is a generous Giver, and selfish getting is sin. God laughs in the sunshine and sings through the throats of birds. They who neither laugh nor sing are out of tune with the Infinite. God has exercised all his ingenuity in making the world a pleasant place. Those who find no pleasure and give none offer Him a constant affront. However precise their conduct, their spirits are an offense. . . . Woe to you, Scribes and Pharisees. You are painfully careful to give exactly one-tenth your incomes to the Temple, figuring down to fractions of pennies. But you neglect the weightier matters of the law—the supreme obligation to leave the world a little more cheerful because you have passed through. (75)

In Barton's version, the prodigal's flaws aren't just forgiven as in the Bible; they're exculpated and even celebrated.

In enumerating the advantages of parables over other forms of persuasion, Barton particularly emphasizes their flexibility. Unlike rules, principles, and laws of the sort that Pharisees and scribes invoke, parables allow you to "'put yourself in step with your prospect'" and to "catch the attention of the indifferent" by speaking to their "practical self-concern" (104). Thus, when Jesus finds himself among fishermen, he invites his audience to become "'fishers of men'" (106), and when among farmers, he tells a story about sowing seeds. In Barton's age, when the newly emerging science of market research allowed admen to target ever more precisely the "practical self-concerns" of consumers, this flexibility was a particularly appealing virtue. If the values or products being "pitched" in a given parable or ad were foreign to a given audience, a comfortably familiar story line could go a long way toward disarming them.

In all likelihood, it would not have occurred to Barton to attribute audience resistance to a values conflict. For Bruce Barton, Advertising Man, audiences resist products simply because they don't yet know they need them. This is also the case with his hero, Jesus, who sets out to sell Christianity in an ancient world already awash in religions and sects: "Assuredly there was no demand for a new religion; the world was already oversupplied" (92). But through the use of parables, Jesus could put himself in step with his prospects and offer an appeal that "even the dullest [might] understand . . . , shrewdly calculated to awaken an appetite for more" (108). For Barton, demand drives supply (90). And advertisers create demand, which is infinitely elastic. Christianity, like typewriters, steamships, and sewing machines, is a product that preceded demand into the marketplace. And like trees that fall unheard in the forest, products for which there is no demand have a dubious existence. Only when advertisers create consumers for a product is it robustly real, which is why for Barton, supply is mechanically "produced" while demand is magically "created." And parables, as Barton makes clear, are "the most powerful advertisements of all time" (107) insofar as they allow Christ and advertisers to sell people products before they know they want them. Given that Barton announced earlier in his career that his highest ambition as a writer was "to inspire his readers with *divine discontent*" (*More Power* 117), his affinity for parables, the tool of choice for religious teachers since ancient times, is a natural one.

The last virtue of parables, the one that most strongly recommends them to those marketing alien values, is the one virtue not named by Barton: the power to prescribe while appearing merely to present and thereby to surreptitiously implicate readers/viewers in the construction of their prescriptions. Which is to say, parables are nominally accounts of single instances that serve as "examples" of general principles. In Aristotle's terms, examples are "better-known" cases that clarify for audiences "lesser-known" cases and help them recognize a principle shared by both. Examples are of course chosen on rhetorical grounds in hopes that audiences might extend to the lesser-known cases being exemplified the same acceptance or rejection associated with the better-known examples. What is unique about parables viewed as examples is the extent to which the general principle they supposedly exemplify is actually derived from the single instance they recount. All examples are, in Alexander Gelley's formulation, "derived proleptically" (3) and function as a species of an as-yet unrealized genus. "In this sense example cannot assume a whole on which it draws. Rather it is oriented to the recovery of a lost whole or the discovery of a new one" (3). But parable, considered as a species of exemplification, "both thematizes and occludes a performative or ethical dimension" (20), which is to say, in reading parable, one may pass from example ("it is") to the exemplary ("thou shalt") without acknowledgment.

In describing the three functions served by "particular cases" in argument—as examples, illustrations, or models—Perelman and Olbrechts-Tyteca cite a strikingly relevant case to make their point that the distinction between the singular example and the hortatory exemplar is often tricky.

> On many occasions a speaker will clearly show his intention to present facts as examples, but this is not always the case: Certain American magazines like to describe the career of this or that big businessman, politician, or movie star without explicitly drawing a lesson from it. Are the facts retailed just a contribution to history or a sidelight on it? Are they examples suggesting a spontaneous generalization? Are they illustrations of well-known recipes for social success? Or are the central figures in these narratives put forward as remarkable models to be emulated by the public? It is impossible to be sure. Probably a story of this kind is meant to—and does indeed effectively—fulfil all these roles for different classes of readers. (351)

For at least some audiences, then, what an example assumes—the recipe for success that "everyone knows"—is in fact justified by the particular instance it narrates. The narrative cannot *logically* be a singular instance and stand for a general principle. But through the "ruse" of parabolic discourse, it can function *rhetorically* in just this way, persuading audiences to accept it as actual and universal, a description of how things are and a prescription for how they ought to act. It is the same surreptitious movement from *is* to *ought* perfected by advertising that, according to Judith Williamson, "constantly re-interprets while only claiming to represent realty" (74), addressing us as "consumers [with] . . . certain values, [who] will freely buy things, consume on the basis of those values, and so on," thereby "invit[ing] us 'freely' to create ourselves in accordance with the way in which they have already created us" (42).

Clearly, some parables are more devious than others in their transformation of singulars into universals. In this regard, Barton's supposed model, Jesus Christ, offers a different version of parabolic discourse. Throughout the New Testament, Christ's use of parables, along with his reluctance to perform miracles, frustrates his disciples and members of his audience longing for the certitude of rules and empirical demonstrations of supernatural power. For the biblical Christ, it would appear that the function of parables is not to "put himself in step" with his audiences but to exclude those whose hearts have grown too dull, ears too heavy, and eyes too closed to hear his message (Matt. 13.15) and to speak past them to the spiritually awakened. What Christ requires as a necessary condition for understanding his parables is a belief that Barton would have his parable impose upon his audience.

In what is arguably the most self-conscious of all Christ's parables, the parable of the good Samaritan, his complex rhetorical design is perhaps most clearly visible. The good Samaritan, more than any of his parables, relies on its frame tale for understanding. Christ has just finished telling his disciples how blessed they are to perceive spiritual truths denied to "prophets and kings [who] desired to see what you see and did not see it" (Luke 10.24, RSV) when a lawyer, part of a Pharisee plot to try and "entangle [Christ] in his talk" (Matt. 22.15), stands up to "test" him. The question the lawyer puts to Christ is predictably legalistic. He wants to know the sufficient conditions for inheriting eternal life: "What is written in the law? How do you read?" (Luke 10.26). Christ's straightforward answer—love God with all your might and your neighbor as yourself—disarms the lawyer, who, "desiring to justify himself" (Luke 10.29) and squeeze the last ounce of ambiguity out of the response, demands a legalistic definition of "neighbor." In lieu of telling the lawyer his definition, Christ tells the story of the good Samaritan who rescues the robbery victim after a priest and a Levite pass him by. He then puts the question back to the lawyer: "Which of these three, do you think, proved neighbor to the man . . . ?" (Luke 10.36), forcing the lawyer to answer his own question and impose upon himself the obligation that his quibbles would have obscured.

The parable functions dialogically for Christ as surely as it works monologically for Barton, whose analysis of Christ's use of parables, predictably enough, emphasizes quite a different set of traits. While Christ underscores again and again the power of parables to keep spiritual truths from being understood by the unholy, Barton is most impressed by their capacity to disguise the fact that Christ is saying the same thing over and over again. "The thoughts which Jesus had to give the world were revolutionary, but they were few in number" (*TMNK* 155). By casting these thoughts in the form of parables, Christ could repeat those ideas endlessly—"many stories, many advertisements, but the same big Idea" (156)—and derive that major boon of redundancy known to all advertisers: "'reputation is repetition'" (155). The scandal of parable, that it imposes what it purports to teach, is for Barton its single greatest virtue.

The Second Reformation: CHRIST ENDORSES "SOFT-SELL" OVER "REASON-WHY"!

The rhetorical practices that Barton uses to render his "retelling" of the Gospels persuasive to a modern audience—the conversion of narrative to breaking news, the selective hiding and foregrounding of sources depending on their friendliness to his argument, and the use of parabolic discourse to move seamlessly from example to exemplar—comprise what might be termed a "stealth rhetoric." Such practices in turn characterize the approach of one of two major schools of advertising in his day. Through his use of these covert practices and through his praise of Christ for using them, Barton implicitly valorizes this school; by eschewing a different set of advertising practices in his own narrative and by associating them with Christ's antagonists, meanwhile, Barton marks the other school as deviant. To appreciate what was at stake in this struggle and its centrality to Barton's vision of Christ, a bit of history is required.

There was indeed a deep schism among advertisers of the second and third decades of the twentieth century, between the so-called soft-sell and reason-why approaches to advertising, and while Barton's soft-sell approach was clearly dominant, reason-why advocates were still plentiful and influential. Before looking at the differences in approach, however, it should be noted that the ascendance of the soft-sell or "suggestional" approach represents a second "reformation" of the profession. The first great reformation in advertising took place in the nineteenth century when "scientific" and "professional" practitioners began to nudge aside the magical snake oil salesmen who mostly represented the patent medicine companies that dominated advertising early on. Because of their extravagant markups—the main ingredient was invariably alcohol, which cost little to manufacture and was untaxed—and the low cost of transporting their product, patent medicine manufacturers were among the few with profit margins ample enough to afford the luxury of national marketing. Print ads for patent medicines did little more than replicate their drummers' oral pitches: lavish promises offered with a wink; a smattering of testimonials; a prominent depiction of the product; a portrait, bewhiskered and/or saintly, of the medical doctor/professor/scientist/ savant who supposedly discovered the miracle cure; and a catchphrase or jingle to make it memorable. They gave hope to the afflicted and legitimated tippling among the many "nervous" souls of the day.

The next generation of advertisers, anxious to "professionalize" the field and to distance themselves from their sketchy past, emphasized appeals to reason. In modest, even pedantic, language, they confided in the reader and built trust for the product. Eventually, early "masters of advertising" like George Kennedy and Albert Lasker christened their approach "reason-why" advertising, which quickly became the new orthodoxy. According to reason-why acolyte J. George Frederick, this shift constituted an "epoch-making rebellion in copywriting" (25) that he compared to Martin Luther's Reformation. (If, as Unamuno once claimed, all revolutions in art are made in the name of greater realism, all reformations in the world of advertising are made in the name of greater respect for the consumer.) Loudly rejecting the "time-honored assumption that the public was a mass of dumb, driven sheep," reason-why advocates claimed to appeal only to "reason and intelligence" (25).

But in effect, reason-why advocates simply went from devaluing the public's intelligence to devaluing its virtue. According to Merle Curti:

> Advertising experts of the period [1890–1910], in the main, agreed that the keys to human nature are rationality and a rational understanding of self-interest, an idea associated with classical economic theory. The advertiser should assume that all men are, like himself, rationally out to maximize profits. (339–40)

Reducing rationality to calculative intelligence and narrow self-interest, reason-why advertisers targeted consumers' selfishness rather than their stupidity in pitching their products. And while reason-why advertisers did significantly reduce hyperbole in advertising, it seems likely that the 1908 Food and Drug Act, which made false advertising actionable, had more to do with their newfound restraint than did their oft-professed reverence for consumer intelligence.

Reason-why advertising was self-described as "salesmanship in print" and attempted to replicate in magazines and newspapers the one-on-one meeting between the buyer and the seller. They were, in comparison to their soft-sell rivals, extremely "talky" ads with minimal visual appeal, the equivalent of talking heads in film. If reason-why advertising in many ways worked against its medium, soft-sell or suggestional advertising exploited that medium by grafting highly stylized art and photography onto its copy. Mediacy was no curse for soft-sell advertisers, who welcomed the freedom to persuade by association and impression rather than by logic. Soft-sell advertisers made no pretense of selling a particular product to a particular person by offering persuasive reasons for the purchase. What they sold was not the product per se but an association between the product and some intangible quality desirable to a carefully targeted audience most likely to read a particular magazine. Instead of offering persuasive arguments to "everyman," a soft-sell argument used demographic research to segment the market and identify "the actual preferences . . . [and] measurable habits" of that market segment and then to use "forceful concrete details and pictures [and] attention-arresting stimuli" (Curti 347) to associate a given product with those preferences and habits.

Soft-sell advertisers were the first to address a new class of people, "consumers," in that "buttonholing" manner that greets and confers an identity simultaneously. Advertising, according to Richard Ohmann, became a potent tool for helping members of an emergent professional managerial class (PMC) "fix their bearings in the fluid social space of that moment and to do so to their social advantage" (220). Members of the rapidly expanding PMC sought, on a massive scale, to fit in, to look and behave like each other. Whereas previously one fit in by conforming to dominant mores—MacIntyre's "externalities" or Taylor's "ontic logos"— the PMC was more inclined to seek normalcy in the mirror of advertising. This shift parallels a larger-scale change in thinking about identity noted by philosopher Ian Hacking: "The cardinal concept of the psychology of the Enlightenment had been, simply, human nature. By the end of the nineteenth century, it was being replaced by something different: normal people" (1).

The logic of reason-why advertising reflects its more classical assumptions about human nature. Its ads operate on the basis of traditional Aristotelian rhetoric, making straightforward appeals, either unadorned or incidentally adorned by visuals, to known audiences. Its structures are essentially enthymematic and move from better-known premises (for example, a common problem and its lamentable consequences) to lesser-known conclusion (a solution in the form of a product, usually with a "revolutionary," heretofore unrevealed ingredient). Its argumentative structure is relatively transparent to those who encounter it. While reason-why advertisers were not above deceit, exaggeration, and omission, theirs was not a "stealth rhetoric." They might sometimes lie, but unlike their soft-sell competitors, their approach lacked the wherewithal to enchant, to create what one soft-sell advocate called "'an invisible cloud of friendly, favorable impressions'" (MacManus, qtd. in Fox 74) around a product.

Bruce Barton's Christ is clearly a messiah of the soft-sell sect. He thus offers no "reason-why" for his faith, preferring the indirection of parables and dramatic, highly visible action over the exposition of ideas. Like a good soft-sell ad campaign, Barton's book offers numerous depictions of one grand notion in a highly visual, presentational mode that is essentially a monologue, an illustration of a single purpose that is opposed by those archvillains the scribes and Pharisees, with their tedious creeds and insidious dogmas, who sound suspiciously like reason-why copywriters.

Jesus Christ: Signifying Magician

Barton's reliance on advertising in his retelling of Christ's life goes beyond borrowing a number of isolated rhetorical strategies from his advertising practices. His text reflects the very dynamic of advertising. And that dynamic, as outlined by Judith Williamson in her fine-grained structuralist analysis, *Decoding Advertisements*, is fundamentally magical. Advertisements, Williamson argues, are magical spaces in which odds and ends of various mythic systems (for example, celebrities from the worlds of sport and entertainment) are put together with products, which then take on meaning from the association. That meaning is in turn transmitted through the product to those who buy and use the product. Or in the language of Saussure utilized by Williamson, within the wholly self-referential space of the ad, there are no signifieds, only signifiers, whose meaning is a function of their arrangement: "[I]t is structure which signifies in ads: not genuinely 'significant' things, but things arranged so as to *transfer* significance from themselves to something else" (168) and ultimately to the consumer. So, in placing Michael Jordan next to a box of breakfast cereal, the significance of Jordan, whose athletic skills are so transcendent that he comes to exemplify not just basketball excellence but the very notion of excellence itself, is transferred to the product. And when we purchase the cereal, his aura is magically transmitted to us who can then "be like Mike," the exemplar of exemplarity.

While Barton lacks the nomenclature of structuralism and semiotics to articulate the ways in which his advertising practices inform his writing practices, his text and his comments on the structure of that text anticipate a number of points Williamson will make about advertising fifty years later. He defines the discursive space of his book in pictorial terms; he empties out his subject, Jesus, of traditional meaning and associates the now free floating signifier with figures from popular myth; he lays story lines from popular narrative over the "tracks" of biblical narratives like a skilled sound engineer laying an advertising jingle over a classical theme; he incorporates messages hostile to his own into his text and co-opts them; and he establishes an elaborate analogy between Christ's relationship to the masses and advertisers' relations to consumers.

Early on in his retelling of Christ's story, thus, Barton announces his intention to create a "portrait" as opposed to a biography "bound by the familiar outline which begins with the song of the angels at Bethlehem and ends with the weeping of the women at the cross" (10). The subject ultimately depicted in Barton's portrait of Christ is an iconic figure, a curious mix of a Hammett or Hemingway code hero and Frederick Taylor's organization man. As such, it exemplifies the heroic ideal of Barton's age. Theodore Greene, using a series of outtakes from *Colliers* magazine (1914–17), has characterized that ideal as follows:

> Once the hero had been selected for leadership in his field, he demonstrated his knowledge that "without organization you never get anywhere on a big job." He knew the necessity for "acceptance of other people's ideas; other people's ways of doing things if such acceptance will bring results." He knew that "the man who works himself is ineffective in great things unless he has the gift to choose the men who can work for him and with him." A just treatment of his men was "the secret of what has been called his knack for 'organization.'" As "a born executive" he did not allow himself to be harassed by details. He remained "a silent man in the background directing vast forces." . . . "You might readily think of him as a machine of a man, with no waste words or motion who was organizing a machine of men." (330–31)

Part Jake Barnes and part Henry Ford, this ideal gets perhaps its fullest expression in Ayn Rand's objectivist *ubermensch*, Howard Roarke—and Bruce Barton's Jesus.

Chapter 1 of *TMNK*, "The Executive," links Barton's Christ to Taylor-esque management ideals, stressing his ability to rally people to a cause, to attract and motivate people by showing faith in them (28). He is, on the one hand, a model of efficiency, resentful of his disciples for "constantly wasting his time" (4) during his quest to "forge . . . an organization that conquered the world," while on the other hand he is a model of patience and restraint in managing his sometimes obtuse disciples. Having done what he can in chapter 1 to glorify Christ the organization man, Barton does what he can in chapter 2 to endow his divine subject with qualities of a mortal hero.

Appropriately, chapter 2 opens with a scene right out of a Zane Grey novel, the moment when the "dude" or the outsider, realizing finally that there exists in the raw West no institutional mechanism for redressing grievances, reluctantly takes matters in his own hands and metes out his own rough justice: Christ throwing moneychangers out of the temple, a scene Barton presents in melodramatic fashion worthy of a first-rate potboiler. The moneychangers are avaricious and fat—one "with the face of a pig leaned gloatingly over his hoard" (34)—engaged in the "ruthless extraction" of money from the widows and orphans who have made their pilgrimage to the temple. The young Christ stands apart, his anger rising while he "half unconsciously" braids some loose cords into a whip. And then, without a word, he starts throwing tables while the crowd "melted back" like dutiful extras in a Western film who cheer while the hero takes on the villains they can only cower before. He then uses his whip to drive the animals out of the temple into the street. And when it's all over, the crowd, as crowds do, offers him no support in his confrontation with the aggrieved "priests and robbers," which is fine with Christ, who backs down his adversaries and denounces their puny social authority in the name of his higher authority: "'*This* is my authority,' he cried. 'It is written, "My house shall be called a house of prayer for all the nations," but ye have made it a den of robbers'" (36).

The composite Christ that emerges from these first two chapters, who is an exaggerated but mostly recognizable version of the biblical Christ, is a figure looking ahead to Clark Kent/Superman, Bruce Wayne/Batman, who will soon entrance mass audiences with their powers of transformation from "mild-mannered" organization men into superheroic, urban versions of Western gunslingers ever ready for single combat. More than mortal, but not quite a god, Barton's Christ is a superhuman man of metal whose arms ripple with "muscles hard as iron" (37), remarkable for "the steel-like hardness of his nerves" (43). And when Jesus heals a sick man, "[i]t was as though health poured out of that strong body into the weak one like the electric current from a dynamo" (45). The picture of Christ that concludes the chapter has all the earmarks of a magazine illustration for an adventure serial: "The straight young man stood inches above [Pilate], bronzed and hard, and clean as the air of his loved mountain and lake" (56).

Not surprisingly, Christ, like the comic book superheroes to follow, is as irresistible as he is unattainable to women, but not because of a developed "feminine" side; quite the contrary, for "weakness does not appeal to [women]" (43). The "very large proportion" of women included among Christ's closest friends is attributed by Barton to the fact "that women are *not* drawn by weakness. . . . [S]ince the world began no power has fastened the affection of women upon a man like manliness. The men who have been women's men in the finest sense, have been the vital, conquering figures of history" (48–49). In this context, it is hard not to hear in Pontius Pilate's "Behold . . . the man!" response to a "bronzed" (56) Christ's approach an echo of this female longing. And according to Barton, Pilate's exclamation offers "a truer portrait than any painter has ever given us" of his hero (56). And the central form of that hero is neither his divinity nor his humanity; it is his virile manhood.

In turning the central figure of Christianity into a macho executive with preternatural PR powers, Barton is doing something advertisers have turned into an art form—incorporating elements "whose actual content and body of thought is hostile to advertising" (Williamson 170)—into his ad. In fact, "the more hostile, the better use advertising can make of it, for its recuperation from criticism then seems all the more miraculous *and* inevitable" (170). Following the same logic that led to the incorporation of "Joe Isuzu" into car ads and "You've come a long way, baby" into cigarette ads, Bruce Barton incorporates Jesus into his advertorial on behalf of ad execs.

Barton utilizes this gap to gain strategy at another level in his account by employing Christ's story to thematize an abiding conflict between advertisers and consumers on the one hand and producers and laborers on the other. The first conflict is between advertisers' magical powers to manipulate consumers and their total dependence on consumers to respond to their magic, while the second centers on a parallel conflict between godlike manufacturers and their continued reliance on increasingly deskilled laborers. The first conflict is thematized in *TMNK* as a conflict between Jesus' power to perform miracles and his need for credulous audiences to witness his performance. The second conflict is thematized as God's reliance on humans to complete his grand design. In both cases, Barton's profound ambivalence toward the masses who make and buy the goods for which he creates demand manifests itself in his story as a schizophrenic attitude toward the multitudes in whose name Christ supposedly died.

Just as products require consumer demand to be real, miracles require credulous audiences to be enacted. The powers of Christ, it turns out, are no different in kind than the powers of marketers. Thus, when Christ revisits his childhood home, Nazareth, Jesus the Son of God is reduced to Mary and Joseph's boy, a mere mortal incapable of performing miracles. The people who had grown up with him were "skeptical; they had heard with cynical scorn the stories of the wonders he had performed in other towns" (46–47), and their skepticism rendered his "miraculous power . . . powerless" (46).

> "He could do there no mighty work," they tell us, "*because of their unbelief.*" Whatever the explanation of his miraculous power may be, it is clear that something big was required of the recipient as well as the giver. Without a belief in health on the part of the sick man, no health was forthcoming. (47)

Later in the book, Barton extends this principle all the way to the top, suggesting that God is as dependent as Christ on human cooperation.

> For if human life has any significance it is this—that God has set going here an experiment to which all His resources are committed. He seeks to develop perfect human beings, superior to circumstance, victorious over Fate. No single kind of human talent or effort can be spared if the experiment is to succeed. The race must be fed and clothed and housed and transported, as well as preached to, and taught and healed. Thus *all* business is his Father's business. All work is worship; all useful service prayer. And whoever works wholeheartedly at any worthy calling is a co-worker with the Almighty in the great enterprise which He has initiated but which He can never finish without the help of men. (179–80)

In saying that "all business is his Father's business," Barton would seem to echo Puritan doctrine by claiming sacred status for the everyday labors of ordinary people. And his lofty estimate of the masses is underscored elsewhere when he notes that "to be sure it was the 'poor' who 'heard him gladly,' and most of his disciples were men and women of the lower classes" (69). But it is finally "the vast dumb multitudes of men" (187) who desert Christ, rendering him powerless by their skepticism, and

Christ's disciples (drawn, it will be recalled, from "the bottom ranks of business") who "never fully understood" (27) his grand design. The "noisy vulgar throng" (51) let Christ down in every key situation. In the opening scene, they refuse his request for food and a bed. After he has cleared the moneychangers out of the temple, they melt away and leave him to face the authorities alone. When he returns home prior to his trial, the locals' disbelief renders him unable to perform miracles. And most clearly in the crucifixion scene at the conclusion of the book: "It was over. The rabble had sickened quickly of its revenge and scattered" (219–20). Only the better sort, the "socially elect" (71), like the centurion with whom Christ feels an "immediate bond of union" (26), thanks to the fact that "[b]oth were executives" (27), maintain symmetrical relations with Christ.

While there is no logical way to reconcile Barton's heroic vision of humanity with his sneering view of the masses, there is an analogical explanation: Christ's view of the ancient masses is equivalent to Barton's view of the modern consumer/producer. On the one hand, guided by Fordist principles of the day, American producers acknowledged their need for labor to realize their organizational visions and ultimately to buy their products. But on the other hand, they aggressively promoted managerial and technological schemes that deskilled and commodified workers. During the same period, advertisers like Barton simultaneously venerated and duped audiences by engaging in soft-sell advertising that stimulated the masses' generalized "wants" and "divine discontents" on the sly. Producers and advertisers alike were thus totally dependent on masses of people whose actions they set out to reduce to motions and whom they largely envisioned to be "more 'irrational' than 'rational'" (Curti 347), victims of their own desires. In this context, advertisers' repeated claims of "scientific" mastery over their audiences may be seen as less an exercise in self-aggrandizement than an act of whistling past the graveyard. The greater the hubris of scientific advertisers and managers, the more schizophrenic their relationship with those whose belief and cooperation they desperately needed to realize their designs. It is a problem that proves to be chronic for later success rhetoricians who must persuade mass audiences that heroic and exceptional capacities can be accessed via miraculous three- to twelve-step algorithms.

Burke and Barton: Mystery and Mystification

However useful Burke's approach is in understanding all the texts collected here under the success rhetoric rubric, it is particularly useful in understanding Burke's contemporary, Bruce Barton. Both men were witness to what Hugh Dalziel Duncan called "perhaps ... *the* representative American act" of the modern era, "the rise of the once humble businessman to power" (*Communication* 110). In fact, Duncan cites "the business 'gospel' of Bruce Barton" (111) as among the age's most important strategies for naming business relationships and calls upon critics to codify such strategies as expressions of Burke's "equipment for living." Moreover, both writers tend to find traces of myth and religion in the realm of commerce and to understand social and business hierarchies in terms of religious hierarchies. Against this common backdrop, the very different conclusions they reach stand out in particularly clear relief.

Burke's most salient treatment of the relationship between religious and secular hierarchies, and perhaps his most trenchant gloss on the underlying logic of *TMNK*, appears in a 1951 presentation he made to a Ford Foundation symposium on "Organizational Behavior." The purpose of Burke's presentation is to understand social behavior in the context of symbolic, as opposed to biological or material, motivation. So understood, all human forms of organization are ultimately seen as deriving from religious hierarchies. In that spirit, Burke proceeds to construct an origin myth for secular hierarchy patterned after Christian myth, which is to say, in the beginning there is a unifying principle containing numerous imaginative possibilities that can be realized only one at a time. The process of realizing one imaginative possibility at the expense of all others Burke earlier termed "bureaucratizing the imaginative" (*ATH* 225). Every enactment of this process was seen as a reenactment of the Fall.

In his 1951 presentation, Burke shifts his emphasis from an "idealist" perspective on the process, emphasizing the lapse from ideal to real, to a more pragmatic perspective, which allows him to acknowledge some of the more fortunate elements of this Fall. Hence his adoption of "hierarchy," which he defines in *Rhetoric of Motives* as "the old eulogistic word for bureaucracy" (118), to describe the organization resulting from the movement from ideal to real. What distinguishes bureaucracy from hierarchy is the retention in the latter of "imaginative" traces in the form of a principle of gradation. A hierarchy, thus, entails more than just a sense of regularity. "It also involves a distribution of authority. And such mutuality of rule and service, with its uncertain dividing line between loyalty and servitude, takes roughly a pyramidal or hierarchal form" (*P&C* 276).

With hierarchy, and its ordinal distribution of people into ranks and classes, comes the sense of mystery. "(Owing to their different modes of living and livelihood, classes of people become 'mysteries' to one another)" (*P&C* 276). In ancient times, it fell to priests to intermediate between the people and their mysteries. In fulfilling their office, they served "in part to promote cohesion among disparate classes, and in part to perpetuate ways that, while favoring some at the expense of others, may at times thereby endanger the prosperity of the tribe as a whole" (276). The first office would be filled by reminding people of the principle of gradation on which their ranks and classes rest. The second office would be filled by identifying the hierarchal principle with those who occupied the topmost ranks of the hierarchy (compare *RM* 141). Today "[t]he normal priestly function of partly upholding and partly transcending the Mysteries of class, is distributed among many kinds of symbol-users (particularly educators, legislators, journalists, advertising men, and artists)" (*P&C* 276).

There can be little doubt about which of the two priestly functions, upholding or transcending the status quo, journalist and advertising man Bruce Barton is primarily concerned to serve. For Barton, the better sort, the "socially elect," represent the essence of the hierarchy, while the rabble appear to be its accidents. Barton's socially elect, like the Puritan elect, turn out to be nearer to God than thee, and the hierarchy they happen to find themselves atop is the one true hierarchy, an identification that is fundamentally at odds with Burke's notion of a healthy hierarchy. For Burke, no hierarchy is truly complete

> in the mere arrangement whereby each rank is overlord to its underlings and underling to its overlords. It is complete only when each rank accepts the *principle of gradation itself*, and in thus "universalizing" the principle, makes a spiritual reversal of the ranks just as meaningful as their actual material arrangement. (*RM* 138)

Given that Christianity explicitly acknowledges a "last shall be first" principle of hierarchy, Barton's equation of social and spiritual rank seems particularly perverse but hardly surprising, given the delicate balancing act performed by latter-day priests who must call "upon images surviving from an earlier social order . . . [that] have their appeal precisely by reason of their remoteness" (*P&C* 277) and combine them with "images more in tune with the times" (277) in order to revivify a sense of mystery in contemporary audiences. In adapting ancient spiritual images (for example, his treatment of Satan) for contemporary secular audiences, Barton will, in the name of plausibility if nothing else, be more sedulous to uphold than to transcend the status quo.

From the foregoing discussion, it should be clear that Burke's critical vocabulary is well adapted to Barton's rhetorical project and that he anticipates Barton's role and function in general terms. In turn, it is clear that Barton falls short of Burke's priestly ideal, which calls for a middle way between inflating (mystifying) and dismissing (debunking) mystery, a process of "contemplation and sufferance . . . best adapted to the recognition and acceptance of a social form inevitable to social order" (*P&C* 294). To properly understand social hierarchy for Burke is to understand that while hierarchy in general is inevitable, no "particular hierarchy is inevitable" (*RM* 141), a principle Barton clearly violates by equating a particular social order with a spiritual model.

But that said, a Burkean treatment of Barton should be guided by the same principles that Barton appears to fall so short of. Burke's comedic approach, with its emphasis on "contemplation and sufferance," calls for cajolery rather than debunking. How that principle might be applied to Barton can be glimpsed in a couple of comments Burke makes about modern consumer culture. While Burke would surely question Barton's attempts to arouse a sense of "divine discontent" (compare Burke's dismissive reference to the "cult of endless *streben*" in *Faust*), Burke's goal of "maximum consciousness" encourages one to view even the pursuit of commodities as "a mode of transcendence that is genuine, but inferior" (192). And Burke imagines that even advertisers who engage in "the avid imagining of reasons why our citizenry should intensely yearn for all sorts of manufactured and 'processed' things (a narrow but unending succession of ends)" (15) are capable of helping us envisage "all the different ways in which it is thought, the world itself might end" (16), thereby restoring an eschatological vision of the sort Barton systematically avoids.

Burke cites another example of "genuine" if "inferior" transcendence, and in the process demonstrates an acute understanding of soft-sell advertising logic, in a Chrysler ad he finds in *Nation's Business*. The ad touts the car's "'Unseen Value,'" which is said to be "'far more real and far more vital to the car-owner than the iron, rubber, steel and glass of which the car is made,'" and bids the reader to "'look beyond the assembling line and search for the impelling aims and ideals of the organization'" (*ATH* 91). In Chrysler's ad, Burke sees a commercial version of "transubstantiation, the business parallel for the Church as the body of Christ, [which] arises when Unseen Value is incorporated in the body of a Chrysler car" (91). What Burke, tongue in cheek, suggests the Chrysler ad is doing is of course exactly the sort of thing that Barton claims with a totally straight face to do—give corporations a "soul" and link them to the "great river of eternity." But again, Burke does not flatly reject such claims; he merely tweaks and deflates them, using his comic frame to deal with oppositions between the ideal ("Christ," "divine discontent") and the actual ("Chrysler," "unending succession of ends"). Seeing the putative opposites "in terms of" each other à la a pun or a trope (Christ/Chrysler) results in each one rounding off ("both-and") rather than excluding ("either-or") the other. This is the heart of comedy.

Occupational Psychosis: Every Adman a God

Occupational psychosis, it will be recalled, is a term Burke borrows from Dewey to describe the process by which "a society's patterns of thought are shaped by the patterns of livelihood" (*PLF* 315). And while he assures us that he and Dewey do not use psychosis in its "psychiatric" sense, Burke certainly uses the term elsewhere to denote dysfunctional behaviors. For example, those who confuse secular hierarchies for their religious models display "undue acquiescence" (*P&C* 291) to the magic of rank and its insignia, and those who are blind to abuses of special interests are said to be afflicted with "hierarchal psychosis" (291). And "competitive psychosis" that emerges under free market capitalism is said to be "best revealed in the professionalization of sports, and in the flourishing of success literature during the late-lamented New Era" (*P&C* 41). Those afflicted with occupational psychosis, meanwhile, may be so thoroughly shaped by their patterns of livelihood as to enfeeble their capacity to "discount" terminologies.

"Discounting" is Burke's primary hermeneutical instrument, a merger "of interpretation and critique" (Crusius 125) through which we modify what is immediately before us by referring it to what we imagine to be below the surface or beyond the range of our perception. In the case of human communication, discounting is a way of correcting for distortions necessarily arising from "efficiency": "A man cannot say everything at once. Thus, his statements are necessarily 'efficient' in our sense; they throw strong light upon something, and in the process cast other things into the shadows" (*ATH* 248). When a friend tells us we look good, we discount the statement by calculating what other sentiments this particular person in this particular situation might be choosing not to pass along to us and modify our understanding of the sentiment accordingly. To discount is to consider not just the sense of words but the circumstances surrounding their utterance and the circumstances in which they are customarily used.

On a larger scale, we must discount terms when they move from one realm—"orientation" or "terministic screen"—to another. As noted earlier with regard to the behaviorists, problems in discounting are particularly acute when a specialized terminology is extended to the everyday. But in every instance, specialists in one field will have difficulty getting beyond the terminologies through which they filter the world to properly discount terms from another realm. In this regard, Burke mentions Marx's contention that historians and philosophers tend to privilege ideas over the material basis of history because they are in effect idea specialists. He also mentions Bacon's "reverse application" of the principle in "Idols of the Cave" where Bacon discusses scientific specialists who take up philosophy and "'distort and color'" their contemplations in obedience to their "'former fancies'" (*RM* 133). In the language of discounting, those who are occupationally psychotic incline toward 100 percent discounts, essentially "massacr[ing]" (*ATH* 246) the terms they import and emptying them out of their original meaning so as to impose the sense of their occupational "fancies" on them. One can point to a long line of humorous grotesques in literature who exemplify the malady, from *Tristram Shandy*'s intrepid Uncle Toby to *Catch-22*'s obsessive surgeons for whom all symptoms point toward the organ of their specialty and for whom all cures require the removal of said organ.

The tendency toward occupational psychosis is accelerated under capitalism, according to Burke, who identifies the tendency with a "'Faustian' concept of effort that went with the rise of business effort" (*ATH* 158). The latter "one-track efficiency" is contrasted to the "classical notion that one developed himself by the harmonious apportionment of many different ingredients [as opposed to Faustian] development [which] meant the intensification of some one peculiarity or aptitude" (158). Clearly, the art of discounting is more likely to flourish within an ethos of "harmonious apportionment" than within one stressing "one-track efficiency." Moreover, capitalism's tendency to intensify specialization is exacerbated, according to Burke, by the concurrent movement from God's Law to natural law to the law of the market (*GM* 92), from "monotheism" to "monetarism." Following the inexorable logic of Occam's Law of Parsimony, capitalism's search for an ever simpler, more neutral, and fungible ground of motivation lands finally on money, a pure abstraction with no inherent qualities, a "universal idiom" to which all diverse human values may be reduced. In turn, "the rationale of money had much to do with the innovation, specialization, diversification, partialization, and classification of economic motives" (115). Money functions as a "god term" for industrial capitalism by motivating people to perform mindless, narrowly repetitive tasks and by providing them with a new "scale to rate the rationality of the act" (333), not to mention a new "principle of gradation." A wage, with its quantity of promises for the future, moved people on a massive scale to live vicariously in anticipation of what was to come, a sense of anticipation fed most relentlessly and ingeniously by advertising.

Meanwhile, occupational specialization, which under capitalism seems almost predestined to become occupational psychosis, eventually runs afoul of Burke's paradox of substance. That paradox rests on the necessity of defining what a thing *is* "in terms of" *what it is not*. It is a central concept, perhaps *the* central concept, running through Burke, lending his work what Frank Lentricchia calls its "air of indelible self-difference" (*Criticism* 29). For Burke, definition is a matter not of distilling something down to its purely intrinsic essence, though he acknowledges an intrinsic dimension, but of locating an entity within a web of extrinsic relationships with which it is "identified." In matters of personal identity, thus, Burke moves very quickly beyond the intrinsic dimension of that identity to "scenic equivalents" of identity, including profession and vocation. In this context, occupational psychosis can be understood as a futile attempt to escape the paradox of substance, to render personal identity homologous with professional identity, thereby limiting one's moral and social responsibilities to one's professional obligations.

Which brings us back to Bruce Barton, Advertising Man, and his project to ethicize his occupational psychosis. Oddly enough, Burke's most useful commentary on such a project occurs in a discussion of Franz Kafka. Certainly one could be excused for not noticing that Kafka and Barton were contemporaries. And it might also escape one's notice that both dealt with similar matters—parallels between religious and secular hierarchies. But Burke's analysis of Kafka reminds us of their commonalities and the usefulness of Kafka as an ironic gloss on Barton.

By the lights of Burke's reading, Kafka's *The Castle* can be understood as an uncanny mirror reversal of *TMNK*, particularly in its treatment of divinity. Where Barton's God is the heroic, paternal figure who enlists our aid in his heroic struggle, Kafka's God is some mysterious official who just happens, fortuitously it would appear, to sit atop a hierarchy notable mostly for the "dinginess" of those persons who occupy its highly stratified ranks.

It is a hierarchy of "suits," to use a contemporary metonymic reduction that Kafka would surely savor. And its reigning figure "is a nonentity in the sense that he manifests no *intrinsic properties* fitting him to represent the religious motive; yet the mysteries of rank endow him with 'reverence' anyhow. Indeed, his very unfitness as a vicar perversely suggests the dignifying effect of the office itself" (*RM* 237).

Kafka's deity personifies the vanity of human attempts to craft gods from mortals. The paltriness of his God, argues Max Brod in explaining why he calls Kafka a "religious humorist," is a testament to our inability to "'overcome the incommensurability of earthly and religious aims'" (qtd. in *RM* 243). In Kafka's thoroughly bureaucratized hierarchy, the divinity is a default personage—whoever happens to occupy the highest rung of officialdom. There is no ruling principle, no spiritual ground through which one might make sense of the order or endow any of the activities with value. The only glamour that attaches to the reigning official derives not from any exalted intrinsic qualities he might possess but rather solely from his occupation of the loftiest spot. He is a divine monarch after belief in an ontic logos has lapsed. The hierarchy he rules, meanwhile, is purely a matter of *status*, where "top" means "opposite of bottom." Period. It is a monument to the failures of the human imagination, afflicted with occupational psychosis such that "the terms of the social order incongruously shape our idea of God, inviting men to conceive of communication with God after the analogy of their worldly embarrassments" (*RM* 234).

While Kafka's text explores the calamities that arise from the failure of an impoverished human imagination to conceive a spiritual realm "different in kind" from the earthly, Barton's book enthusiastically enumerates the differences in degree between quasi-divine executives and the rabble. Barton's Jesus is an irresistible, charismatic figure, whose "God was no Bureau, no Rule Maker, no Accountant" (72) and whose identity is almost entirely self-determined. In violation of Burke's paradox of substance, Barton's Jesus aims to be wholly defined by intrinsic qualities and not to be governed by "authorities and precepts" of a hierarchy that contains him or dependent on the masses who surround him. And whereas Kafka's religious humor ironically reduces God to the merely human, Barton "elevates" Christ to the level of the superhuman. He transforms Jesus into a secular hero who ends up looking more like Superman than Achilles, let alone Buddha. For Barton, the secular and divine realms appear to be not only commensurable but also co-extensive and permeable;

in fact, the religious appears to be little more than the "earthly plus," a quantitatively distinct region of the "newest," "greatest," and "biggest," as devoid of mystery as an advertisement for the latest breakthrough in, say, "auto protectant technology."

Barton's conversion of Christ into a secular superhero is, in turn, a violation of a second fundamental principle of Burke's philosophy, the paradox of purity: "We confront this paradox when deriving the nature of the human person from God as 'super-person,' as 'pure,' or 'absolute' person, since God as a superperson would be impersonal—and the impersonal would be synonymous with the negation of personality" (*GM* 35). This is to say, Burke here acknowledges the matter of absolute "incommensurability of earthly and spiritual aims" in the context of heroic individuals. We can never hope to *be* such a figure and "can *possess only in attenuated form*" (*ATH* 268) those qualities that make the figure heroic in the first place. Thus, the example of Christ will be followed by the "truly religious man," not in hopes of *becoming* Christ, but only in the hope of possessing "a vicarious share in Christ's perfection. . . . He wanted to be as near like his hero as possible within his human limitations" (268). When the religious emphasis shifts to a secular one, meanwhile, Burke suggests that a corresponding shift in perspective must take place: "[I]nsofar as the ideal of heroism becomes secularized we hold that a corresponding shift to comedy must take place" (268).[3]

Insofar as Barton never manages a comedic perspective on the ideal of heroism, he never manages to create either a plausible secular hero or an awe-inspiring divinity. What he attempts instead is what Burke describes as "the perfecting or absolutizing" (*P&C* 292) of a secular term of a secular-divine analogy. And perfectionism or "end-of-the-line speculation" (292) of this sort, however natural the impulse to do it, never turns out well in Burke, who recommends getting off before the end of any line, the last stop where all the cults and psychoses await us.

3 The Profession of Success: From Carnegie to Nixon

In retrospect, Bruce Barton is both one of the last of his kind and a precursor of things to come. For all his rhetorical sophistication, he is one of the last of the amateurs in a field that is increasingly dominated by professionals: the consultants, preachers, therapists, media personalities, columnists, "career coaches," and sundry other success mavens whose livelihoods derive almost exclusively from their ability to persuade their audiences that they know how to help them succeed. Having themselves enjoyed relatively modest, if any, success in other lines of work, tens of thousands of people today make a living helping others succeed. There have been, to be sure, accounts written by (or for) various business superstars—Trump, Gates, Iacocca, Welch, and others—detailing their surefooted ascent to fortune in the worlds of real estate or electronics with a few nuggets of wisdom and advice thrown in along the way. But these tomes fall closer to the category of celebrity bios than pieces of success rhetoric per se, which is to say, they are read and listened to mostly, as opposed to partially, for magical reasons: by ingesting the career of Lee Iacocca, consumers of such fare vicariously *become* Lee Iacocca. The attraction of such books is clearly the attraction that Kenneth Burke once attributed to "inspirational literature": "[T]he reader, while reading it, is . . . living in the aura of success. What he wants is easy success; and he gets it in symbolic form by the mere reading itself" (*PLF* 299).

In some important respects, those who follow Barton appear to have less in common with him than with some of his predecessors, people like Elbert Hubbard and Russell Conwell. Those who succeed Barton, like those who preceded him, tend to share an ideology that resonates more with New Thought theology than with Barton's liberal Christian theology.

And Barton's successors will follow the path of his predecessors in transforming themselves from mere authors into performers on a national stage. But still, the differences in degree between those pioneers in the field and their more recent avatars are sufficiently great to place them in a different category. Latter-day success rhetoricians—the Dale Carnegies, Napoleon Hills, Norman Vincent Peales, Tom Peterses, Tony Robbinses, M. Scott Pecks, and Stephen Coveys—are to their originals as media conglomerates are to vaudeville acts. One can trace through their lineage the emergence of the success professional culminating in "the guru," a figure so exemplary that he becomes, following the logic of Burke's "paradox of purity," a higher-order being different in kind from those who would measure themselves by his example.

"If You're So Rich, Why Aren't You Smart?": Deskilling Success

Unlike the earlier business religionists, latter-day success professionals enjoy a superstar status reserved for sports figures and evangelists in Barton's day. They are not the mere amanuenses of others' success tales forced to borrow their legitimacy from religious figures like Christ. Rather, in the tradition of Colonel Sanders, each is the brand name for his or her own success recipe. The origins of this status, like the origins of any mythic hero, are murky. How, after all, does one explain a Tony Robbins? Robbins enjoys (or "enjoyed"—like so many of the gurus his star has faded in the new century) to an unparalleled degree that condition of tautological bliss first remarked by Daniel Boorstin—the state of being well-known for well-knownness. All his fame and fortune derive from his success at signifying success. Because he is a success, because he exemplifies so perfectly so many themes of the American success myth, people buy his books and his video- and audiotapes and attend his seminars, thereby making him "successful." The great mystery remains, of course, where did that success, upon which all his success is built, originate? Like a Derridean signifier, Robbins apparently possesses no such origin. He exemplifies a metaphysic not of presence but of absence. One attempting to make sense of his story will only encounter another story; rags-to-riches jostles with the frog prince jostles with *Fountainhead* to account for the phenomenon "Tony Robbins." In turn, Robbins's message is as insubstantial as his persona; it comprises little more than an odd lot of signifiers, a space not unlike Judith Williamson's space of advertising, where various fragments of sundry American myths and lore modify each other without necessarily signifying anything outside their space. Perhaps better than any of his peers, Robbins illustrates the success professional's version of a hermeneutic circle, one whose spirit was so economically captured in the old *Saturday Night Live* skit where the putative "guru" urges his audience to "Buy my book, *How to Get Other People to Buy Your Book for $50!* For only $50!"

Again, the contrast with Barton is striking. Barton not only earned his reputation and most of his fortune in a field other than the success profession but also sold a relatively paltry number of books and, more important, failed to exploit his status as a success professional by "extending his brand." While *The Man Nobody Knows* was indeed the best-selling nonfiction book of 1926 and eventually sold over a quarter-million copies, his subsequent books did not do nearly so well, and he never became a household name outside New York. While he did cash in his celebrity for a successful run for the House of Representatives fourteen years later, he was soon out of office. His book sales and unremarkable political success make for relatively small beer in the success business, where one's books must sell in the millions and spinoff profits must eventually dwarf royalty income for one to be considered a "player" in the field. In effect, Barton was first and last an "advertising man" who happened to do other things, including writing about the relationship between success in business and religion. Success rhetoric as a field in itself remained to be established by those who would follow.

And also in contrast to his successors, Barton's books are less about how to succeed than they are defenses of certain ways of succeeding. He offers aspirants more information about who they need to be than about what they need to do in order to make it. He mostly reassures them that the sorts of success they seek are legitimated not only by the lives of latter-day business legends and political luminaries he invokes but also by Jesus Christ, whose own life turns out to be a sort of prequel to the lives of Barton's secular heroes. In the process, he speaks less as a professional success rhetorician than as a champion of business as a worthy profession, even a "calling." He sought professional legitimation by connecting the present to larger times and "the great spirits of the past" ("Human" 67). Representing an emergent profession embarrassingly dependent on market forces for its success, Bruce Barton followed the path of so many other professional apologists in inventing "a culture with roots in a classic past" (Larson xv).

Barton's immediate successors, meanwhile, spend little time fretting over justifications for their notions of success (indeed, "fretting" in any form is anathema to Barton's successors) and focus almost exclusively on the means of acquiring what all are assumed to seek—success, which is increasingly synonymous with money. While later success professionals will, to be sure, invoke weighty moral concerns and cite various important thinkers who have reflected on larger questions, such musings are typically brief and superficial, nearly always restricted to prefaces and introductions. They are ritual nods to convention, cursory preludes to lengthy lists of techniques and procedures and rules of behavior guaranteed to move one ahead in whatever endeavor one may find oneself engaged, from raising chinchillas or manufacturing cheese snacks to "closing the deal." They speak not as outsiders seeking to justify a place in a hierarchy whose ruling principles may be hostile to their endeavors but as "experts" secure within their professional niche. Their role is not to inspire any "endless *streben*" or stir up any "divine discontent" but to advise people on how to nudge past the competition in the pursuit of rewards that are always finally, and unapologetically, financial.[1]

Perhaps because Barton's work appears at the very beginnings of twentieth-century success ideology, it has about it the feel of an origin myth, possessing heroic qualities little in evidence among his successors' works. It is not so much the replicable behaviors of Barton's Christ that make for success; it is his inimitable capacity for outsized, even miraculous, deeds, his resolution and courage, his certitude and his willingness to commit even physical violence in the name of his beliefs. He represents, in brief, a number of virtues that would not necessarily serve one well in mid-twentieth-century corporate America. Barton's antinomian hero disappears from success rhetoric until Tom Peters and Rob Waterman's *In Search of Excellence*, where he resurfaces in the form of the shadowy men/gods who found excellent companies by breaking all the rules, even those promulgated by the authors.

If Barton demands authenticity and heroic resolve of "executives," his immediate successors ask little more of their readers than a sincere commitment to a handful of vaguely worded principles. To borrow from one of the many mechanical analogies favored by Norman Vincent Peale, one learns to "lubricate" (19) one's mind with positive suggestions that take the "scratchiness" out of one's personality and leave one capable of passing efficiently through life free of friction. It is not so much that one must strive hard and work long hours like the virtuous yeomen of nineteenth-century success handbooks or strenuously oppose the dogma and rigidities of received value systems as in Barton. One must merely "believe" strenuously and sincerely in one's capacity to succeed. And in case one is unsure how to go about doing this, there are always rules, steps, and inspiring anecdotes to guide one.

A defining moment in this new manner of thinking about success occurs in Peale's "thrilling story of my friends Maurice and Mary Alice Flint" (134). According to Peale, this once hapless couple failed at virtually everything they turned their hands to, all the while blaming their problems on "'dirty deals' other people had given them" (135), in violation of positive thinking's most hallowed principles. Indeed, Peale considered Maurice "one of the most negative persons I have ever encountered" (134). But then "Maurice Flint really took to the faith idea" (135), particularly the notion that "if you have 'faith as a grain of mustard seed, nothing is impossible'" (135). Eventually, Maurice strengthens his wavering faith by carrying around an actual mustard seed, fished by Mary Alice out of a pickle jar. But he kept losing the tiny seed until finally, against the advice of a "supposed expert," he succeeded in encasing the seed in a plastic ball. Through the offices of Peale and his friend Walter Hoving, president of Bonwit Teller, the Flints began marketing the mustard seed, which "sold like hot cakes" (136). By 1952, when Peale recounts their story, the couple had opened a factory to mass produce the incredibly popular "Flint Mustard Seed Remembrancer."

What is particularly striking about this tale in the context of the history of success rhetoric—beyond its anachronistic acknowledgment of chance's role in achieving success—is that it offers a rare example of a success rhetorician relating a tale in which he spawns a success in the field of success rhetoric. The Flints' success is not just an effect of Peale's teaching in a different domain; it is of the same order as Peale's teaching. Their success lies exclusively in selling a success aid to others. While the mustard seed may be seen as an expression of religious faith, it is clear that its primary significance to Peale and to the Flints is as an emblem of faith in oneself. It functions for them as a magical talisman that gives one sufficient faith in oneself to achieve otherwise impossible deeds, such as building a factory to produce plastic-embalmed mustard seeds. By replicating himself in the Flints, Peale is taking a critical step on the path to professionalizing his field. He is engaging in what Magali Sarfatti Larson calls the "production of professional producers" (17) of domain-specific expertise and technology.

Of course in Peale's case, one needs to substitute "faith," or its contemporary secular cognate, "empowerment," for "expertise" to make the analogy work, but clearly by replicating himself in the Flints, Peale has established that he is selling an "alienable" commodity with a value in the marketplace. And while the Flints offer the most striking instance of "producing producers" within a professional line, Peale's books are replete with examples of his disciples saving lost souls using the master's techniques. And Carnegie, of course, maintained an enormous staff of professionals to oversee and run his seminars, produce his course materials, and market his program. In their production and organization of other success professionals, Carnegie and Peale anticipate the present-day guru distribution system, though today's gurus have the luxury of "outsourcing" their wares through an army of consultants, corporate trainers, and human resource specialists who purchase and reproduce the gurus' techniques, seminars, tapes, and books.

Commodifying the notion of success allows Carnegie and Peale to treat it like any other good and to produce, package, and market it for mass consumption in a manner unforeseen by Barton. Whereas Barton's Christ relies primarily on intuition, charisma, and decisive action (not to mention Barton's page-turning prose) to mesmerize his audiences into success, Carnegie and Peale routinize their procedures and sell them as products. In Carnegie's mind, what he had managed to do was to operationalize a notion he attributes to John D. Rockefeller: "'The ability to deal with people is as purchasable a commodity as sugar or coffee'" (13). More pointedly, the value Rockefeller placed on that ability— "'And I will pay more for that ability ... than for any other under the sun'" (13)—surely encouraged Carnegie to set up shop and start selling his success techniques. The problem was how best to pitch so remarkably uninspiring a vision to audiences in search of inspiration.

By the Book: Scripture as Textbook

The "Flint Mustard Seed Remembrancer" exemplifies one such pitch. It is a notable model insofar as it managed simultaneously to invoke a matter of "ultimate concern," religious faith, at the same time that it converted that concern to a commercial product devoid of doctrinal substance. The Flints, with a little help from Bonwit Teller, quite literally commodified and secularized faith, a process since perfected by gurus, while ensuring that the commodity remained aloof from doctrinal strife that might limit its market appeal. The mustard seed could signify capitalist faith or Catholic faith, a junior high romance or an act of martyrdom. It stands in the same relationship to particular religious faiths as success rhetoric stands in relationship to particular business fields. The mustard seed perfectly emblemizes the characteristic mix of religious exuberance and ideological vacuity that marks the discourse of midcentury success rhetoric.

The substitution of mustard seeds for crosses on various forms of personal adornment throughout the 1950s also says much about the American religious temperament of the time, a temperament nicely captured in what Harold Bloom calls a "notorious" remark by then President Eisenhower that "the United States was and had to be a religious nation, and that he didn't care what religion it had, as long as it had one" (49). In such a setting, religious doctrines and corporate philosophies could readily merge with one another while clergymen like Peale could become corporate advisers as readily as a businessman like Dale Carnegie could become a source of spiritual solace to many of the nation's faithful. While this tendency to put one's faith in faith without worrying overmuch about the specifics of doctrine is especially pronounced during this period, its roots in American religious tradition are deep.

In the words of Richard Hofsteader, "The essence of American denominationalism is that churches became *voluntary* organizations" (82) and as such have, since their earliest days, relied on marketing techniques to procure the new members necessary to survival. From eighteenth-century "lay exhorters," commissioned by churches to go out among the masses as did the legendary Yankee traders of the day and convert people to the tenets of the "true faith," to today's televangelists, the tendency to package religious doctrine as a salable product has always characterized evangelical American churches. When Billy Sunday defended his fabulous wealth against those who criticized him for the cost of his revivals by declaring that "'[w]hat I'm paid for my work makes it only about $2 a soul, and I get less proportionately for the number I convert than any other living evangelist'" (qtd. in Hofsteader 115), he could count on a sympathetic response from audiences accustomed to measuring religious institutions by congregation size and conversions. In such a setting, "lubricating" church doctrine to minimize the friction between the secular and the spiritual recommends itself to church figures like Peale for many of the same reasons that lubricating the personality through self-effacement and subscription to scrupulously inoffensive beliefs recommends itself in the workplace.

All of this goes a long way toward explaining why Carnegie and Peale could blandly assume that their audiences would require little in the way of justification for their apparent commodification of spiritual matters and human relations. And indeed, their self-presentations are remarkably free of the various rhetorical gambits used by Barton, such as parabolic argument, a stress on the "news value" of the subject, or the seductively engrossing dramatic narrative, let alone explicit defense or justification for their methods. And certainly no one would ever attribute their wondrous book sales to their relentlessly insipid prose. There are few passages in their books notable for stylistic felicity or distinctive voice, even fewer distinctive characters, and the events they recount tend to be both highly predictable and barely plausible. They foreground the very redundancies Barton works so assiduously to disguise. Their books are as far removed from Barton's dramatic "portrait" of Christ as chemistry textbooks are from bodice-rippers.

Indeed, the books closest in substance and spirit to *How to Win Friends and Influence People* and *The Power of Positive Thinking* are textbooks that introduce readers to an unfamiliar but well-established field, offering an overview of settled matters and a tour of the axiomatic principles and unassailable procedures of a "normal science." There is little theory to be found in these books (Carnegie and Peale view theorizing as only marginally more tolerable than fretting), and if there are anomalies and controversies that might threaten the ruling paradigm, they are never mentioned. While Barton too exhibited little patience for those who resorted to theory or dogma, he at least dramatized the agon between Christ's intuitive approach and the more prescriptive "theoretical" approaches of his old antagonists the scribes and Pharisees.

In addition to their imperturbable tone, absence of drama, and attention to coverage of fundamentals, the authors also ape several formal devices of textbooks. Thus, in *How to Win Friends and Influence People,* Carnegie includes a chapter on how to read his book and suggests within that chapter that his student/reader treat it as a *"handbook on human relations"* (58). Early on, he suggests that the function of his book is not to impart knowledge but to influence behavior and refers to it as an *"action* book" (18) as opposed to a mere knowledge book. Peale meanwhile refers to *The Power of Positive Thinking* as a "practical, direct-action, personal-improvement manual" (xii) and as such a member of the same family as the Bible, which he calls "the textbook of spiritual science" (44).

In Burke's treatment of "traditional principles of rhetoric" (*RM* 49–180), his discussion of Cicero is particularly salient to the textbook strategy employed by Peale and Carnegie. After identifying the three styles of oratory enumerated by Cicero, "the grandiloquent, plain, and tempered" (*RM* 73), along with his three "offices" of rhetoric—to teach, to please, and to move—Burke notes Cicero's claim that "the plain style is best for teaching" (73). While any piece of oratory is ultimately motivated by a desire to move the audience to action, Cicero recommends "that the orator should call as much attention to his use of instruction as possible, but should thoroughly though unnoticeably infuse his speech with the other two functions" (*RM* 74). While Carnegie and Peale do in fact announce their intent to move their audiences to act, their version of action mostly concerns their audience's ability to follow instructions and thereby better manipulate the behaviors of others—which is to say, their version of "acting" is in Burke's nomenclature "sheer motion (what the behaviorists would call a Response to a Stimulus)" (*GM* xx). Moreover, references to actually moving people are as rare in their writing as instances of grandiloquence; mostly their books are taken up with matters of instruction written in a studiously plain style. Their textbook prose imposes more than induces consent. It exemplifies the use of "tonalities" that suggest they are "speaking *in conclusion*" (*RM* 98) even when justification may be called for, a tendency Burke sees in teachers who use "subtle tonalities to *suggest* a set of judgments," which, if "explicitly mustered," would allow students to critically question them (98). Peale and Carnegie are free to adopt this strategy and eschew grandiloquence mostly because today, "purposes indigenous to the monetary rationale are so thoroughly built into [our] productive and distributive system . . . [that] a relatively high proportion of interest in purely 'neutral' terminologies of motives can be consistent with equally intense ambition" (*RM* 96). Speaking to audiences thoroughly conditioned by "the monetary rationale," Peale and Carnegie need only enumerate the steps for gaining material advantage in the blandest, most neutral of terminologies to "inspire" and stimulate a feverish response.

The studiously neutral textbook prose style of Carnegie and Peale contrasts markedly with Barton's use of scenic construction, narrative tension, and pronounced point of view. Keeping Barton in mind, consider a typical "scene" in Peale. The setting is a golf club locker room. Some friends have organized a golf outing to cheer up "George." We never know what George's problem is or anything particular about any of the actors in the scene. After one brief paragraph of background, the scene reaches its "climactic" moment:

> Finally one of the men arose to go. He knew about difficulties, for he'd had plenty himself, but he had found some vital answers to *his*

problems. He stood hesitantly, then laid his hand on his friend's shoulder. "George," he said, "I hope you won't think I am preaching at you. Really, I'm not, but I would like to suggest something. It's the way I got through my difficulties. It really works if you work at it, and it's this. 'Why not draw upon that Higher Power?'" (213)

Later, offstage, George apparently follows his friend's advice and becomes "a healthy, happy man" (213).

Peale's scene floats insubstantially before us, imparting little sense of a particular time or place. And his characters, as Wendy Kaminer suggests, "All . . . sound alike; that is, they sound like Peale" (51). There is no "rising action" here; we go directly from the "crisis" to the denouement in the form of an omniscient voiceover offering up a two-sentence declaration of the resolution. It has the feel of those old cartoon strip advertisements for the Charles Atlas course featuring the 90-pound weakling morphing into a 190-pound bully-beater in the course of two panels; one goes instantly from lamentable problem to resounding solution, the closest thing to a crisis being the hero's willingness to "gamble a stamp" and send away for the course. The arduous process of getting from "here" to "there," the actual sweat and exercise required to produce those muscles, remains as mysterious a process as George's discovery of a discretely amorphous "Higher Power." And the only advice Peale ever offers on the latter process—don't try too hard, remain positive at all times, count on divine guidance—is not so much designed to teach one how to tap into those powers as to reassure one that such powers are always available for tapping into.

Peale's anecdote is right out of the allegorical or homiletic tradition in which everything points outside itself to something else; nothing that is being related matters for its own sake, only for the sake of the meaning it points to. In Perelman and Olbrechts-Tyteca's terms, this anecdote, and virtually all the anecdotes recounted in Peale and Carnegie, take the form of "illustrations" or repetitions of a general principle at a slightly more particular level. There is little ambiguity here of the sort one finds in Barton's parables between example and exemplary. A potentially subversive principle or moral is never "piggybacked" onto a compelling narrative designed to distract one from the ruse. The efficacy of Peale's illustrations is unaffected by implausibility because they do not, contra Barton's parables, serve an evidentiary function. They serve only to clarify—like graphic illustrations in a textbook.

By the same token, while Barton uses the Bible to legitimate his viewpoint, Carnegie and Peale cite few sources other than their own experience or those reported to them by their legions of important and influential friends and former students. To the extent that textual sources are cited, they tend either to be other of their own works, popular magazines like *Reader's Digest*, or other works of inspirational literature. Peale, like Barton, recommends a number of biblical one-liners to keep in mind, but they are mantras far removed from their context of situation and often used to ends remote from their original function. In Peale and Carnegie, we see the beginnings of the trend in success rhetoric to begin feeding upon itself and to support its claims and prescriptions with equally dubious claims and prescriptions from other works of success rhetoric, usually the authors' own. If one wishes, for example, to discover how "George" tapped into a Higher Power, Peale recommends another of his books in a footnote. The primary function of text, here and elsewhere in Peale's and Carnegie's work, is transitive. One is not invited to linger over or to reflect on the prose. One is marched briskly to the next lesson and to other services and courses bearing the author's brand. The text advertises in the act of advising.

For all that their books appear to be motivated by a desire to set their readers in Skinnerian motion, Carnegie and Peale are obsessed by the need for their subjects to "act" voluntarily. As Carnegie reminds his readers ad nauseam, the procedures he recommends are neither complex nor novel, but they entail a fundamental change in identity. "I'm talking about a new way of life. Let me repeat. *I am talking about a new way of life*" (39). It is not enough merely to smile perpetually, forever see things from every other person's point of view, avoid negative thoughts, and fill your mind with self-affirmations——one must do all this *sincerely*, because THIS IS WHO YOU ARE. Like an American tourist overcoming language barriers by increasing the volume, Carnegie resorts to pure exhortation when it comes to the one thing technique cannot do—render his version of a suitable self sincere (though both authors hint that by feigning the prescribed behaviors long enough and heartily enough, one may achieve a perfectly serviceable ersatz sincerity).

Like Barton, Carnegie and Peale also draw extensively on advertising logic to construct their books, though in their case, the model is not so much the print or radio ad as it is that curious hybrid of overt instruction and covert seduction, the infomercial. Or perhaps more accurately, one can probably trace the origins of TV infomercials to books like *The*

Power of Positive Thinking and *How to Win Friends and Influence People.* The primary tool of the infomercial is redundancy, typically in the form of endless testimonials by satisfied clients who have gone from rags to riches in the same instant and mysterious manner that "George" discovered a Higher Power. Often shot against the background of rolling blue waves and wide beaches, the success guru, deeply tanned and wearing beach attire, will repeat his own inspirational story, tick off the three, five, or seven "keys" to his program, and then introduce a lineup of excessively grateful clients who will repeat, sometimes tearfully, the basic formula and their tales of economic and spiritual salvation. But invariably, one is led by the advice in the infomercial to the need for more advice; one must purchase another book, series of audiotapes or videocassettes, CDs, or personal planner or attend a series of classes or seminars to assure the sort of success seen on the infomercial. Just call the pulsating 800 number at the bottom of the screen. The infomercial is above all else a teaser, an extended stay in the company of magical success that remains tantalizingly close but just out of reach. One needs that next level of advice, ultimately perhaps even some sort of direct contact with the guru, to ensure one's own success.

Hence the success textbook/infomercials of Peale and Carnegie. Each chapter features an important behavioral principle ("How to Break the Worry Habit," "Six Ways to Make People Like You") that is briefly explicated and amply illustrated with a series of anecdotal testimonials, then concludes with a prescriptive summary. While ostensibly self-sufficient, the chapters often allude to other helpful information available from the author. In some instances, the chapter may take one right up to the very edge of the method's vanishing point, that elusive state of sincerity—*Let me repeat. I am talking about a new way of life.* While such moments are typically underscored by repetition, capitalization, or italics, the essence of sincerity remains forever ineffable. And just as the makers of infomercials favor lush settings in which to make their pitches, Peale and Carnegie like to feature themselves in resort settings like the Royal Hawaiian Hotel on whose balcony Peale reports writing *The Power of Positive Thinking*:

> The air is laden with the aroma of exotic flowers. . . . The incredible blue ocean surrounding these islands stretches way to the horizon. The white waves are surging in, and the Hawaiians and my fellow visitors are riding gracefully on surfboards and outrigger canoes. . . . It has an incredibly healing effect on me as I sit here writing about the power generated in a peaceful mind. (24–25)

It is just one of an endless succession of lush and privileged sites—boardrooms, CEO offices and conference rooms, luxury liners, banquet halls, hotel suites, Florida beaches, beautiful homes, golf courses, and locker rooms—from which Peale and Carnegie, always in the company of successful and important people, draw their inspiration. Like Barton's Christ, they are most at home amongst the elite, though they also exude that same folksy ordinariness, that quality of incredible "approachability," that Barton attributes to Christ.

The texts of Peale and Carnegie are, in sum, what Carnegie calls "action books," meant not to be read so much as put into practice. One either skips all the blather about technique and lives vicariously for the nonce in the "aura of success" comprising the scene of their books, or one studies, memorizes, and applies their lessons with quick-twitch alacrity: "(1) PRAYERIZE (2) PICTURIZE (3) ACTUALIZE" (Peale 45). What one does not do is enjoy for its own sake or reflect upon or critically question their writing, not because they have, like Barton, utilized shrewd rhetorical strategies to disguise and soften their messages but because such perspectives have been ruled out of bounds as species of "negative" thinking that threaten to limit one's power and popularity.

The Perennial Success Ideology: New Thought

The rhetorical and stylistic differences between Barton on the one hand and Carnegie and Peale on the other can be traced to the deeper immersion of the latter two in New Thought theology. These differences are most clearly manifested in their treatment of sin and consequently of the agency and function of Christ. While Barton does not tarry over questions of evil, he does acknowledge that God will need our help if the "experiment to which all His resources are committed" (179), the perfection of the human species, is to succeed. For Barton, we are en route to perfection but not yet there, and the obstacles to the attainment of that perfection are formidable, the outcome is in doubt, and considerable heroic resolve, exemplified by Christ, is demanded of those who would triumph over circumstance.

The devolution of Barton's liberal Christianity into the nominally Christian New Thought, or "mind cure" beliefs of Peale and Carnegie, is marked in the latter by the virtual disappearance of Christ, or any other sort of intermediary between man and God. According to Donald Meyer in *The Positive Thinkers*, any sort of intercession between God and man was unnecessary in mind cure theology because according to their view,

"It was not simply that men could know God as Mind; men were actually individualizations of God. Individualizations of the Divine Mind, they themselves were wholly mind" (77). As such, we are wholly lacking in singularity or personality, and Christ was little more than a vaporous principle. He became "*the* Christ" or the principle of God's mind in motion, a sort of divine current that passes from God, the infinite power source, to us, his numberless human outlets.

> Neither the sacrificial intercessor of orthodoxy nor the perfect moral preceptor of liberalism, neither God-man nor man-God, "the Christ," by being a principle, not a man of any sort of all, perhaps most radically shifted religious orientation by dissolving the sense of time organized around a historical life in favor of a timeless truth. (79)

While Meyer is critical of Barton for "[d]omesticating Christianity to the Chamber of Commerce, [and] enlisting Jesus Christ into the ranks of Madison Avenue" (177), he applauds the "antinomian" strain in Barton's thinking and his advocacy for "the power of personal existence, which was to say, of individual creative energy and self-transformation" (178) over New Thought's more ethereal version of power. In a world where legions of New Thoughters busily tune themselves to the infinite à la Ralph Waldo Trine or gratefully swoon to the "Gospel of Relaxation" à la Annie Payson Call or obsessively repeat the New Thought mantra "Every day in every way, I get better and better," Barton's Christ looks like a Calvinist relic.

Peale's descent from New Thought, meanwhile, could hardly be more direct. Take, for example, his notion of "power." It clearly owes far more to the likes of Call, Trine, and Haddock than to, say, Nietzsche. The key to power for Peale is a peaceful mind, and "the chief struggle in gaining mental peace is the effort of revamping your thinking to the relaxed attitude of acceptance of God's gift of peace" (16), most reliably attained through therapeutic church attendance, "the scientific use of prayer and relaxation" (81), and, as in the case of "George," a round of golf. Following his favorite mechanical model, Peale recommends studying "prayer from an efficiency point of view. Usually the emphasis is entirely religious though no cleavage exists between the two concepts" (43). Efficient prayer involves a process not unlike changing the oil in your car. Peale advocates that one first "practice emptying the mind" of any thoughts whatsoever and then filling it with "creative and healthy thoughts" (18) whose presence will force negative thoughts to "struggle for admission" (19). Or,

"Prayerize. Picturize. Actualize." All of this sounds like it was lifted straight from mind cure economist Henry Wood, who championed a technique he called "Mental Photography" whereby "'we must refuse mental standing-room to discord. . . . Think no evil, and have eyes only for the good'" (qtd. in Meyer 109).

Later on, Peale assures us that "[e]very great personality I have ever known, and I have known many, who has demonstrated the capacity for prodigious work has been a person in tune with the Infinite" (32).[2] His failure even to mention here Ralph Waldo Trine, whose name is synonymous with the notion of being "in tune with the Infinite," is more likely a sign of Peale's confidence that his audience knows the allusion than of a failure to credit an important source. Later he tells us that he believes "that prayer is a sending out of vibrations from one person to another and to God. All of the universe is in vibration. . . . [I]n this process you awaken vibrations in the universe through which God brings to pass the good objectives prayed for" (49–50). With this sort of scientific prayer at your command, who needs Jesus for salvation? Or for that matter, sacrifice, humility, or good works?

Underlying this notion of tuning oneself to the vibrations of the Infinite is a notion dear to New Thoughters and their guru descendants, the belief in an abundance theology. At the heart of abundance theology is the rejection of the "illusory" notion of scarcity or lack. Whether we are talking about the material bounty that comes of "scientific" prayer in Peale (46) or the seemingly limitless influence and control over people that comes of yielding your will to the world in Carnegie, the belief in abundance both ensures their disciples a major return on their investment of time and energy and reassures them that those returns need not come at the expense of others locked into some dreary version of the zero-sum game.[3] In the words of H. Emilie Cady: "One of the unerring truths in the universe is that there is already provided a lavish abundance for every human want. In other words, the supply of every good always awaits the demand" (65–66).

In this vein, Peale exhorts his readers "to expect, not to doubt. In so doing you bring everything into the realm of possibility" (86). Carnegie, meanwhile, says that his "sole purpose" in writing *How to Win Friends and Influence People* is to help people "discover, develop and profit by [their] dormant and unused assets" (18). We all have these latent resources, and when we tap into them they always lead us to new bounty. In typical Carnegie fashion, he delivers abundance doctrines sans the metaphysics, stressing the "magic" (one of his favorite words) of his formula rather than the theology. The Carnegie disciple sacrifices ego to will and becomes an egoless, disembodied revenant, a smile floating through life, endlessly converting self-erasure into power over others in a kind of weird psychic version of cold fusion.

While Carnegie's links to New Thought are partially camouflaged by the ostensibly secular nature of his system, one can see a clear connection between his thinking and New Thought doctrine in the matter of appearance and reality. In New Thought, everything—subject, object, God, humanity, past, present, and future—is Mind and as such susceptible to mental control. To the extent that any cogent notion of reality requires the existence of a realm independent of the perceiver's control—hence Burke's equation of his system to "metabiology" in *Permanence and Change*—New Thought turns everything into appearance that can be willed away or modified to suit the perceiver. The most striking declaration of this appearance/reality equivalence in Carnegie occurs in the context of remarks about the joys of mental illness:

> [I]nsane people are happier than you and I. Many enjoy being insane. Why shouldn't they? They have solved their problems. They will write you a check for a million dollars, or give you a letter of introduction to the Aga Khan. They have found in a dream world of their own creation the feeling of importance which they so deeply desired. (35)

For Carnegie, it turns out, happiness truly *is* the condition of being perpetually deceived. While he acknowledges the delusional nature of "insane" happiness, Carnegie ultimately treats it as functionally equivalent—indeed, superior—to the sort of happiness enjoyed by the sane.

Carnegie's thinking here is very much in line with that strain of "pragmatic" idealism that runs so strongly through New Thought. In the words of Ralph Waldo Trine, "'[A]dequacy for everyday life here and now must be the test of all true religion'" (qtd. in Weiss 137). Carnegie too attempts to balance an idealistic belief in the malleability of reality with a utilitarian belief that all value resides in effects. Having reduced the many physical entities to the one Mind, thereby rendering it all permeable and tractable, the tribes of New Thought must at some point effect an about-face and smuggle in through the backdoor an individual subject capable of manipulating that dreamlike reality to his or her own egoistic ends. Carnegie, who has little patience for metaphysics, devotes a good deal more attention to the techniques of manipulation than to the tractable nature of the universe, but such a universe must exist for his techniques to work.

Carnegie's opportunistic outlook is nowhere more evident than when he deals with the problem of evil—or more accurately, when he deals with the opportunities evil affords those resourceful enough to take advantage of others' lapses. Indeed, Carnegie's entire philosophy rests on a recognition of innate depravity coupled with a willingness to use that recognition to one's advantage. Thus the reader is told, "When dealing with people, let us remember we are not dealing with creatures of logic. We are dealing with creatures of emotion, creatures bristling with prejudices and motivated by pride and vanity" (28); and, "Few people are logical. Most of us are prejudiced and biased. Most of us are blighted with preconceived notions, with jealousy, suspicion, fear, envy, and pride" (120); and (upon hoodwinking a policeman into letting him off after being caught with his dog off the leash a second time in Central Park), "That policeman, being human, wanted a feeling of importance; so when I began to condemn myself, the only way he could nourish his self-esteem was to take the magnanimous attitude of showing mercy" (129); and, most famously, "People are not interested in you. They are not interested in me. They are interested in themselves—morning, noon, and after dinner" (62). Carnegie never suggests that these flaws are corrigible, or even that correcting them might be desirable. He is simply passing along information about the human condition so that his readers can put it to use in the furtherance of their own agendas.

The ethical position that emerges from all this is typical of any moral scheme conjured up out of a hedonic calculus—utterly incoherent. One can make no sort of categorical statement about how everyone ought to act without queering the game. All Carnegie's imperatives are aimed only at those shrewd enough to seek an edge in the contest for influence. The worst thing that could ever happen to Carnegie would be if everyone were to follow his advice. In a world full of Carnegian opportunists falling all over each other in an effort to be more interested in the other than the other is in them, no one can be influenced or manipulated by anyone else, no matter how egregiously obsequious. Then again, a world full of totally lapsed or totally saintly folk would be equally bad for business. A world of universally lapsed souls giving free rein to their pride, vanity, self-absorption, and emotion would mean a world void of listeners and "pigeons" in the con game of life; and in a world full of saintly folk, there would be perfect reciprocity and no profit at the margins.

In Peale's theology, meanwhile, there are no dark nights of the soul, no horrifying revelations of absolute otherness that shatter people's conventional perceptions and transform their values. While nominally a "Higher Power," Peale's God is in fact an anthropomorphic creation, a friendly deity that Peale urges his readers to think of as a "partner, as a close associate" (45). Thus, one of the most frequently cited of his numerous biblical mantras (along with "all things are possible to him that believeth" [Mark 9.23]) is taken from Romans 8.31: "If God be for us, who can be against us?" (KJV). It is clear that by "us," Peale has in mind that subset of believers shrewd enough to read his books. And it is equally clear that God's being "for" us includes divine backing for our profit-making ventures. And Peale's God responds to human depravity not with wrathful judgment but with unanswered prayers and financial ruin. Peale's God, it would appear, is created out of the same "embarrassments" of human aspiration as Kafka's God—sans the ironies.

Given New Thoughters' solipsistic worldview and their belief in an abundance theology, the role of human labor in attaining success is unclear. Work is neither a consequence of the Fall nor a calling. In the case of Peale and Carnegie, it looks something like sport, a characterization anticipated perhaps most acutely in Max Weber's critique of modern life:

> [T]he idea of duty in one's calling prowls about our lives like the ghost of dead religious beliefs. Where the fulfillment of the calling cannot directly be related to the highest spiritual and cultural values, or when, on the other hand it need not be felt simply as economic compulsion, the individual generally abandons the attempt to justify it at all. In the field of its highest development, in the United States, the pursuit of wealth, stripped of its religious and ethical meaning, tends to become associated with purely mundane passions, which often actually give it the character of sport. (182)

Hence Carnegie's admonition to "[m]ake a lively game out of mastering these rules" (58), a practice he later illustrates in his account of an encounter with a bored post office clerk. While waiting in a line, Carnegie decides he will make the clerk like him. So he compliments the man on his fine head of hair and gets the desired result. Subsequently he imagines the fellow preening before a mirror, admiring his most excellent hair, "walking on air" (99) as he goes home to tell his wife about the compliment. And when someone later asks Carnegie what he hoped to get out this ploy, he is quick to condemn those who live only to "screw something out of the other person" (99). Carnegie "ethicizes" his act by making it an end in itself; but as such it seems less selfless than senseless.

Peale, meanwhile, draws heavily on the world of sport for his examples and anecdotes. Thus, he learns not to overestimate obstacles from a philosopher/golf companion who teaches him that "'the rough is only mental'" (110), in life as well as on the course. At another point he cautions his readers that "[a]s an athlete goes stale, so does the individual" (38). And in his treatment of romantic love, Peale stresses the gamelike qualities of lovers' pursuit of their prey. Thus, when a woman desperate to attract a husband seeks Peale's counsel, he advises her to smile more, avoid nagging, get a new dress and hairdo, and wear perfume (92).

Gary Wills relates this gamelike quality in Peale's work to the nature of the theological shift he represents. According to Wills, Peale is attempting to reposition American religion and take it from its traditional role as "religion of the 'deserving poor' . . . to the religion of the undeserving rich—for those uneasy because they no longer wear cloth coats" (154). The pervasive anxiety that Peale laments in *Power* is attributed to people's unease over their own good fortune. To soothe the middle-class consciousness, Peale distracts them from the larger context that defines their activity and stresses techniques for efficient action: "[O]ne can only learn . . . passivity toward affluence if the system blessing the nation is kept beyond question. If a man is always discussing the rules of the game, trying to change or improve them, he cannot relax into contentment with his lot" (154). To the extent that one can enjoy and effectively participate in any game, one must forbear questioning the inevitably arbitrary grounds by which winners and losers are determined. In Peale's world, where everything and everyone is appearance, readily vanquished by a positive attitude, readily manipulated by a smile, everything is necessarily a game. And perhaps no figure in American history better understood that game than the subject of Wills's remarks, Peale's confidant, Richard Milhous Nixon.

"I'm Like Ike": Richard Nixon's Life Between Quotation Marks

Written at the apogee of Peale's and Carnegie's influence, Richard Nixon's *Six Crises* exemplifies American success ideology at midcentury. It is a book written in the wake of the author's loss to John Kennedy in 1960 and just prior to his California gubernatorial defeat in 1962. Reissued during his second campaign for president in 1968, the book defies easy summary. It is full of disproportionate and contradictory judgments, astonishing confessions—some deliberate, many more apparently inadvertent—and a self-consciousness about mythic and historical patterns and of the author's place within those patterns seldom found outside *Lives of the Saints*. It is less a "mainstream" work of contemporary success rhetoric than an anthology of major themes of American success rhetoric. And like Barton, but unlike most contemporary versions of success rhetoric, Nixon's focus is on the exceptional case—his own.

What the author offers his readers is a "portrait" of his own life not unlike Barton's "portrait" of Christ. While his narrative follows a nominally linear pattern, Nixon is highly selective in his choice of crises and in the "central form" of his subject. Nixon's "portrait" of an American success turns out on closer examination to be a pentimento with multiple successive portraits layered onto one canvas. One can, thus, read *Six Crises* almost in the manner of an archeologist, working one's way down through all possible variants of America's success myths preserved in different layers of Nixon's persona.

At successive levels of Nixon's book one finds him: celebrating the yeoman's dream in the form of wistful remembrances of his childhood home in rural Yorba Linda, California, where young Richard hears his future in the sound of distant trains passing in the night and imbibes simple values from his Quaker mother; hailing his Algeresque rise from the son of a failed farmer/grocer to a not inconsiderable political prominence (and suitably modest wealth), thanks chiefly to his "iron butt" and an abundance of pluck; limning the exploits of his executive superhero's *mano a mano* facedown of the free market's most sinister foes—Communist spies, lawless rioters, and liberals; unwittingly revealing a Carnegie Man's penchant for duping foes through self-effacement, gamesmanship, and the relentless deferral of personal satisfaction for careerist ends; and perennially aspiring to that state of Pealean bliss and certitude that comes from always thinking positively of others (even one's numerous, powerful, and motivelessly malicious enemies), making the best of one's circumstances (however chronically unjust), and always remembering to thank a Higher Power for granting one the extraordinary gifts necessary to triumph over demonic foes and impossible situations. Though to be sure, Nixon achieves nirvana not through scientific prayer or tuning himself to the Infinite but by practicing The Gospel of Relaxation with a Yeoman's Twist—he continually works himself into a state of ecstatic exhaustion: "[I]n preparing to meet a crisis, the more I worked the sharper and quicker my mental reactions became" (43).

No wonder that Gary Wills says of Nixon that

[w]hat is best and weakest in America goes out to reciprocating strength and deficiencies in Richard Nixon. In the dialogue of such a ruler with the ruled—traced in air as it were, between them as they try to communicate—an older America can be seen struggling back toward life, an older set of hopes and doubts. (ix)

And little wonder too that when two of America's most important contemporary novelists, Robert Coover and Phillip Roth, set out to capture the American *weltanschauung* in the 1970s with *The Public Burning* and *Our Gang*, respectively, they put Richard Nixon at the center of their works, allowing him to narrate large portions of their tales, even incorporating characteristic phrases and words from Nixon's own written record, in all likelihood because, as Roth himself once opined, much of this stuff is beyond authorial imagining.

The rhetorical design of Nixon's book is shrewd, if sometimes heavy-handed. To understand that design, one needs to reflect briefly on the book's function. In its own way, it too is a product of the same advertising logic that characterizes the work of Peale, Carnegie, and Barton. In Nixon's case, *Six Crises* is part of a marketing campaign designed to recuperate his image for future political races. Having lost the presidency in 1960 and having not yet declared his candidacy for the governorship of California in 1962, Nixon was at the time he wrote the book enjoying the status of "stealth" candidate, taking maximum advantage of a brief hiatus from a lifetime, nonstop political career to depoliticize his image. It was a rare opportunity for Nixon to momentarily "rise above the fray" and plausibly suggest, as he had so often implausibly insisted, that he had no venal motives for his action, in this case writing a book. He could then present himself as being simultaneously disinterested in political office and sufficiently statesmanlike to become an irresistible choice for political office.

According to his introductory chapter, Nixon writes the book for posterity. It is intended to serve as a self-help guide for politicians in the art of dealing with crises, an idea, we are told, that was suggested to him by some helpful Northwestern University political scientists (xxv). In fact, the book is a celebration of the triumphs of Richard Nixon over a series of stacked decks, Communist conspiracies, and partisan enemies, particularly in the press. The common reader, it is left unsaid, could no more hope to emulate Nixon's superhuman performances in any of these crises than he or she could hope to turn water into wine. In the end, it is neither self-help book nor campaign biography so much as a work of "auto-hagiography," an advertisement for the self that links Nixon's moment in history to Barton's "great river of eternity" as surely as Nixon's exaggerated, both arms extended, "double-V" for victory pose linked him iconically to the man who had popularized the gesture, General Dwight David Eisenhower.

Structurally, *Six Crises* follows the pattern of a bildungsroman with each crisis representing a stage of growth in the author's professional life. Or, as Gary Wills describes it, "The book is a report card on the student's progress. Mistakes on one crisis are corrected in the next, as if we were moving from semester to semester" (164). Everything in the book is part of a "larger pattern," patterns, like plots, being something of an obsession with Nixon, starting with the title, which echoes Walter Bedell Smith's *Eisenhower's Six Great Decisions*, a book about the man in whose shadow Nixon languished for so many years. Modesty, presumably, prevented Nixon from dubbing his six crises "great," one of the few signs that being forced to write his own encomium may have inhibited him in any way. But each of the six—the Hiss investigation, the Checkers speech, the "kitchen debate" with Khrushchev, the Caracas riots, the Eisenhower heart attacks, and the loss to Kennedy—turns out on closer inspection to be incredibly significant, and not just for Richard Nixon but for his family, his party, his country, and ultimately for world peace.

But through it all, as Wills suggests, "[t]here is a genius of deflation that follows Nixon about" (6). Take, for example, the case of Nixon's relationship with Eisenhower, a relationship that Nixon returns to obsessively throughout *Six Crises*. The complexity of that relationship is labyrinthine. Wills likens it to "a Calvinist's relation to God, or Ahab's to the whale—awe and fascination soured with fear and a desire to supplant; along with a knowledge, nonetheless, that whatever nobility one may aspire to will come from the attention of the Great One" (117). In the context of Nixon's hopes for political recuperation that above all else motivates *Six Crises*, he must try to at once step out from Ike's shadow and distance himself from the public's perception that he was Ike's messenger boy, "Tricky Dick" the party hack to the general's statesman, while at the same time reminding us of his links to Ike's aura, borrowing all the charisma he can from that linkage. He must be a rugged individualist—just like the general. What results from these contradictory impulses is more often than not at least mildly puzzling.

Typically, Nixon relies on tacit identifications between himself and Eisenhower, apparently hoping that his readers will notice similarities between the two unbidden. This is the apparent motivation behind Nixon's copycat book title and his tendency to imitate, covertly, incidents from Smith's book, such as his description of Ike's decision to launch the D-Day invasion:

> The silence lasted for a full five minutes while the General sat on a sofa before the bookcase which filled the end of the room. I never realized before the loneliness and isolation of a commander at a time when such a momentous decision has to be taken, with full knowledge that failure or success rests on his judgment alone. He sat there quietly, not getting up to pace with quick strides as he often does. He was tense, weighing every consideration of weather as he had been briefed to do during the dry runs since April, weighing them with those other imponderables.
>
> Finally he looked up and the tension was gone from his face.
>
> He said briskly, "Well, we'll go." (55)

The similarities between this scene and the following one, depicting the eve of Nixon's fateful Checkers speech, are not, I would submit, gratuitous.

> After the four [advisers] had left the room, I sat alone for another two hours and reviewed the entire situation. I realized that although others could help direct my thinking, the final decision in a crisis of this magnitude must nor represent the lowest common denominator of a collective judgment; it must be made alone by the individual primarily involved.
>
> The range and scope of this crisis began to fall into a pattern. It was, of course, an acute personal crisis. I realized that my decision affected not only me and my future but also my wife, my daughters, my parents and other members of my family. . . . What I did would also affect Eisenhower . . . the Republican Party and the millions of its members . . . [a]nd most important of all . . . the future of my country and the cause of peace and freedom for the world. (101–2)

The rhetorical danger Nixon faces here is of a piece with the sorts of danger encountered by Bruce Barton in his attempt to link the exploits of steel magnates with the accomplishments of a religious savior. Consciousness of the D-Day scene, slyly invoked to ennoble the Checkers scene, inevitably "deflates" it in that the similarities mostly serve to underscore discrepancies between the two scenes. Ike's decision to commit millions of troops to an inevitably bloody and decisive battle upon which the "peace and freedom for the world" quite literally depended is made with heroic ease, five minutes of silence concluding in the simple declarative "Well, we'll do it." Nixon, meanwhile, natters on for nearly a page in a prose style more reminiscent of Ike's own inimitable "Eisenhowerese" than Smith's plain style, using *gradatio* or "swelling effect" to bloat a small beer slush fund imbroglio into a global crisis. His earnest invocation of a guiding "pattern" conjures up memories of an adolescent dance student counting the steps half aloud to himself, unsuccessfully feigning interest in his date, sweating like a stoat the whole while.[4]

While Nixon elaborately foregrounds various "textbook" devices that remind us of his book's supposed educational function and tie it to the Carnegie/Peale tradition of success books—he attaches previews of important lessons learned to each chapter heading and minutely reviews his performance at the conclusion of each chapter—there is a dramatic presence to Nixon's narrative entirely absent in Carnegie and Peale. While the latter simply tag their illustrative anecdotes onto their a priori principles, Nixon dramatizes his "discovery" of the appropriate principle of crisis behavior in each chapter, working back from the event to the principle. Nixon's inductive approach, while certainly more engaging, raises issues of plausibility that are circumvented in the deductive approach. In particular, sincerity is a problem only for Peale's and Carnegie's readers who must learn to be sincere, to really mean it when they practice positive thinking or the arts of influence; in Nixon, the sincerity problem shifts to the narrator, whose heroic deeds form the basis for the conclusions and whose sensibility infuses the entire account. In Carnegie and Peale, it is sometimes difficult to believe in the efficacy of the message; in Nixon, it is often difficult to believe in the sincerity of the messenger.

To be sure, Nixon directly addresses the sincerity problem in his narrative, and his solution here as in so many other cases is to will it away. Thus, in preparing to give the Checkers speech, Nixon tells how he writes several outlines, throwing each away in turn, and then neither reads nor memorizes his talk so that it would "have the spark of spontaneity so essential for a television audience" (113). For Nixon, as for the disciples of Peale and Carnegie, sincerity is a quality of self-presentation acquired by "technique." Spontaneity is a way of acting for Nixon, an attribute acquired through practice, rehearsal, and endless preparation. The spectacular failure of Nixon to appear at all "spontaneous," authentic, or sincere on television throughout his political life is a tribute to difficulties finessed in Peale and Carnegie but unavoidable in dramatic presentation. Probably no one in American political history seemed more self-conscious than Richard Nixon—or less self-aware. Forever plotting to present an image consistent with whatever exigency he dealt with in the moment, Nixon seemed forever unaware that all that plotting would inevitably surface in his manner of presentation.[5] Another disadvantage of Nixon's first-person, dramatic mode of presentation has to do with the difficulty he has convincing us of the great significance of the events he describes. Whereas the events and people depicted in Peale and Carnegie are likely to seem lilliputian after the fact, it is relatively easy in the act of reading about them to forget one's sense of scale and to get involved in the winning or losing of whatever game is being played, whether it be making a fortune off mustard seeds embalmed in plastic or shining on a postal clerk. What matters are their protagonists' successes and how they achieve them, not the "rules of the game" or the significance of the outcome. With Nixon, on the other hand, the reader is never allowed to forget the relationship between the events being recounted and the grand patterns that endow those events with significance. In Nixon's account, as in the accounts of the free market fundamentalists noted by Gary Wills, "myth replaces history" (Wills 513). On virtually every page, Nixon self-consciously substitutes myth for history, reordering quotidian events to fit into larger patterns, all of which renders him irresistible to postmodern writers. Nixon's embarrassingly obtrusive, unreliable narrator torturing the events of his life into myths of universal significance is the very stuff of late-twentieth-century fabulism.[6]

The dominant pattern informing every event and character in *Six Crises* is the mammoth struggle between Good (Republicans, objectivity, obsessive exertion, free markets, and so on) and Evil (liberals, biased media, outside agitators, managed economies, Russia, and so on). Gary Wills argues that Nixon's tendency to complicate and magnify seemingly straightforward matters is a function of his religious fundamentalism (32). Hofsteader's description of American fundamentalist thinking, meanwhile, nicely glosses Nixon's thought processes. According to Hofsteader, American fundamentalism

is essentially Manichean; it looks upon the world as an arena for conflict between absolute good and absolute evil, and accordingly

> it scorns compromises (who would compromise with Satan?) and can tolerate no ambiguities. . . . The issues of the actual world are hence transformed into a spiritual Armageddon, an ultimate reality, in which any reference to day-to-day actualities has the character of an allegorical illustration and not of the empirical evidence that ordinary men offer for ordinary conclusions. (135)

The design of Nixon's book speaks to problems of verisimilitude raised by the above tendency in his thinking. In particular, placing the Hiss case, which so flagrantly violates any sense of verisimilitude, at the beginning of *Six Crises* prepares the reader for willing suspensions of disbelief on a heroic scale. Replete with spies and betrayers, plots and lies and coverups, consummate performances delivered under oath, and secret papers hidden in a pumpkin, the Hiss case renders the notion of a "secret pattern"— any sort of pattern that might make sense of these strange events—irresistibly attractive.

In offering up his version of a secret pattern to make sense of the Hiss case, Nixon, as he is wont to do, buys some credibility for his interpretation by initially attributing it to someone else. Thus he quotes Whitaker Chambers, himself no mean mythologizer, calling the Hiss case a "'tragedy of history'" in which the "'two irreconcilable faiths of our time, Communism and Freedom, came to grips in the person of two conscious and resolute men'" (66). Had Nixon stopped there (and how often the student of Richard Nixon's life and writing is tempted to invoke that phrase), Nixon would have been guilty of only a minor breach of excess, borrowing another participant's bloated account of things to puff his own role. But, inevitably, he forges on, introducing into Whitaker's Manichean conflict between Communism and Freedom a third party, his own particular bête noire, liberalism:

> In this sentence [Chambers] compressed whole chapters of world history: the rise, development, and—as some would argue—the partial decay of the philosophy called "liberalism"; the parallel emergence of a heresy called Communism; the assumption of world leadership by two superpowers, America and Russia, each wedded to a competing faith and each strengthened and yet limited thereby; and finally, the present confrontation of these two faiths and these two superpowers at specific times and places in every part of the world. The issue at stake, to put it starkly, is this: whose hand will write the next several chapters of human history? (66)

Perhaps unpersuaded that his readers will catch the full import of his point here, Nixon goes on to make the connection between Communism and liberalism "perfectly clear":

> Hiss was clearly the symbol of a considerable number of perfectly loyal citizens whose theaters of operation are the nation's mass media and universities, its scholarly foundations and its government bureaucracies. This group likes to throw the cloak of liberalism around all its beliefs. . . . They are not Communists; they are not even remotely disloyal; and give or take a normal dose of human fallibility, they are neither dishonest nor dishonorable. (72)

This is vintage Nixon. Reassuring his readers about liberals, who are, after all, *not* dishonest and *not* disloyal—"not even remotely"—and not really Communists, Nixon manages to render liberalism (not to mention universities, government bodies, and members of the media) a sinister force, ripening in the dark like so many poisonous mushrooms. The pattern Nixon invokes, like all the patterns he invokes, simultaneously legitimates his own self-interests, demonizes those who would oppose those interests, and turns him into a selfless tool of destiny.

In the end, Richard Nixon is less a proponent of any particular myth of success than he is a student of all such myths, a myth consumer who tries a number on for size. As such, he embodies the contradictions within each and among all of the various ideologies. Believing all of them, he is unable to persuade his readers that he sincerely holds to any of them. He invokes each myth in its turn as the situation dictates to put the best possible "spin" on his actions. There is, however, one myth to which Nixon keeps returning in the apparent hope that his reader will see it as his core—the myth of the common man, the people about whom Nixon likes to quote Abraham Lincoln: "He must love them because he made so many of them." That this is the "real" Nixon is testified to by the fact that in those rare moments when he can break free of the journalists and the television people and the public personality they have constructed for him and make unmediated contact with other common people, they invariably applaud him and recognize him as their own.

The implausibility of this vision is confirmed not just by the implausibility of the scenes Nixon conjures up in *Six Crises* but by history, by the later Nixon, the lonely figure in a suit wandering at night through crowds of raggedly dressed protesters gathered around the Lincoln Memorial, unsuccessfully attempting to make contact and somehow win them over to his administration's bombing policies. In the end, his resentment toward being forever underestimated by politicians, historians, and journalists wins out over his need to be loved by the people. He is reduced finally to writing his own countermyth, *Six Crises*, which stresses not his ordinariness but his extraordinary capacity for transcendence. Richard Nixon cannot finally live outside a set of quotation marks, some myth of his or another's making, anymore than he can stop himself from putting quotation marks around any vaguely colloquial word or phrase of the sort common folk might actually use.

4 | The Business-Religion Anoints Its Own: Enter the Gurus

Tom Peters and Robert Waterman's 1982 bestseller *In Search of Excellence: Lessons from America's Best Run Companies* (*ISOE*) sold nearly three times as many copies (1,160,491) in one year as any of the "business list" bestsellers of the previous four years (Huczynski 41). Ostensibly a "business" book—and compared to the likes of Carnegie and Peale, it is both more "businesslike" and more clearly business focused—*ISOE* quickly crossed over into the general trade market and eventually sold more than six million copies. John Micklethwait and Adrian Wooldridge, staff editors for the respected British trade magazine *The Economist* and authors of *The Witch Doctors: Making Sense of the Management Gurus*, subsequently depicted *ISOE* as a catalyst in the guru management movement:

> Ever since *In Search of Excellence*, the guru industry has boomed. Some $750 million worth of business books are currently sold in America alone every year, and the market for audio—and video-tapes, courses and seminars is even bigger. Not only are the latest theories such as reengineering more rapidly and zealously applied than their predecessors, but the wealth and status accruing to those who promote them have increased exponentially. (6)

The sudden popularity of management guru books generally and *ISOE* specifically is not hard to explain. Certainly it has something to do with the ancient rhetorical principle of *kairos*, or "timeliness." In its broadest sense, *kairos* is in Cynthia Sheard's words "the ancient term for the sum total of '*contexts*,' both spatial . . . and temporal . . . that influence the translation of thought into language and meaning in any rhetorical situation" (291). In the "extraverbal sphere," the rapidly growing proportion of the American people invested in the stock market would certainly account for much of the public's growing fascination with the workings of business. While investing is purely a spectator sport for many Americans, a significant minority of the American middle class does actively manage its investments, and a majority of us have, willy-nilly, wagered heavily on the market through retirement accounts and take a more than passing interest in the fate of our holdings. Moreover, despite all the recent attention given to reengineering, downsizing, and "rightsizing," managerial jobs comprise an ever larger portion of the workforce. According to Micklethwait and Wooldridge, "Of the 8 million new jobs created in America in 1991–95, 60 percent belonged to the category of 'managers and other professionals,' now the largest group in the workforce" (8).

And as anyone who has ever served as a manager in either the private or public sector can attest, few jobs leave one feeling more anxious, bewildered, and in need of reassurance than one involving the management of people, particularly when one is working in a middling position in a "service" enterprise (the fastest growing sort of position in the fastest growing sector of the economy). Often the institutional goals one serves are affected by a bewildering number of variables, many of which are not obviously under one's control. One's role in achieving, or not achieving, those goals is thus frequently murky. If any sort of accountability system is in place to measure what one has ostensibly been doing, it all too often rests on dubious outcomes far downstream from one's day-to-day concerns. In turn, institutional objectives change frequently, not always, it would appear, for rational reasons. And everyone who reports to the typical middle manager performs similarly mysterious tasks, usually out of the manager's sight and control. Being evaluated and evaluating others in such an environment can, thus, be excruciatingly difficult and raise numerous anxieties.

Management literature is one of the few places managers and administrators can turn to find reinforcement for their conviction that theirs is a difficult lot and reassurances that many others are similarly afflicted. Nonacademic management writers appear to be especially sensitive to the dilemmas facing contemporary managers and especially adept at speaking to their need for reassurance at a time when, according to business scholar Andrzej Huczynski, "their assessment of themselves is . . . under downward pressure. A similar low assessment tends to be made of them as individuals, and of management as a profession" (171–72). In a world where the term "bureaucrat," never a particularly felicitous descriptor, has taken on increasingly dyslogistic overtones and has been extended to include just about anyone who does not actually produce or sell a material good of some sort, it is little wonder that managers' self-esteem is felt to be "under downward pressure" and in need of some uplift.

Which is exactly what *ISOE* did and at exactly the right time. The month the book was published, unemployment in America reached a post-Depression high of 10 percent even as inflation spiraled upward, a dismaying turn of events that required economists to invent a new term: "stagflation." Business magazines were running cover stories on the failure of American business and its managers to keep pace with Japanese methods, particularly Total Quality Management, which, to make matters worse, the Japanese had picked up from American Edward Deming. The negative direction of economic change was compounded by the dizzying pace of that change. By 1982, we were halfway through a twenty-five-year-long corporate feeding frenzy that would see two-thirds of the firms listed on the Fortune 500 in 1970 disappear into insolvency or the maws of bigger corporate fish. Traditional approaches had difficulty describing, let alone solving, the new sets of problems facing management. And through it all, business academics were, in the view of most practitioners, notoriously unhelpful, resolutely focused on the intricacies of structure and strategy, ignoring the mysteries of people management. These "soft side" matters were left largely to psychologists and nonacademic analysts, some of whom donned the mantle of the guru—none more enthusiastically than Tom Peters.

However important all these "extraverbal factors," the links between *ISOE* and a canonical textual source were perhaps even more crucial to its "translation of thought into language." Specifically, *ISOE* is replete with echoes from the speeches of Ronald Reagan, the "Great Communicator." Reagan, it will be recalled, swept to the presidency in 1980 declaring "a new morning for America" after a decade of political scandals, economic disasters, international embarrassments, hostage crises, and the badly mangled conclusion of a woefully mismanaged, morally bankrupt, and interminable war. And all that was needed to achieve this "new morning," Reagan assured and reassured his audiences, was to call upon the native genius and heroism of the American people. According to Reagan, America was great because "we unleashed the energy and individual genius of man to a greater extent than has ever been done before" (Reagan 242). And if we are to do so again, we must encourage the cultivation of "heroes" (243) and our native "genius for leaders" (220) among ordinary American citizens by bringing government "closer to the people" (257) and by getting rid of "centralized bureaucracy, of government by a self-anointed elite" (200). Regulation and "slavish adherence to abstraction" (186) must give way to common sense, flexibility, and a more pragmatic view of managing America's affairs.

And above all, Americans were encouraged to "believe" their way out of their current crisis and a "new kind of defeatism" (271) that Reagan characterized as spiritual malaise. If ever America had a leader who subscribed to New Thought's abundance theology, it was Ronald Reagan. Whatever injustices and inequities (not to mention massive federal debt) we might have to endure in the short run to cultivate our productive champions—"The production of America is the possession of those who build, serve, create and produce" (264)—such trifles would be more than justified by our bounteous future when we would, "with God's help," at last become "as a city upon a hill with the eyes of all people upon us" (201). Keep government off the back of our heroes, and they would produce bounties that "trickle down" from the city on the hill to the unheroic masses outside the gates as surely as water runs downhill to the sea, as surely as Bruce Barton's giants will walk the earth when unfettered competition prevails.[1]

When Peters and Waterman subsequently called upon American business to ignore the foreign models being urged upon them by academics and journalists and to follow the example of native models already achieving excellence, their gospel ("There is good news from America" [xxiii]) was bound to be well received in an embattled business community already looking to Reagan as its savior. The readers of *ISOE* would have already heard in the speeches of Ronald Reagan, not to mention the books, essays, and media commentaries by members of the burgeoning neoconservative movement, that American enterprise was beset by too many abstractions, rules, and regulations (exemplified in *ISOE* by "faddish" matrix management systems [49] and the American military structure in Vietnam [29] and personified by ITT CEO Harold Geneen [29]) that prevented companies from maximizing the productive capacities of their individual workers. And always, the search for excellence leads Peters and Waterman back to the individual worker, management "champion," or customer. Corporations, like government, must get "closer to the people" and let the will of customers, rather than some organization chart, guide their decisions.

In Search of Excellent Rhetoric

Beyond good timing and the opportunistic borrowing of already popular political ideas, *ISOE* is a remarkably astute rhetoric book, which is to say, the authors do not merely use rhetoric to persuade (*rhetorica utens*), they teach managers rhetorical principles (*rhetorica docens*) that will make them better managers. In the process, the authors reject modernist management theory, exemplified by Alfred Chandler's magisterial *Strategy and Structure*, whose thesis they reduce to: "Get the strategic plan down on paper . . . [and] the right organization structure will pop out with ease, grace, and beauty" (4). They instead counsel managers to begin with people and a corporate culture that stresses "the status of the individual employee" (261). Structure will follow in unanticipated ways. The authors also reject the modernist notion that meaning follows function and charge managers and companies to "make meanings for people" (29) by dreaming up "a special language" reflecting a "true people orientation" (260). "Corny" language, "hoopla" (240), and gamesmanship are all recommended in pursuit of "Productivity through People" (235–78).[2]

Perhaps the first hint that *ISOE* is more rhetorically sophisticated than its predecessors occurs early in chapter 1 with an illustration from the well-known painting by surrealist René Magritte, *Ceci n'est pas une pipe* (This is not a pipe). The painting, it will be recalled, features a series of primitivist representations of tobacco pipes with the title written out in script immediately below each representation. The point the authors make with Magritte is the fairly pedestrian one that "[t]he picture of the thing is not the thing. . . . [A]n organization chart is not a company, nor a new strategy an automatic answer to corporate grief" (3). They do not tarry over the illustration, quickly leaving Magritte behind to critique American companies' fascination with organizational charts and strategic solutions to management problems and their differences with Chandler. But the image of the "pipe" that is not a pipe may well be a more apt emblem of the authors' enterprise than their own treatment of it suggests.

What Magritte's painting exemplifies is the capacity of representations to comment on the nature of representation in the act of representing. It "problematizes" our normal processing of images and our standard assumption that the medium is neutral or transparent and not implicated in the message. The way Magritte's pipe is represented is unavoidably a part of the pipe's meaning. This foregrounding of medium and its attendant complication of the message, a tendency we associate with postmodernism, is a tendency sometimes exhibited by Peters and Waterman's book, where questions about the nature of representation are often raised by its manner of representing its subject. Or, to use earlier invoked terms, the lessons about rhetoric that *ISOE* offers to business (*rhetorica docens*) are implicit in the way it represents business (*rhetorica utens*). The sound management advice offered in *ISOE* turns out also to be sound rhetorical advice, and the authors' excellent companies often appear to follow the same precepts that guide the construction of their own excellent text.

The most fundamental expression of this equivalence is found in the authors' functional definition of management. According to Peters and Waterman, the most important function good managers and excellent companies perform for those they employ, besides making meaning for them, is to "create a sense of highly valued purpose" (51), using stories and myths that provide "uplift and idealism" (282) in such a way as to override the "important contradictions" (285) that inevitably beset corporate life. In other words, the function of management for Peters and Waterman is more than anything a rhetorical function having to do with articulation, motivation, persuasion, and identification, sometimes at the expense of planning, logic, and organization. And like the managers they describe throughout the book, the authors create meaning and a sense of purpose for their readers, the millions of beleaguered American managers held responsible for the collapse of American business, by telling stories that uplift even as they disguise manifold contradictions in the authors' approach. Thus, the simultaneous "loose tight" properties of well-managed companies (318–27) that allow them to finesse the inevitable contradictions of corporate behavior are in turn manifest in the prose of *ISOE*, which combines a "tight" global structure, built around eight principles, with a loose, anecdotal texture that distracts one from the inevitable contradictions and considerable overlap among the principles. Moreover, the authors, like their "champion" managers, are unafraid to let a good deal of redundancy loose in their message, not to mention "hokey" or "cornball" prose in order to "celebrate" their subject with the same "evangelist[ic]" (288) fervor that they attribute to good managers.

Academe v. the Gurus: The Not-So-Great Debate

ISOE's stress on the rhetorical dimension of management caused many in the popular press and in academe to dismiss the book out of hand. The popular press, most notably in cover stories in *Newsweek* and *Business Week*, emphasized the failure of most companies featured in *ISOE* to remain "excellent" as time went on. Academic critics, meanwhile, focused on *ISOE*'s methodological flaws and lack of rigor. To better understand both the thrust of these academic critiques and the reasons for their ineffectuality, let us turn to a 1991 *Management Decision* critique of *ISOE*.

The four authors of this piece, while they offer some astute and surely valid criticisms of the book, do so from a very narrow perspective. They largely ignore the rhetorical dimension of the book, other than to express their dismay that it obviously "struck a responsive chord in managers who daily face the tough competitive struggles typically denied the academic researcher" (Capon et al. 18). The academic authors' focus on quantification and their failure to explore the appeal of *ISOE* would in turn appear to corroborate one of *ISOE*'s major arguments: that the numerical exactitude and methodological rigor beloved of academics come at a steep price. In the words of John Steinbruner cited by Peters and Waterman: "'If quantitative precision is demanded, it is gained, in the current state of things, only by so reducing the scope of what is analyzed that most of the important problems remain external to the analysis'" (44).

While a lack of "quantitative precision" is ostensibly the major failing of *ISOE* identified in the *Management Decision* piece, it begins by cataloguing the failures of five of *ISOE*'s "excellent" companies during the previous decade and by citing six other articles purporting to show how "ephemeral" excellence has proven to be. Fair enough. But a few pages later, the authors claim that they "have not concerned [them]selves with the fact that several 'excellent' firms have deteriorated in performance post publication of Peters and Waterman's book" (19), thereby telling us that they are not telling us what they have told us three times.

Having undermined the ethos of *ISOE*, the authors turn to its logos. They establish that *ISOE*'s eight "relatively soft, multidimensional, and overlapping" (15) principles need some bolstering, which they provide by considering presumably "harder" items from another study and "13 strategy items" ignored in *ISOE*. At this point, the authors share a dilemma with their readers. "Should we dismiss the work because of its scientific failings and move onto other more respectable academic pastures, or should we attempt to test, in as rigorous a way as we are able, the propositions that so many managers have apparently accepted?" (18). Citing "the responsibility of academic business researchers to the business community" (18), the authors plunge on, resolutely ignoring *ISOE*'s rhetorical appeal in the name of demonstrating its "scientific failings."

Not surprisingly, further analysis turns up further shortcomings. *ISOE*'s eight "redundant" principles are boiled down to two factors—maintaining an open entrepreneurial climate and choosing businesses related to one another in various ways (19)—and its linkage of success to organizational design is challenged: "A more parsimonious explanation is that firms that spend big on R&D [research and development] reap big rewards in terms of new products developed" (19), thereby reaffirming the traditional academic business focus on strategy over design and "climate."

In the face of all this academic hardware—parsimony, rigor, "multivariate F-tests," "varimax rotation," "scree criterion," and so on—*ISOE* does indeed come up looking more than a little squishy and unreliable. But given the audience, the "business community," putatively being served by these academic "business researchers," one would have to question their essay on rhetorical grounds, beginning with their implied criticism of the "many managers" gullible enough to fall for *ISOE*'s unscientific reasoning. Clearly, in fact, such managers are not their primary audience. The article speaks past practitioners to address other academics, permanent residents of those "more respectable academic pastures," who alone might question the authors' decision to pursue a lowlife subject like *ISOE*. While the article surely represents a responsible piece of research by the standards of the authors' discipline, and while it surely points up a number of legitimate shortcomings in *ISOE*, their argument is, in Burkean terms, less a comic critique than an exercise in debunking. Operating within one domain, they offer no discount on terms from another domain and concede nothing to the "context of situation" that might account for terminological differences between the two domains. Consequently, they use narrow, quantitative standards of truth to dismiss absolutely ideas that may better deserve "cajolery."

To the extent that this academic response to guru culture is typical, the failure of academics to slow, let alone stem, the tide of guru effusions is unsurprising. Peters and Waterman appear to have grasped a basic rhetorical principle that eludes their academic critics. To wit: truthful arguments (by the standards of a given community) are not necessarily effective arguments (by the standards of another community). And any attempt to divide truth off from effect, Hans Blumenberg reminds us, is doomed insofar as "the rhetorical effect is not an alternative that one can choose instead of an insight that one could *also* have, but an alternative to definitive evidence that one cannot have, or *cannot* have yet, or at any rate cannot have here and now" (436). As economist Dierdre (née Donald) McCloskey has repeatedly suggested, academics operating in sciencelike ways maintain a misplaced faith in the universality of quantitative analysis and its ability to trump "softer" arguments: "Numbers are believed to be objective, intersubjective, conclusive. Most people, and even most economists, believe that once you have reduced a question to numbers, you have taken it out of human hands" (141).

Inevitably, however, questions of value creep back into the academics' equations. Thus, for example, when *ISOE*'s methodology is said to contain a sufficient number of flaws of sufficient magnitude to be deemed statistically "significant," McCloskey's ur-question—"How large is large?"—is evaded, and the inescapably rhetorical notion of "significance" is converted into a positive term on the order of a "house" or a "horse." For Burke, it should be remembered, "nothing is more rhetorical in nature than a deliberation as to what is too much or too little, too early or too late; in such controversies, rhetoricians are forever 'proving opposites'" (*RM* 45). Positivists insulate themselves against the embarrassment of "proving opposites" by designating a threshold beyond which all is by definition "too much." But in the process, they rule fundamental questions of value out of play by simply pushing the debate back one step and presenting as fait accompli a threshold that is itself arguably "too much or too little." Likewise, the lack of rigor imputed to Peters and Waterman begs the question, "Just what *is* rigor"? According to historian of mathematics Morris Kline, "'There is no rigorous definition of rigor. A proof is accepted if it obtains the endorsement of the leading specialists of the moment. But no standard is universally acceptable today'" (qtd. in McCloskey 32).

All of which is not to suggest that quantification is or should be considered inherently less persuasive than other forms of evidence. It is to suggest that in many nonacademic communities, quantification lacks the evidentiary sovereignty that it possesses in many academic communities and by itself rarely wins the assent of nonacademics. In attempting to persuade nonacademics, researchers need to acknowledge and accommodate such differences. For example, the "scene" of argument varies dramatically between the two realms: academic arguments typically take place on the pages of academic journals, and the outcome is typically a corrected version (and seldom is the correction dramatic) of a given audience's (and seldom is the audience very large) understanding; business arguments are typically elaborated in meeting rooms, memos, and e-mails and typically result in a decision and an action or series of acts whose consequences may or may not be proportionate to the thoroughness of the argument. Academic arguments may take years to go from inception to reception and may never again be cited, let alone acted upon. Business arguments, meanwhile, must be conceived and acted on or dismissed much more quickly. In classical rhetorical terms that Burke borrows from Augustine, academic arguments are mostly designed "to bend" (*flectere*) an audience's attitude, while business arguments are designed mostly "to move" (*movere*) an audience to act (*RM* 52).[3] By the same token, the conditions under which arguments are read and received vary dramatically. In a classic 1975 *Harvard Business Review* article, "The Manager's Job: Folklore and Fact," Henry Mintzberg, who set aside the rational model of managerial behavior and looked at managers' actual day-to-day functioning, concluded that they spend on average about nine minutes on each task in a day, less time than the average academic will spend reading and grading a single three-page student essay.

Clearly, Peters and Waterman took the scene of business persuasion into account in writing their book, both in the advice they offer managers and in the way they compose their text. Thus, for example, they applaud Hewlett Packard at one point for "'suboptimizing'" (112) their operation by settling for less than maximum economies of scale. While an HP executive objected to their use of the term, it turns out to be a species of thinking long adhered to by large corporations of the sort *ISOE* appeals to. Dubbed "bounded rationality" by Herbert Simon, such thinking rules real but low probability risks out of play, even when they may have catastrophic consequences. Mary Douglas and Aaron Wildavsky summarize Simon's thinking:

> The operational rule of industrial firms that enables them to act is precisely to avoid attempting to know too much about future consequences. Limiting data, not expanding them, is their guide. Most possible alternatives and consequences are ignored. If there is any finding that has been amply documented in studies of decision making by large-scale organizations of the hierarchical kind, it is that most alternatives most of the time are not considered as candidates for adoption. Only a few ideas—those best known and closest to existing programs—are given attention. (93)

In both the advice that it offers and in the manner that it offers that advice, *ISOE* acknowledges the above principle. Hence Peters and Waterman's promotion of various simplifying devices such as story, information chunking, redundancy, imagery, and a folksy manner of delivery to make meaning for their employees; the authors use the same devices in constructing their message for their readers. They urge companies to "stick to their knitting" (292–305) and tend to those businesses they know best while they themselves offer advice in the form of self-evident "motherhoods" (xiii); they urge businesses not to be first to market but to be safely second, advice they implicitly follow by collecting their principles ad hoc from excellent companies rather than trying to dream them up a priori. While there is certainly a place for academic critics, playing Socrates to the gurus' Callicles, to point up the compromises inherent in such advice, the gurus' ability to adapt their prose and message to audience circumstances should not go unremarked. And neither should the costs, measured in time, required to optimize decisions and to read discipline-specific arguments using terms and rules of evidence alien to their audience be ignored.

To sum up, *ISOE*'s academic critics are handicapped in the battle for the attention of the business community by their compulsion to focus on "hard" rather than "soft" matters and to concede little to that audience's circumstances. But however perversely inappropriate this rhetorical strategy may be for the critics' putative audience of managers, it is considerably sounder for their real audience—the readers not of *Business Week* but of *Management Decision*. For the latter audience, the academics' nod to their "service" function, their "responsibility to the business community," will be immediately recognized as ceremonial. Academic reputations, as Magali Larson reminds us, are otherwise made: "The main instrument of professional advancement, much more than the profession of altruism, is the capacity to claim esoteric and identifiable skills—that is, to create and control a cognitive and technical basis" (180). And among "academics—especially in elite institutions where 'publish or perish' is the rule"—the reigning attitude toward one's clients is one of "indifference" (188). According to Larson, any profession, but especially the academic profession, defines itself "as *an occupation which tends to be colleague-oriented* rather than client-oriented," and anyone "'who stakes all upon his reputation with his clients-patients, students, 'cases'" is likely to be labeled "a quack" (226). The true professional is a self-sufficient, fully autonomous individual, beholden only to professional canons.

ISOE's critics are then righter than they realize to stress the divergent interests of "managers who daily face the tough competitive struggles" and those of "academic researchers" far removed from such struggles. Indeed, the growing awareness of such divergences helps explain why "[c]onsultancies have replaced Oxbridge and the Ivy League as the nurseries of the powerful. Indeed students from the latter jostle to get into the former, and with good reason" (Micklethwait and Wooldridge 45). Most gurus, including Peters and Waterman who worked for the noted incubator of Fortune 500 CEOs Mckinsey & Company, start out in consulting firms, which have nudged universities aside as the primary legitimation sites in the realm of management. Understanding the historical reasons behind the origins of consultancies and their eventual eclipse of universities helps explain why their approach differs so dramatically from that of academics.

As it turns out, the $15 billion a year (in 1996) consulting industry was born out of the accounting industry. At first glance, accounting, until very recently the grayest and most prosaic of business practices, may appear to be an anomalous source for the most flamboyant and glamorous of business professions. In fact, the move by accounting firms into consulting practices was, says Larson, necessitated precisely by their highly bureaucratized function.

> The large and autonomous professional firms bureaucratize, thereby tending to stress specialization and contributing to the routinization of techniques. They also appear to be pioneers in opening up new areas of practice: in accountancy, for instance, the "big eight" which dominate the field compensate for routinization by "moving into new areas of uncertainty" such as management analysis. (204)

Within every profession, Larson argues, there is a need to balance the "codification" of professional skills, which allows them to be disseminated, and the "indetermination" of those same skills, which ensures that they remain sufficiently esoteric to justify practitioners' status and fees (204). Any profession that can be reduced to algorithms will not long remain a profession. Because accounting was widely perceived to be just such a highly routinized profession, it made good sense for it to incorporate management consultants into its practice. And it made equally good sense for consultants to become "un-accountants," to endorse non-rationalistic management philosophies and to de-emphasize routinized and determinate practices. Operating under the aegis of the most sober and reliable sorts of firms (at least until the firewall supposedly separating accounting and consulting divisions proved to be flimsier than the emperor's new suit), consultants have been free not to worry about the parsimony of their explanations, the reliability of their data, the rigor of their methodologies, and so on. The latter concerns are consigned to the province of academics, not to mention the legions of bean counters occupying the lower floors of their office towers. They are licensed by their professional function to "think outside the box." Little wonder that their primary competitors in academe, whose own legitimation needs pull them in exactly the opposite direction, have had such a hard time gaining any traction in the business community.

A final note on the relationship between management gurus and their academic critics concerns the role of prediction in the two realms. As noted above, Peters and Waterman's critics simultaneously gloat about the inaccuracy of the authors' predictions even as they claim not to hold them accountable for those inaccuracies. One need not look far for the reasons behind their disingenuous approach. To challenge directly Peters and Waterman's undeniably lamentable record of prognostication would raise obvious, and no doubt embarrassing, questions about the critics' own capacity to predict. On this score, the record is clear. No one can predict economic behavior or corporate success. Economists can seldom agree about what has happened or is happening at any given moment of economic history, let alone predict the future. (Hence Harry Truman's famous declaration he was inclined to remove one hand from every White House economic adviser in order to forestall the inevitable "On the other hand . . ." that accompanied all economic advice.) Thus too, McCloskey, quoting Ludwig Von Mises, reminds us that "predicting the economic future is . . . 'beyond the power of any mortal man'" (15).[4]

Gurus, to be sure, are considerably more resourceful than their academic counterparts when it comes to papering over their lamentable records of prediction. And they have managed this feat largely by turning to their most venerable strategy: gap to gain. After being exposed as a lousy prognosticator in the late 1980s, Tom Peters promptly wrote a series of books enthroning change—ever accelerating, unpredictable change generated by turbo-capitalism and technology—as the élan vital of commerce. He also refashioned management as the art of thriving on chaos rather than on prediction and control. He is the poster boy for Thomas Frank's contention that "[m]anagement theory expresses a virtually unanimous hostility not only to 'the past' itself, but to just about any of the operations of memory" (243). In a world where change is instantaneous, discontinuous, and relentless, where causes are gone by the time anyone figures out where to look for them and where nothing could be done in time to make a difference anyway, the business of prediction is best left to the Jeanne Dixons of the world. And anyone who infers anything of predictive value in the work of the guru and holds him or her responsible for the failure of that prediction is, as they used to say, "So yesterday."

Guru Ventriloquists and Academic Dummies:
The Darker Side of *ISOE*

According to Kenneth Burke, there is inevitably an element of advantage-seeking in all rhetoric, but the quest for "local advantage" (*RM* 61) is tempered as one moves up the hierarchy of rhetorical motives by an increasing element of "self-interference" (269) that universalizes the advantage sought and transforms ulterior motives ("cunning") into "ultimate" motives associated with pure persuasion, of the sort familiar to writers who experience self-interference

> when a book, having been developed so far, sets up demands of its own, demands conditioned by the parts already written, so that the book becomes to an extent something not foreseen by its author, and requires him to interfere with his original intentions. We here confront an "ultimate" motive (as distinct from an "ulterior" one). (*RM* 269)

This principle of self-interference, meanwhile, is a manifestation of the more fundamental Burkean notion of "recalcitrance" (*P&C* 255–61). At levels below the ultimate, in the positive and the dialectic orders, recalcitrance comes from without in the form of nature's unwillingness to confirm a hypothesis, an audience's unwillingness to accept an argument without modification, or a citizenry's rejection of an ideology based on its inability to produce and distribute goods adequately. The concept of recalcitrance is central to Burke's realism and serves to distinguish rhetoric from magic "in the discredited sense of that term" (*RM* 42). While the former involves the use of language to "*induce action in people*," the latter involves the use of language to "*induce motion in things*" (42). At its most cunning, rhetoric and magic merge and recalcitrance is "disappeared" through lies, deceit, or some rhetorical version of "Shazaam!" All of this is prefatory to a consideration of *ISOE*'s version of magic, which involves retrofitting sources to make them say what is required by the authors' argument and their pursuit of local advantage.

The first instance of questionable attribution in *ISOE* arises, ironically enough, from Peters and Waterman's use of the concept "fundamental attribution error" (FAE), which sets out to explain why causal interpretations are so often flawed. To be fair, FAE is not an easy notion to pin down. Like any powerful concept used in a variety of domains, it may be expressed and understood differently according to circumstances. In the hands of Peters and Waterman, FAE turns out to be a valuable resource for "positive reinforcement" (58) and as such a tool their corporate readers may use to advance their interests.

> The fundamental attribution error that so intrigues the psychologists is that we typically treat any success as our own and any failure as the system's. If anything goes well, it is quite clear that "I make it happen," "I am talented," and so on. If anything bad happens, "It's them," "It's the system." Once again, the implications for organizing are clear. People tune out if they feel they are failing, because "the system" is to blame. They tune in when the system leads them to believe they are successful. (58)

This definition is not only inconsistent with its putative source but is also internally inconsistent. If people attribute all success to themselves and all failure to "the system," how can an ostensibly dysfunctional system strengthen their belief in themselves by seconding their faulty attributions? Individuals appear to possess the illusion *ISOE* would have the system foster.

But quibbles about internal consistency aside, *ISOE*'s definition of FAE diverges sharply from that offered by its supposed source, psychologist Lee Ross, who defines FAE in "The Intuitive Psychologist and His Shortcomings" as "the tendency for attributers to underestimate the impact of situational factors and to overestimate the role of dispositional factors in controlling behavior" (183). Ross specifically rejects the notion "that we typically treat any success as our own and any failure as the system's," a view he credits to a rival faction of researchers, proponents of "ego-defensive biases" (181). The latter, says Ross, argue that "actors . . . attribute 'success' to their own efforts, abilities, or dispositions while attributing 'failure' to luck, task difficulty or other external factors" (182), an argument that he and others "have experienced little difficulty in challenging" (182). While FAE *might* result in someone claiming undue credit for a success, it might just as easily go the other way, as in the case of teachers who overestimated their impact on students' *failures* (182).

Not only do Peters and Waterman misrepresent FAE, they arguably fall prey to two of its corollaries and thus "commit" them as well. The first corollary noted by Ross involves a propensity for agents to overemphasize "the influence of salient extrinsic rewards and constraints" at the expense of "intrinsically motivated behavior" (185). Insofar as Peters and Waterman tout "hoopla" and other nonmonetary incentives (that is, extrinsic rewards that cost the company nothing) as essential to the production of a turned-on workforce and mostly ignore intrinsic motivation beyond the control of management, they would appear to commit the very sin predicted by this corollary. The second corollary, noted by Richard Gerrig (59), suggests that FAE is more pronounced among *observers* of an action than among participants—which is to say, FAE would predict that Peters and Waterman, who as consultants are outside observers par excellence, would be more inclined than participants to credit business success or failure to individuals. So when one executive responds to their eight principles by declaring that "'every one of the eight is about people'" (39), the authors are overjoyed. And their boundless faith in human agency leads them to underestimate the importance of circumstance and chance to success and thus to make those bold predictions that eventually provide so much fodder for their critics.

However flagrantly Peters and Waterman ignore the "recalcitrance" of FAE in turning it to their own ends, their misuse of psychologist Ernest Becker's *Denial of Death* is even more flagrant. In fact, Becker's appearance in *ISOE* follows the logic of those advertisements Williamson cites that delight in featuring elements hostile to the advertiser's message. It is impossible to imagine, thus, that Ernest Becker, who died in 1973, would have been pleased to serve as "a major supporting theoretical position, albeit one ignored by most management analysts" (*ISOE* xxi), for Peters and Waterman.

What particularly recommends Becker to the authors of *ISOE* is, in their words, his contention that "man . . . needs both to be a part of something and to stick out. He needs at one and the same time to be a conforming member of a winning team and to be a star in his own right" (xxi). In their first one-sentence summary of Becker, the authors appear to strain, but not to rend, credulity. It is the second sentence, with its barely submerged sports metaphors of "teams" and "stars," that will cause anyone familiar with Becker to demur. And it gets worse. Later they quote Becker on the matter of transcendence, which he sees grounded in our "creatureliness" that "leads us urgently to 'seek transcendence,' 'avoid isolation,' and 'above all fear helplessness'" (59). According to the authors, "The organizational implications of this line of reasoning are inescapable, although with a potential dark side (e.g., we'll do almost anything to seek transcendence)" (59). What is clear from even a superficial reading of Becker is that it is this "potential dark side" of our need to transcend mortality that consumes him. And what Peters and Waterman blandly refer to as our need "both to be a part of something and to stick out" is a central problematic in Becker, who, according to Sam Keen in his 1997 foreword to *The Denial of Death*, never came to terms with his

> radical conclusion that it is our altruistic motives that turn the world into a charnel house—our desire to merge with a larger whole, to dedicate our lives to a higher cause, to serve cosmic powers—[which] poses a disturbing and revolutionary question to every individual and nation. At what cost do we purchase the assurance that we are heroic? No doubt, one of the reasons Becker has never found a mass audience is because he shames us with the knowledge of how easily we will shed blood to purchase the assurance of our own righteousness. (xiv)

There are instances, Becker claims, of "ignoble heroics of whole societies: it can be the viciously destructive heroics of Hitler's Germany or the plain debasing and silly heroics of the acquisition and display of consumer goods, the piling up of money and privileges that now characterizes whole ways of life, capitalist and Soviet" (7). Indeed, societies routinely erect elaborate artifices that distract their denizens from death and invite them to evade growth. Here Becker cites Kierkegaard's notion of the "lies of character," a form of bad faith resting on the denial of possibility, causing "men" to

> follow out the styles of automatic and uncritical living in which they were conditioned as children. They are "inauthentic" ... one-dimensional men totally immersed in the fictional games being played in their society, unable to transcend their social conditioning; the corporation men in the West, the bureaucrats in the East ... (73)

One must go "through" such trivial forms of transcendence, Becker says, to arrive at authentically heroic transcendence. But unlike Peters and Waterman, who fear that we might opt out of these games altogether, Becker's gravest fear is that we will linger forever within these "fictions," entranced and trivialized by them, capable neither of solitude nor of healthier forms of affiliation.

To return to *ISOE* after an extended stay in Becker's text is a jarring experience. Becker's dysfunctional behaviors are transformed by *ISOE* into opportunities corporate America can exploit by creating myths and cultures that will insulate us from the very dread that Becker sees as a prerequisite for salvation. Peters and Waterman co-opt Becker's central project, which calls on us to reject the many easy forms of ready-made transcendence and to open ourselves up to "the rumble of panic underneath everything" (Becker 284). In their hands, our desire for pre-fab identities, our need to believe in the conceit that "heroism" is synonymous with doing an institution's bidding, and our longing to tranquilize ourselves against the possibility of meaninglessness are rhetorical tools they use to win readers over to ideas antithetical to Becker's.

Given the eschatological tone of Becker's project, *ISOE*'s discussion of "value" seems particularly perverse. Thus, at the conclusion of their chapter on motivation, the authors pause to wonder what values they are celebrating.

> Maybe, for one, we might suggest simply "to be the best" in any area as James Brian Quinn says, or to "be true to our aesthetic," as Walter Hoving said of himself and Tiffany's. Perhaps it's Ray Kroc of McDonald's seeing "beauty in a hamburger bun"... or "Forty-eight-hour parts service anywhere in the world" at Caterpillar. (85–86)

Anything, it turns out, that is as far removed as possible from that "rumble of panic beneath everything." Indeed, what Peters and Waterman's ideal companies seem to require of their workers is a form of Kierkegaard's "'Philistinism [that] tranquilizes itself in the trivial'" (Becker 74), as exemplified by some major "heroes" of *ISOE* including Ray Kroc fetishizing a hamburger bun; a Proctor and Gamble executive rendered apoplectic by a suggestion that P&G's pursuit of perfect toilet paper might be a bit misplaced (xix); the Honda factory worker aligning the windshield wipers on every car each night (37); or the Frito-Lay employees fixated on the production and on-time delivery of zero-defect cheese snacks (45). It is a line of heroes descended less from Captain Ahab than from Captain Queeg, afflicted not by hubris or monomania but by some virulent strain of obsessive-compulsive disorder.

One final bit of magic Peters and Waterman perform upon their sources concerns the legendary "Hawthorne effects": "For us, the very important message of the research that these actions spawned, and a theme we shall return to continually in the book, is that it is *attention to employees*, not work conditions per se, that has the dominant impact on productivity" (5–6). In fact, the authors trace their roots in management theory to Elton Mayo, the "father" of Hawthorne effects. And in doing so, they are righter than they know. As Richard Gillespie meticulously documents in his *Manufacturing Knowledge: A History of the Hawthorne Experiments*, Mayo himself was a consummate magician when it came to overcoming recalcitrant data. The data on which his conclusions were drawn were gathered in a highly selective fashion from relatively meager sources (eight workers, two of whom were fired midway through the trials for being "uncooperative" [62]). Moreover, Mayo neither designed nor oversaw the experiments. Rather, he was brought in from Harvard late in the day to spin the findings—he was notorious for his management-friendly views—and to lend them an air of academic legitimacy, which he promptly did. In drawing his conclusions, Mayo proved to be particularly adept at "transform[ing] any challenge by workers of managerial control into evidence of psychiatric disturbance" (73). And most famously, Mayo found that high productivity could be magically induced by manifesting a "caring" attitude toward workers that need not be translated into decent pay or humane work conditions or any other costly "variable" his analysis kept carefully out of play. The fact that the Hawthorne myth is so widely believed may mitigate Peters and Waterman's uncritical use of it. But given the centrality of that myth to their book's thesis, the impact of this particular distortion is significant.

Prometheus v. the "Knitting Needles": The Creation Contradiction

Beyond their tendency to ignore the recalcitrance of their materials, *ISOE*'s authors also tend to finesse a number of significant contradictions. Of all those contradictions, the most significant involves the origins of excellent companies. "How did these companies get the way they are?" (26) the authors ask early on. After initially rejecting Great Man views of history, they reluctantly admit that "associated with almost every excellent company was a strong leader (or two) who seemed to have a lot to do with making the company excellent in the first place" (26). These "strong leaders" prove to be embarrassing on many levels. The glimpses we get of the various founders suggest that they are intolerant, demanding, and inflexible souls prone to surrounding themselves with yea-sayers. The scenes from corporate mythology that sustain their memory feature them cutting locks off doors and sweeping papers off desks, scolding those who violate the letter of company laws and punishing failure. They are, in sum, the "nexus of unfreedom," remote and arbitrary adult authorities of the sort found in fairy tale, not the beneficent boosters *ISOE*'s corporate culture seems to call for.

The contradictions manifest in *ISOE*'s founding figures can be understood as an instance of Burke's "paradox of purity," which says that any entity in its pure or "absolute" form is different in kind from all impure versions of the entity (*GM* 35). *ISOE*'s founders personify their corporations; they embody the absolute principle that their minions identify with or participate in but are never synonymous with. And they violate with impunity *ISOE*'s eight governing principles. They cannot, after all, "stick to their knitting" in the absence of needles and yarn. They must first procure the means of production, a Promethean act inconsistent with calls to stay close to one's customers and to be willing to be "second to market" with a new product. Unlike their minions who dither back and forth between their need to "stick out" and to "fit in," founders seek only to stick out, thereby lending their prestige to the heroic side of the paradox Peters and Waterman borrow from Becker and making explicit an assumption implicit throughout *ISOE*: Individualism is the ultimate value, personified by superordinate founders and, eventually, by Tom Peters.

ISOE's ambivalence toward Promethean originators carries over to its treatment of lesser creators. Creation is invariably associated with subversion. Excellent companies consign their most creative projects to "skunkworks," which are "don't ask, don't tell" operations often conducted in remote, locked rooms on workers' personal time under the paternal protection of "project champions," benign senior executives close enough to the founder's vision to distinguish between permissible and impermissible transgressions of his spirit. Creativity requires "cabals," carried out by "wild ducks" (222). The avuncular corporation winks at such operations, thereby salvaging the sanctity of the founder's originary act even as it acknowledges the need to have its young continually transgress the limits of that vision.

The ambivalence that Peters and Waterman find in corporate attitudes toward original acts is in turn evident in their own attitudes toward authorship. The source of the authors' authorial ambivalence lies in their split allegiances to their two distinct audiences: individual managers and corporate America. While promising managers radical solutions to their problems underwritten by out-of-the-box thinkers like Ernest Becker, they must stay within the comfort zone of those in upper management primarily responsible for gurus' success.

Take, for example, the vulgar matter of earnings. According to recent book cover blurbs on *ISOE*, it has sold nearly 6 million copies since 1982. Assuming that royalties on the book averaged around $1.80 per copy (15 percent at $12 average list price), Tom Peters, the true guru of the pair, would have earned about $5.4 million. But even if one attributes the bulk of those sales to individual managers, Peters's overall wealth derives from corporate America. Thus, in 1995 alone, Tom Peters was estimated to have given sixty seminars, typically sponsored directly or indirectly by corporations, at $60,000 per seminar for a total of about $3.6 million (Micklethwait and Wooldridge 6). Even after expenses, Peters's seminar earnings would soon dwarf his royalty earnings. Indeed, given the time and effort it takes to produce a book and its relatively modest return, it is something of a "loss leader," an advertisement used to extend the author's brand name, not unlike the "2,500 free baseball caps" once offered at Tom Peters's Web site.[5]

All of this helps explain why consulting firm CSC Index and two of its consultants spent nearly $1 million buying 40,000 copies of the consultants' book from bookstores used by the *New York Times* to compile its bestseller list, thereby setting in motion one of those self-fulfilling prophecies so beloved by gurus. The book's strong initial sales generated a "buzz" that promoted further book sales, generated new business for CSC, and emboldened the authors to boost their seminar price to the quasi-guru level of $30,000 (Micklethwait and Wooldridge 24). After *Business Week* outed the authors on August 7, 1995, book sales and reputations suffered, but CSC's "reengineering" movement continued to flourish.

What the above scheme illustrates and what *ISOE*'s rhetorical strategies suggest is that "staying close to one's customers" is as important for writers as for managers. And for gurus, clearly, their primary customers are not the managers or general readers of their books but the corporate leaders who buy "hot" books in large lots for their employees and underwrite gurus' considerably more lucrative ancillary ventures (consultancies, workshops, tapes, and keynote addresses). In sum, creativity is a dangerous topic in corporate America. Thinking outside the box is encouraged so long as innovators limit their thinking to the quest for zero-defect processes and the perfection of predetermined ends and resist the temptation to dream up new ends or apply ethical standards to those ends. (At one point, the only such point I can find in the book, the Peters and Waterman sneak up on an ethical issue—toxic shock caused by defective feminine hygiene products—but only by way of saluting the offending company's quick PR response to the crisis [190].) To the extent that corporate America redefines or reevaluates its ends, the impetus should come from the gods of the marketplace, from customers, especially "'lead users'" (200) of the products, not research and development departments where people strive purposefully to excogitate new ends.

All the contradictions that characterize *ISOE*'s treatment of creativity are in turn personified by Tom Peters, who sells himself on his dust jackets and his Web site as "a champion of bold failures, prince of disorder, professional loudmouth," and, most provocatively, in an October 1997 *Reason* interview, "half an asshole" (44) (as opposed, according to Peters, to "total assholes" like Tony Robbins). But for all his bold and disarmingly self-deprecating allusions to himself, Peters is finally, as he notes on his Web site, "a corporate cheerleader and lover of markets" and an unlikely revolutionary. Politically, his seeming liberalism turns out on closer inspection to be a libertarianism—a label he eschews—limited to the protection of individual rights (he claims in his *Reason* interview to have made the largest single contribution in the history of the American Civil Liberties Union to the protection of First Amendment rights), not the promotion of social justice. He is corporate America's licensed fool, free to say the unspeakable so long as he excepts his sovereign and flatters the authority that grants him his license and pays for his stage.

Stephen Covey's Seven Habits: The Automation of Virtue

If *The Witch Doctors'* authors are nonplussed by *ISOE*'s successes, they are clearly flummoxed by the worldwide fascination with Stephen Covey's *7 Habits of Highly Effective People: Powerful Lessons in Personal Change*, which they include in their final chapter, "A Walk on the Wild Side," a survey of "the strange but annoyingly wealthy creatures" (304) who inhabit the "unmapped regions" between management and quackery. They are sufficiently puzzled by his appeal to visit the Stephen Covey Leadership Center in Provo, Utah, which they describe as "an archipelago of small islands of Coveyism: in one building Covey's lieutenants plan his campaign in the American South; in another they wonder how he will conquer the Asian market; in yet another they produce books, magazines, videotapes, and personal organizers" (305) that generated nearly $100 million in 1996 (306). They are aghast at the style of *7 Habits* and wonder aloud how "you can really take seriously a man who claims, straight-faced, to have identified 'the universal value system of all mankind'" (306). But, in the end, Micklethwait and Wooldridge admire Covey for the consistent application of his deep religious beliefs and the extremely efficient way in which he operates his business. Moreover, compared to his peers, Covey is "alarmingly well qualified" (309) by virtue of his doctorate and his Harvard MBA.

In the midst of their somewhat grudging recital of Covey's academic credentials, Micklethwait and Wooldridge note that while doing his Ph.D. thesis ("American Success Literature since 1776"), Covey discovered that, for the first 150 years of the Republic, most success literature concentrated on questions of character. But shortly after the Second World War people became more interested in superficial things such as appearance and style. (307)

This is a lapse that *7 Habits* was supposedly written to correct. Here the authors are paraphrasing Covey's own account of *7 Habits*' origins in chapter 1, where he tells the story of his adolescent son's puzzling failures in school and in sports and of Covey's ill-advised attempts to solve the problem by using "positive mental attitude techniques" (17). Eventually, Covey has an "Aha" experience—the first of many—and recognizes that his unsuccessful solution is a product of the dreaded "Personality Ethic," a witch's brew of "social image consciousness, techniques and quick fixes" (18) promoted by contemporary success literature and contrary to the sturdier "Character Ethic" of previous centuries. All this he has learned from a study of "literally hundreds of books, articles, and essays in fields such as self-improvement, popular psychology and self-help" (18) that led to *7 Habits*.

The first curious and slightly troubling aspect of this account concerns Covey's failure to evidence his voluminous research in his book. Benjamin Franklin is the only significant figure in that history to receive more than passing reference. And one is hard-pressed to discover a Ph.D. thesis on the topic of American success literature since 1776 that Covey might have written. Indeed, the only dissertation attributed by *Dissertation Abstracts* to Covey is a 1976 thesis entitled "Effects of Human Relations Training on the Social, Emotional, and Moral Development of Students, with Emphasis on Human Relations Training Based on Religious Principles," which earned him a doctor of religious education degree from Brigham Young University's Department of Church History and Doctrine. Covey's dissertation bibliography lists 117 sources, only one of which, Richard Huber's *American Idea of Success*, clearly belongs to the scholarship on success literature. And it is from Huber that Covey borrows, without attribution, the distinction between the "Character Ethic" and the "Personality Ethic" (Huber 226) and the analysis that gives rise to the distinction. In fairness, Covey himself does not seem ever to have claimed a Ph.D. His bios always refer simply to his "doctorate" in an unnamed field. Moreover, he is careful in *7 Habits* to refer to his study of American success literature as simply that, a "study" (18), or, as in his unpaginated acknowledgments, a review done "as part of a doctoral program."

What is particularly curious about Covey's claim to have undertaken so exhaustive a study of success in America, other than the scant evidences of those labors, is that the clearest precedent in the literature of success for this sort of claim was made by Dale Carnegie, who is cited by Huber as one of the perpetrators of the shift from Character to Personality Ethic (226). In *How to Win Friends and Influence People*, thus, Carnegie claims to have "read everything I could find on [human relations] . . . from Dorothy Dix [to] William James" (14) and to have hired a full-time researcher to assist him.

While Covey would have us believe that his researches yielded radically different results from those produced by Carnegie, there are other significant parallels between the two. Both men, for example, write their books on the textbook model. Covey includes "application suggestions" at the end of each chapter and a section on "How to Use this Book" (59–60), which advises readers of the need to review earlier principles at each new stage. And Covey, like Carnegie, touts the importance of teaching his book's lessons to others, preferably within forty-eight hours of learning them (60). Covey's narrator, meanwhile, assumes the second-person imperative address of textbooks, advertising, and hypnosis: "Clear your mind of everything except what you will read and what I will invite you to do. . . . Just focus with me and really open your mind" (96). At other times, he interrupts his account of an affirming anecdote or a recitation of terms to hector his reader in the manner of a nineteenth-century schoolmaster: "Mark it down, asterisk it, circle it, underline it. *Without involvement, no commitment*" (143).

The style of *7 Habits*, meanwhile, is as sober as a religious tract, less spirited even than the prose of Peale or Carnegie. While Covey refers often to his family and to personal experiences, the book is strangely impersonal in tone. The narrator is always "Stephen," grave, thoughtful, the one whom others seek out for wisdom and advice. Those around him, meanwhile, are insubstantial figures, rarely named and even more rarely given any lines to speak. And what lines they do recite are all delivered in the register of Covey and serve invariably to present "Stephen" with problems to solve. There is little of Peters and Waterman's wit here, none of the sometimes mildly profane, audacious assertions or bold predictions and almost no sense of the narrator as anything other than a source of solutions. And outside a botany textbook, it is hard to imagine another book with as many taxonomies and lists as *7 Habits*.

This last point is worthy of further consideration insofar as Covey's persuasive appeal depends greatly on his extensive use of taxonomies, flow charts, and lists—of elements, stages, factors, and criteria. They combine to lend his system an air of exactitude and gravitas that places it beyond the scrum of lighter weight, less systematic approaches promoted by his rivals. They also combine to render thoughtful critique a vertiginous, if not impossible, project. Before one can connect one claim to another, one must first traverse a seemingly endless number of lists full of nonparallel, vague, and overlapping items. (Thus, under the heading "natural laws" or "principles"—the two may or may not be synonymous—presented on page 34, Covey includes "fairness," "human dignity," "potential," and "encouragement" and leaves open the possibility of numberless additions.) And besides the seven habits, issued in the form of commandments— be proactive; begin with the end in mind; put first things first; think "win/ win"; seek first to understand, then to be understood; synergize; sharpen the saw—Covey includes at least forty-two other lists enumerating elements of his system. The lists range from the three elements of each habit (47) to the four elements of our "life center" (109); from ten alternative "centers" to the eleventh, and ideal, principle-centered life (111–16); and include forty categories of effect derived from the impact of the ten alternative centers on the four elements of our life center (119–21), and so on. By the time one makes it from one claim to the next supposedly related claim, the prior claim is a distant memory.

The squeak of marker pens on newsprint and the ghosts of overheads hover about Covey's book. It has about it the indelible feel of the workshop presentation that participants will leave feeling satisfied that they got "tons of information" to go with their inspirational charge. Moreover, by breaking everything down into atomic elements, Covey renders his system extraordinarily simple at every given moment. Only if one tries to connect the dots comprising Covey's system is one likely to be frustrated. And on this score at least, Covey's otherwise omniscient narrator is of little help. Seldom does he discuss the relationships among the many parts of his system. One is left to imagine what, if any, relation exists between a particular mode of thinking (right- or left-brained) and one's place on the "maturity continuum," or between one's "social map" and one's "life center." In the act of exhaustively spatializing and mapping virtue, Covey leaves little room for his reader to interrogate or discuss a system whose origins remain utterly mysterious. In its entirety, *7 Habits* is like a schematic drawing of an extremely complex, wondrous machine capable of performing miraculous acts—but representable only in its unassembled state.

And for all the apparent specificity of these lists, there is a gnawing sense of vagueness about them. Indeed, this lack of specificity is the one feature that most clearly distinguishes Covey's "habits" from the virtues preached by the long-ignored advocates of the "Character Ethic" he is supposedly resurrecting. Despite Covey's final declaration that "correct principles are natural laws, and that God, the Creator and Father of us all, is the source of them" (319), few readers who stay with him to the end would be able to name many, if any, acts proscribed or prescribed by such laws. This confusion owes much to his tendency to state laws in titular form—if "human dignity" is a law, how does one obey it? And on the rare occasions when Covey speaks of laws in any active way, he favors agricultural analogies that describe invariant natural processes rather than purposive human acts. Thus, he solemnly tells us, you must sow before you can reap (21), or you must plant a crop before you harvest it (51), advice that leaves us a great deal of latitude as to what to plant and when to sow. Clearly, this vagueness of reference offers some local rhetorical advantage insofar as it allows each of Covey's readers ample room to plug in their particular values and then, presumably with the assistance of a Quad II Organizer (150) available from Franklin Covey Inc., to chug away, planning and prioritizing their day.

But to be fair to Covey, the agenda he lays out for his readers in the early chapters is a formidable one by guru standards, requiring "inside-out" change. Each one of us must make ourselves over into a better person before we can hope to make ourselves over into a more successful one. And "better" persons, it would appear, are above all else those who can subject their desires to their values—whatever those values might be—utilizing Covey's all-encompassing method for chastening wayward impulses. But before analyzing the intricate system of laws, principles, values, and habits that comprise Covey's approach, we need to return to his earlier mentioned dissertation on human relations training and consider more carefully the religious principles and values that he lays claim to there. Written some thirteen years before *7 Habits*, Covey's dissertation offers glimpses into the mysterious sources of his system and the logic of that system that the book itself is considerably more reticent about.

The Guru in Waiting: Covey Ante-"Stephen"

Whatever the dissertation may reveal about the sources of Covey's system, it offers few hints of the blockbuster bestseller to come.[6] It has about it the air of a dutifully conducted school exercise chosen as much because it could be carried out and written up in the time available as because it promised to advance a field. It describes a one-semester experiment in which Covey tests two versions of human relations training—a traditional secular approach and a "stewardship" approach based on Mormon education principles—on two upper-division BYU business courses enrolling 222 students ("Effects" 83). Two lab sections comprised the experimental group, and two other lab sections comprised the control (84). Students were exposed to the different approaches in fourteen weekly two-hour labs. At the conclusion of the course, the effect was measured by a survey given to all subjects who in two iterations of the same survey first self-reported their progress and then commented on their peers' progress.

Even at first blush, the experiment appears doomed. One is not surprised to learn ultimately that neither form of human relations training showed any significant impact on the subjects. It is hard to imagine that fourteen two-hour labs would significantly change any given group's expressed values, let alone subjects' behaviors. And this was hardly any given—or broadly representative—group. It was more than 80 percent male (83) and, given the demographics of BYU, was surely very white. These were junior/senior business and communication majors, nearly all of whom would have been deeply committed to the tenets of Mormonism—at the time of the experiment, entrance to BYU was tied to recommendations from local bishops attesting to the solidity of the applicant's faith (Mauss 178). As Covey himself notes, a third of the students would probably have completed a two-year mission for their church ("Effects" 129). As he belatedly confesses in his "Explanation for Lack of Statistical Significance": "When one stands back to gain a perspective regarding the impact of one two-hour lab experience in a fourteen-week period with very limited exposure to spiritual principles, it becomes fairly apparent why there was little reportable change in attitudes and behavior" (129).

However flawed Covey's dissertation might be, it affords one a clear understanding of certain values that remain elusive in his later work. Underlying those values is a theological vision that will sound familiar to anyone who has followed the history of success rhetoric in twentieth-century America. According to Covey's summary of Latter-day Saints (LDS) doctrine:

> [M]an is a spirit child of God, The Eternal Father, and earned the right through obedience to come to earth life to obtain a body and to receive and live the gospel. Through his obedience and diligence in obeying the laws and principles and ordinances of the gospel, he

will grow and develop according to the divine celestial pattern and will eventually become capable of not only living with his Father in Heaven, but becoming like his Father in Heaven. ("Effect" 57)

Unlike humanistic doctrines stressing the discovery of godhead within, the "LDS view ... would be far more literal ...; that is, that man literally is a god in embryo. The process of becoming like God and eventually becoming a god is largely one of overcoming and obeying" (58).

For all that Covey decries the "individual fulfillment school of religious education" ("Effect" 58), there remain significant residues of New Thought in his thinking here. In particular, Covey's assertion that "man literally is a god in embryo" is consonant with New Thought belief that human beings are "individualizations" of God's mind. While New Thought stops short of saying humans are literally gods, it does contend that humans are "in no tension with god" (Meyer 77), thereby rendering the divine and human realms continuous as opposed to incommensurable. This belief in the continuity of the human and divine renders Christ's role problematic in New Thought and subsequently in Covey. If Christ's role is to intermediate between the human and divine, what is left for him to do after the two realms are merged? The New Thought solution is to treat Christ more as an abstraction or principle than as an individual man/ god, a solution Covey appears to follow. Thus, "the Savior and Redeemer" is a "perfect model" or "exemplar" whose gospel is a "celestial law" ("Effects" 57) and whose human suffering is, like the figure of the cross in Mormon iconography, notable mostly by its absence. In his study of American religion, Harold Bloom puts the matter more bluntly: "So extraordinarily intense is the mediation of the corporately structured LDS church that Jesus becomes pragmatically unnecessary in the work of salvation" (123).

But whatever the links between Covey and New Thought, sharp differences remain. One does not, after all, "relax" one's way into grace in the sterner vision of Stephen Covey. The words "obedience" and "obeying" appear four times in the passage from Covey's dissertation cited above. Indeed, Christ is exemplary because of his "obedience and development," not his love and sacrifice. In turn, the research questionnaire that Covey's subjects used to self-report their "social, emotional, and moral" progress is heavily skewed toward matters of obedience. Of thirty items on the questionnaire, twelve appear to deal explicitly with matters of obedience and discipline, including everything from avoiding pornography to fulfilling a church calling.[7]

The concept of "moral development" that emerges from Covey's dissertation has little to do with choice and judgment. Even the concept of "problem solving" as it is operationalized on Covey's questionnaire involves the ability to "work well with others" (151). It is not surprising, thus, when we turn to *7 Habits* to find Covey denouncing "the current social paradigm [that] enthrones independence" (50), calling instead for his readers to be "interdependent" people. (Curiously, he lashes out seventeen pages later against the "current social paradigm [that] tells us we are largely determined by conditioning and conditions," suggesting either that he is confused or that those unnamed souls who construct social paradigms are having it both ways on a grand scale.) Interdependence and independence are not, of course, mutually exclusive ends, and Covey in fact sees independence as a necessary condition for interdependence, a position seemingly consistent with dialogic views of human relationships.

But Covey's peculiar notion of independence would seem to leave his thinking far removed from people like Bakhtin and Buber. Independence in Covey is less about autonomy than it is about forbearance. It typically refers to one's "private victories" over desire and emotion, not one's critical questioning of general principles or social institutions. Independence mostly means that one is free "from" temptations, including the temptation to deviate from authority, rather than free "to" question and reject norms and mores or to exercise one's judgment. If interdependence is to work in any strong sense, one's model for human interaction will need to be along the lines of Rorty's "conversation of mankind" or the "Burkean parlor" where the independence of those who participate rests on their mutual ability to modify each others' beliefs. Within an inflexible hierarchy where the institution is always right and some people are in fact primus inter pares, "interdependence" will serve simply as a euphemism for acquiescence to the status quo.

The nature of the environment within which individuals might ideally practice Covey's seven habits gets little explicit attention in his book. Society and politics are hardly mentioned, except as corrupting forces, while businesses and families are dealt with as mostly the sum of their individual characters insofar as those characters are either corrupted by social conditioning or saved by principle-centered conditioning, the triumph of which results in a condition resembling what Thomas Frank has dubbed "inner Taylorism" (185). Covey's version, derived from his definition of "discipline," involves devotion "to a superordinate goal or a person who represents that goal" (148). The nature of these superordinate persons and goals that comprise the larger context for Covey's spiral of individual growth requires a further detour, this time into the Mormon doctrines that explicitly inform Covey's dissertation and tacitly inform his book.

The Mormon Way of Knowing

In the process of using LDS doctrine as a "terministic screen" for understanding and critiquing Covey, some criticism of the Mormon Church seems implicit. Indeed, Alan Wolfe, in a withering review of Covey's *7 Habits of Highly Effective Families*, cites LDS doctrine as an insidious and covert element of Covey's thinking. While the following analysis of links between Covey and LDS doctrines is also critical, an initial caveat is required. A number of problematic issues in Covey will be traced to his theology, but criticism of such links is not intended to extend to his religious beliefs *qua religious beliefs*. The application of theological principles to corporate management or political governance is fraught with peril, no matter what religious doctrines are brought to bear. Any religious hierarchy will in the end prove to be problematic for civic or commercial enterprises requiring compromise and commitment to secular ends. What might be judged a mere inconsistency in the application of secular principles may look like gross hypocrisy in the application of religious principles. Moreover, most religions find themselves wedded to at least a few principles that are difficult to "stretch" casuistically to new social realities, causing considerable anxiety among and beyond the faithful. And most church hierarchies do not translate well to secular contexts. Mormonism is unique among religions for the visibility of its problematic doctrines more than for the dangers they pose to secular life.

That said, any non-Mormon who attempts to connect Covey's book to Covey's religious beliefs will do so with significant misgivings. Even a cursory review of the literature on Mormonism shows how difficult trustworthy sources are to identify. Given both the influence and singularity of Mormonism in American society, surprisingly few academic presses—the notable exception being the University of Illinois Press—feature critical studies of Mormonism on their lists. For example, most of the 750 books, microforms, and videos that appeared in response to a "keyword" search of "Mormon" in my university's library (in a state where 6 percent of the population is Mormon) are church histories, historical accounts of key events in Mormon history, family records and diaries, and various biographies and interviews with prominent church members. A large portion of these studies were published by a handful of presses in Salt Lake City, and few appear to have been peer reviewed. The rest tend to wobble between extremes: a few conspiracy theorists linger lovingly over the church's presumed promotion of polygamy or its lengthening corporate tentacles, while many true believers defend the faith with arguments borrowed from what Mormon sociologist Armand Mauss calls the "particularistic indoctrination" (97) of the Mormon Church Education System. While many speak on behalf of the church in publications sold through church-owned bookstores, the status of these authors in relation to the church itself is often unclear.

The reasons for this confusion are many. First, there is the matter of the long history of suspicion on the part of non-Mormons and longer-established religions toward the peculiarities of Mormon doctrine, beginning with the church's unlikely founder and first prophet and extending to some of its more controversial doctrines. Moreover, there is the whole puzzling matter (to the outsider at least) of the church hierarchy, whose uppermost reaches are closed to members and nonmembers alike. And apropos of the church's suspicion of intellectuals generally and "priestcraft" specifically, the members of that hierarchy are laypersons with backgrounds mostly in applied fields that leave them ill-equipped to articulate complex and nuanced theological doctrines. In fact, little is made in Mormonism of the distinction between the "laity and the clergy (terms almost never used in Mormon parlance)" (Mauss 160). Consequently, as Mauss goes on to suggest, "there is a sense in which every Mormon is his or her own theologian" (160). While at least some of that theology will reflect official doctrine, it is equally likely to include a generous portion of "folk wisdom that might have no basis in official doctrine" (160). And "there is in Mormonism no tradition of canon law and thus no a priori basis for assigning or denying legitimacy to any of the acts or statements of the church leaders at any level" (161). Because church leaders make all major decisions in secret and offer their conclusions in unanimous voice with no dissent or opposition, one is never privy to their reasoning. While this process befits decisions made on the basis of faith and revelation, it renders full understanding, let alone critique, difficult. Even so adept a hermeneuticist as Harold Bloom, who is not unsympathetic toward Mormonism, which he calls a "variety of the American Religion," or Joseph Smith, whom he calls "an authentic prophet" (95), throws up his hands before the perplexities of LDS theology, declaring it to be "so jerry-built that no one can hope to get it straight" (68).[8]

The elusive nature of Mormon doctrine can doubtless be attributed in part to its relatively recent and rocky beginning. Born as an institution in a skeptical age, Mormonism has difficulty consigning its origins to the mists of myth and ancient history. Mormonism, says Protestant theologian Martin Marty, has "no place to hide. What can be sequestered in Mormon archives and put beyond the range of historians can often be approached by sources outside them. . . . There is little protection for Mormon sacredness" (174). We know far more about the origins of the church and about the foibles of its founders than we could possibly know about early Christianity. And in the case of Joseph Smith, whose prophecies form the basis of the church, questions of credulity are particularly acute. According to Richard and Joan Ostling, "Book of Mormon apologists have a much tougher job than apologists for the Bible. Not a single person, place, or event unique to Joseph Smith's 'gold Bible' has ever been proven to exist" (259). Moreover, the existence of the "gold Bible" itself, the basis for Smith's prophecies, has never been independently confirmed. This is not to say that the roots of Mormonism are fraudulent. But because it has "no place to hide," it must rely to an unusual degree, even by theological standards, on personal authority and faith to support its truth claims and beliefs.

In the end, the Mormon faithful base their belief more on the writer or revelator than on the writing or revelation. Or as Mormon lore, if not always church doctrine, would have it, "'[W]hen the prophet speaks, the debate is over'" (Ostling 368). The provisional status of text and doctrine is underscored by the church's frequent editing of the Book of Mormon, a process closely monitored by disaffected Mormons Jerald and Sandra Tanner: "Their specialty is showing changes and alleging contradictions in what holds itself to be God's one truth faith—for example, their *3,913 Changes in the Book of Mormon*" (Ostling 348). However single-minded their critique, the Tanners are viewed as "dedicated, meticulous, and rarely inaccurate" (348).

In Mormon theology, the revelations of "latter-day saints" do indeed trump the revelations of earlier seers. Perhaps in part because of the extreme vulnerability of its earliest prophecies and doctrines, the church tends to equate sacredness less with origins and "first things" than with progress. Indeed, they embrace a doctrine of change and progress, the theological version of Covey's spiral of growth, as exuberant as any guru's. Even God, according to early-nineteenth-century Mormon apostle John A. Widstoe, is considered to be "engaged from the beginning . . . in progressive development, and infinite as God is, he must have been less powerful in the past than he is today" (23–24). Every day, in every way, the faithful and their deity get better and better. But while today's prophets are free to modify the words of past prophets, the church labors to ensure that latter-day revelations do not discredit its much revered prophets.

To illustrate the process by which church doctrine has been changed without rejecting earlier doctrines or tarnishing the doctrines' promulgators, consider the church's rejection of polygamy, a practice grounded in official doctrine and in the prophecies of Joseph Smith. The change in doctrine was initiated by the church's first president, considered to be the church's "prophet, seer, and revelator" (Ostling 86), and appeared responsive, albeit belatedly, to political pressure. After the illegality of polygamy was upheld in the courts (*US v. Reynolds*, 1879), the doctrine prevented Utah from attaining statehood (ultimately conferred in 1896). But rather than renouncing the offensive doctrine, then President Woodruff simply announced its discontinuation in an 1890 "Manifesto" calling for the suspension of polygamy. There was no indication that the decision was based on a revelation. Eighteen years later, the manifesto was added to the official church Doctrines and Covenants after its official status had been called into question during Senate hearings for Senator-Elect (and high-ranking church official) Reed Smoot (Ostling 84). None of the original doctrines justifying the practice were amended. Even after the manifesto was added to the Doctrines and Covenants, polygamy was apparently tolerated by high church officials, causing many of the faithful to complain about the "'pretzled language' [that] became common public discourse on the subject of plural marriage" (Ostling 89).

As the preceding scenario suggests, Mormonism's view of truth can be surprisingly supple, especially in light of the rigid stance the church often assumes on social, political, and moral issues. According to the Ostlings, "for Mormons history—and truth, which is supposedly embedded in history—is dynamic and fluid. There is nothing quite like what the poet T. S. Eliot called 'the still point of the turning world.' As Mark P. Leone writes in *Roots of Modern Mormonism*, in Mormonism truth is not absolute or fixed; it is changeable, flexible, and additive" (249). And it does not appear that the church requires these new truths to be reconciled with existing truth.

One of the fundamental challenges facing a nonbeliever attempting to understand Mormonism is this seemingly paradoxical belief in moral absolutism on the one hand and cognitive relativism on the other. If God is in fact unfinished and non-absolute, how can moral laws grounded in such a deity be viewed as absolute natural laws? If the basis of the faith is revelation, and yet all the revelations by which one has lived one's life and on which one has based one's faith may be superseded by contemporary revelations, and if the texts that embody those revelations may be modified continuously, where does one's faith reside? Again, what mediates all these apparent contradictions is the church leadership, which has, according to LDS scholar Philip Barlow, "direct experience with God" (43) and thus can see past the corrupted truth of texts, even the most venerable and sacred of texts, including the Bible, and glimpse absolutes bare.

Which brings us back to that larger context within which Covey's individuals will undertake their "spiral of growth." To the extent that this context derives from Covey's religious faith, one might expect that it would be extremely hierarchical and resistant to change. Those in the uppermost reaches of the hierarchy—being literally nearer to God—would be *essentially* different from those below. One's place in the actual material arrangement of the hierarchy is more crucial in determining the validity of one's enlightenment than is the consistency of that enlightenment with existing doctrine. Hence the importance of obedience and the willingness of the faithful to accept abrupt reversals of policy and principle from above and to live with the contradictions that inevitably attend such reversals. In such a world, the power of persuasion is ultimately trumped by the powers of revelation.

How Absolute Beliefs Survive Relativist Understandings

While Covey is considerably more circumspect about the origins of his hierarchy in *7 Habits* than in his dissertation, he makes clear throughout the book that it is absolute in nature. The ruling principles of that hierarchy are not corrigible, according to Covey, who quotes Cecil B. DeMille on the subject: "'It is impossible for us to break the law. We can only break ourselves against the law'" (33). Why then do people fail to acknowledge these universal truths and hence fail to grow and develop in accordance with them? Certainly the plants that Covey cites as exemplary subjects of natural law follow those laws universally and assiduously—why don't we? And why do we seem to disagree so vehemently over the precise nature of those laws? Clearly we live in a fallen world; so what theodicy rationalizes that world? This brings us to Covey's notion of "paradigms," a key intervening variable in his system.

As it turns out, "the reality of . . . principles or natural laws becomes obvious to anyone who thinks deeply and examines the cycles of social history" (*7 Habits* 34). All societies that have followed them have flourished; all that ignored them have disintegrated. The problem is that some of us have been victims of inadequate "paradigms," which Covey defines as the "maps" (23) or "subjective realiti[es]" (33), that connect perceivers to perceived. It is these bad maps that cause us to misread the never-changing territory and to disagree about principles. But those differences have no effect on the principles themselves. "Although people may argue about how these principles are defined or manifested or achieved, there seems to be an innate consciousness and awareness that they exist" (35). Of course, at this point some may wonder just what these principles could possibly *be* apart from their "definitions, manifestations, or achievements," or where they might reside when at home, or what effect these mute, extraverbal apparitions could possibly have on the resolution of human differences and the reform of faulty paradigms.

This brings us to the "other" side of Stephen Covey, the cognitive relativist and subjectivist par excellence. To illustrate how our subjective realities, our "maps," may interfere with our perception of objective reality, Covey offers an extended discussion of an experience he had with the well-known "old woman-young woman" drawing during a class at the Harvard Business School. His instructor showed half the class a drawing of a young woman and half the class a drawing of an older woman, both modeled on the picture that can be seen either way (26–46). When the entire class was finally shown the latter drawing, those who had first seen the drawing of the young woman also "saw" her in the ambiguous drawing, while the rest of the class continued to "see" the older woman they had been shown. According to Covey, a fierce debate ensued, illustrating, he says, that "two people can see the same thing, disagree, and yet both be right. It's not logical; it's psychological" (27).

Ultimately, the members of the class, "through continued calm, respectful and specific communication" (28), were able to recognize the fundamental ambiguity of the optical illusion. They saw "reality." But what is still problematic by the end of the anecdote, and what remains problematic to the end of *7 Habits*, is the status of interpretation in relation to reality. If faulty paradigms necessarily distort our vision of reality, and a true vision of reality is a necessary precondition for correcting our paradigms (and in turn for morally correct behavior), how do we ever break out of the circle? The example of the ambiguous drawing offers no decisive guidance on the matter in part because both visions are in effect "true," which allows the participants to reach consensus without either side having to acknowledge being wrong. But what about cases that feature two mutually exclusive visions of reality, each of which is considered "right" by its adherents and "wrong" by its skeptics? And what if a shift in position on the matter entails a reassessment of one's belief system and significant spiritual or material loss? How might Covey respond, say, to a dissident minority within the Catholic Church challenging the Vatican over the exclusion of women from the priesthood? Would people raising the issue be guilty of possessing a faulty paradigm? But if such wrongheaded notions are the product of a faulty paradigm, the holders of these notions necessarily perceive not only the contested reality through that paradigm but the counterarguments of right-minded people like "Stephen" as well. How can right-minded arguments (or exemplary behavior, or any other sort of right-mindedness) ever get through the distorting lens of faulty paradigms when not even Covey's foundational reality, our "innate" awareness of principles, can make it through unscathed? How does one see past one's fallen state when one of the crucial attributes of that state is a fallible mode of understanding?

On the one hand, we find Covey saying that "[t]he principles don't change; our understanding of them does" (123). But on the other hand, it is not clear just how we can access those principles that elude our understanding because "[w]e see the world, not as *it is*, but as *we are*—or, as we are conditioned to see it" (28); because "facts have no meaning whatsoever apart from their interpretation" (29); and because "*[b]eing is seeing*" (32). So, nothing is known apart from interpretation . . . except the certainty that principles exist independently of interpretation? The most direct expression of this conundrum occurs in conjunction with the anecdote of Covey's underperforming son that begins the book. Initially, Covey concludes that if he and his wife "wanted to change the situation, we had to change ourselves. And to change ourselves effectively, we first had to change our perceptions" (18). But then, fourteen pages later, Covey just as emphatically insists that "to see our son differently, Sandra and I had to *be* differently. Our new paradigm was created as we invested in the growth and development of our own character" (32). Throughout most of the rest of the book, changes of character or being (the two seem to be interchangeable) are treated as prior conditions for (or, as in the second sentence of the previous quote, simultaneous occurrence with) changes of interpretation. But, like the optical illusion of the old and young woman, like revelations that do and do not supersede previous doctrine, both possibilities are left open. There is no resolution or synthesis, and the matter is left as vague as the nature of Covey's originating principles.

The Discontinuous Spiral

Somewhere along the path to divinity, about the place where Covey's spiral of growth winds upward from private victories to public ones, one encounters a lacuna. Amidst the blizzard of taxonomies, flow charts, and lists, it is hard to say exactly where this gap lies, but its consequences are clear enough: it annuls the first principle of Covey's "Character Ethic," the law of inside-out development whereby principle-centered personal change is a necessary condition for public success. "*Private victories precede public victories.* You can't invert that process anymore than you can harvest a crop before you plant it. It's inside out" (51). In the opening sections of Covey's book, all attempts to violate this law are attributed to the dreaded "Personality Ethic's" "outside-in" way of doing things. The latter scheme encourages queue jumping, or skipping the initial "private victories" and character building called for by Covey in pursuit of public triumphs. Adherents of the Personality Ethic delude themselves into believing that "something out there—some new planner or seminar . . . will help [them] handle all these pressures in a more efficient way" (41).

For the first one-third or so of *7 Habits*, Covey is unfailingly loyal to the strictures of the Character Ethic. But then, starting with Habit 3, "Put First Things First," where he introduces us to the Quad II Organizer available exclusively from Franklin Covey, he begins moving away, subtly at first but decisively by the end, from the natural law of development that launches him on his quest. All those planners and seminars that Covey tells us in the early going are used by outside-in enthusiasts to solve their problems on the cheap turn out to be the very heart of the matter for most of *7 Habits'* concluding chapters.

More than once, Covey stresses in later chapters the "dramatic, profound" (155) results people experience when using his own fourth-generation planner, citing instances of individuals who take his seminars and experience nearly instantaneous paradigm shifts or entire corporations who over slightly longer periods of time undergo miraculous transformations. Increasingly, the book takes on the character of an infomercial script. We hear all sorts of stories about people who benefit from the wisdom of "Stephen" in such a way as to achieve "public victories," without giving any evidence of having won any private victories over themselves or having achieved any enlightened level of character or principle. It is not even clear that the beneficiaries of Stephen's wisdom in the latter portion of the book keep up with their Quad II planners. One need not, after all, be particularly virtuous to "think win/win" or to practice empathic listening any more than one must be sincere to practice the persona management techniques of Carnegie and Peale, especially when the stress throughout Covey is on the capacity of each technique to maximize return on investment, and every story affirms that public victories require no private sacrifices. So why stress over private victories and all the rigors of those first three stages of the spiral when one can simply hire someone like "Stephen" to come in and help one achieve "win/win" for the cost of a consulting fee?

The dilemma facing Covey here is not unlike the dilemma Burke sees facing strict constructionists of constitutional principles. By declaring his law of development a natural law not open to amendment or alteration and banishing all contraries to the law, Covey is declaring it adequate to and equally efficacious in all circumstances. But as the history of constitutional law would suggest, no principle can survive intact through unforeseeable circumstances. Some "casuistic stretching" will be necessary to fit the principle to the exigencies of the moment, and some incorporation of antagonistic principles into one's ruling principles will be required. But Covey, having left himself no formal machinery for amending his principle and having consigned all opposition to the realm of the illusory, has no choice but to violate that principle when circumstances require compromise. In the end, there is nothing wrong with Covey advising people of possibly flawed characters on how to achieve success. And there is nothing necessarily wrong with people who would achieve success while skipping Covey's notion of virtue. The problem lies in the illusion that one's principle remains intact under these circumstances and thus that those who achieve success have ipso facto achieved sturdy characters, or, to reprise an earlier formula, that one can attain heaven by the same route one uses to reach Philadelphia.

Peters and Covey: What Kinds of Fool Are These?

If Tom Peters dons the motley and takes on the role of corporate America's licensed fool, Stephen Covey would have us believe that he is our holy fool, God's fool, whose piety and obedience have earned him special insight into the affairs of men, viewed sub specie aeternitatis. Traditionally, the role of the licensed fool was to remind a king that he is not a god. By reveling in the physical, the scatological, the reductive, and the humorous, the licensed fool forever keeps the hubris of moral authorities in check. And so it is with Tom Peters, who revels in his profane and zany role and happily reminds us of the close association between the fundamental and the fundament ("half an asshole"). Reluctantly acknowledging the importance of strong founders in the corporate mythos, he nevertheless continues to challenge their hegemony—albeit carefully and in restricted ways—with wit and clandestine action of the sort that one glimpses in the self-conscious construction of his text. The danger of Peters's role is of course that it is not always easy to distinguish the licensed fool from the con man or the more trivial sorts of jokester. One is never sure just how much trust one might place in Peters. He is valuable insofar as he negates and checks certain baleful tendencies in the status quo, but in the end he appears to have little to offer by way of alternatives to that status quo.

The holy fool, on the other hand, reminds us that godhood can shine through mere mortals in the form of divine innocence. Holy fools want nothing of us and remind us every day, through their example, of the sacred. They are people of principle whose spirituality transcends the licensed fool's carnivalesque celebrations of the body. If the licensed fool is, in St. Chrysostom's memorable phrase, "he who gets slapped" for his impertinency, the holy fool is "he who gets crucified to be reborn" for his apostasy. The danger faced by holy fools is the frequent tendency to be confused with natural fools or simpletons—and vice versa. In our eagerness to believe in the existence of holy fools, we may sometimes be a bit too credulous toward candidates for the role. Nowhere is this tendency better illustrated than in Jerzcy Koczinski's *Being There*, a peculiarly postmodern version of the rags-to-riches tale.

Koczinski's protagonist is Chauncey Gardener, the witless, middle-aged bastard son of a wealthy businessman whose garden Chauncey tends, never leaving the confines of his benefactor's home until, at the beginning of the novel, his benefactor dies and Chauncey is cast out into a reality known to him only through a lifetime of addictive television viewing. Wholly by chance (he is also known as "Chance the gardener") and a series of random occurrences, he ascends to the very innermost circles of power, advising presidents and being fawned over by the media, which eagerly report his gardening homilies—gardening being the only thing Chauncey knows anything about—transforming them into profoundly insightful analogies for the state of the economy and the world. He is, in Daniel Boorstin's language, the personification of "image," depthless and perfectly passive like the televised images he ceaselessly watches; he is the tabula rasa on which the media script their desire. He is the natural fool transformed by a media system into a holy one, and as such he anticipates uncannily the career of Stephen Covey. And could anyone who followed those careers or heard the two men offer presidents—fictional in the one case, actual in the other—self-evident advice wrapped in gardening metaphors not find themselves trapped helplessly between laughter and tears?

5 | Academic Border Crossers and Border Guards

In this chapter, I return to a relationship discussed earlier, particularly in the introduction, chapter 1, and chapter 4, between success rhetoric and academic critics. The discussions in the introduction and chapter 1 focused on the failure of humanists generally and rhetoricians particularly to give much critical attention to contemporary success rhetoric. Chapter 4's discussion, meanwhile, focused on an academic article critical of Peters and Waterman's *In Search of Excellence* and why that article would have little influence on practitioners to whom it was ostensibly addressed and how it failed to account for *ISOE*'s appeal to those same practitioners. But while these earlier critiques assumed the *possibility* of successful forays by academics into the popular marketplace, this final chapter revisits that assumption to consider if academics critical of success rhetoric, or any other phenomenon, can voice that criticism in the mainstream without betraying disciplinary assumptions and professional values. In the case of the two academics examined in this chapter, the first, Deborah Tannen, has successfully penetrated popular markets but only, it would appear, by violating some of the same professional decorums that the second, Stanley Fish, says are necessarily violated whenever disciplinary arguments are popularized. In what follows, it will be argued that while Tannen's work may illustrate the dangers of border crossing and thereby offer prima facie support for Fish's theoretical position, that position and the borders it defends are ultimately more porous than Fish would have us believe.

The Delicate Art of Breaking Out Without Selling Out

Whatever her shortcomings as a popularizer of academic thinking, Deborah Tannen clearly is not a member of the one academic group that has in recent years been most successful in gaining the attention of the American people—the far right. The Bennetts, Blooms, D'Souzas, Cheneys, and others, however meager—with the exception of Bloom—their academic bona fides, have lent credence to some extraordinarily reductive views of American culture and history. Unhampered by nagging doubts about the legitimacy of their enterprise, they offer popular audiences reassuringly simple advice without any of the qualification, citation, or parenthetical hand-wringing that attenuate academic claims. Speaking in the unflappably vatic voice of a Stephen Covey, they have improbably succeeded with popular audiences by mourning the ascendance of deviant academic theories produced by writers largely unknown to and almost entirely unread by their audiences. Such unlikely success stories serve as a reminder that some academics enjoy privileged access to routes and relays out of academe and that so long as their messages resonate with those who control the purse strings of bountifully financed institutes and publishing companies on the right, those messages—even obscure and ponderous ones—will be amplified in much the same way guru messages are amplified by corporate America. The nominally liberal Tannen at least demonstrates that such structural advantages are not a necessary condition for border crossing.

Christopher Newfield, in an extended, not unsympathetic critique of Tom Peters, acknowledges the considerable inherent structural advantages enjoyed by conservatives like Peters in appealing to mass audiences:

> We can line up the usual suspects: the servile media, the political and cultural power of capital, the intellectual timidity of the worried, overworked work force facing seemingly irreversible decline, the increased policing of scapegoat groups, and the solidly right wing of most upper management. ("Pleasures" 37)

But, in the end, Newfield attributes Peters's great success less to his well-subsidized bully pulpit than to his tremendous visceral appeal. His message "offers specific steps for more freedom, creativity, and prosperity in the place where you get paid" (37), if not always in the short run—where zany, contrarian thinking in the skunkworks must often yield to bean counters' logic—then surely in the long run. Indeed, the vision of Tom Peters, defiant refugee from corporate America, off on his Vermont farm tending his herd of llamas, seems to hold the same sort of fascination for today's corporate minions that the promise of "mud-daubed huts" and ten-acre plots once held for the American merchant class.

Newfield is unique among academic critics for acknowledging the potential usefulness of Peters's message—in another essay ("Recapturing Academic Business"), he calls on universities to scrap the scientific management model that has reigned in academe since the days of Taylor in favor of something like Peters's liberation management model— and for extending rather than simply debunking Peters's arguments. In effect, Newfield draws up a new map for academics seeking routes to the wider world and calls on them to quit focusing solely on the shortcomings of Peters's model and to adapt his persuasive strategies to their own arguments. He applauds Peters for his appropriation of the "pleasure principle" for the workplace and attempts to transform Peters's microeconomic arguments for corporate excellence into macroeconomic arguments for social justice.

While some of these arguments—for example, Newfield's call for corporations to voluntarily cede authority to noncorporate interests—seem a bit naive, his contention that elements of Peters's corporate vision might be retrofitted to civic and educational institutions deserves consideration, as does his call for scholars to build on the rhetorical stratagems of gurus like Tom Peters to sway public opinion or educate the public on some of the very matters gurus lay claim to. (In the latter regard, it should be noted, Newfield practices what he preaches, organizing his argument guru-style around a series of injunctions followed by elaborations as opposed to, say, a series of claims or questions followed by justifications.)

Whatever the limits of Newfield's model, it does appear to offer would-be guru academics a new, if tentative, map to the "other side." And Deborah Tannen appears to follow that map insofar as she utilizes some of the gurus' favorite rhetorical stratagems in making her own way across the border. Unfortunately, the one strategy that arguably lends Tannen's work its greatest mass appeal is the one that Newfield finds most problematic in Peters—the tendency to ignore larger contexts and to soft-pedal the systemic roots of problems. Particularly in her early work, Tannen reduces systemic problems to individual ones with solutions grounded in individual acts of cognitive will aimed at personal betterment rather than collective expressions of political will aimed at structural modification. And to the extent that she later deviates from this line of thinking, sales of her books appear to suffer.

On the other hand, Tannen's work is clearly grounded in and remains faithful to responsibly done scholarship in her discipline. To be sure, she has been charged by peers with oversimplification, but her reductions appear for the most part to be consistent with prevailing views of many of, if not all of, her peers.[1] And while she certainly reports those views selectively, foregrounding those that might be of most immediate use to her general audience, she does not appear to invent or distort in the manner of mainstream gurus. Whether or not the model of disciplinarity she follows in arriving at or, more important, justifying these truths is viable or not remains a much harder question to answer. For now, we will consider some of the ingredients, rhetorical and historical, of Tannen's successful border crossing in *You Just Don't Understand: Women and Men in Conversation* (*YJDU*) and her less-successful attempt to repeat that journey in *Argument Culture: Moving from Debate to Dialogue* (*AC*).

Ironically, the extended stay of *YJDU* on the *New York Times* bestseller list owes much to its shrewd use of rhetorical devices that Tannen later censors in *AC*. In particular, Tannen clearly invokes a pop culture myth, "The Battle of the Sexes," to frame her argument in *YJDU* and then explicitly rejects such devices in *AC*: "Is it necessary to frame an interchange as a battle to get people interested?" (6). The popular appeal of the battle of the sexes lies in its wondrous capacity for simplification. It reduces the conflicts and tensions that mark the slow and grudging recession of American patriarchy into something on the order of a domestic spat between two sitcom characters who just can't help themselves from seeing the world in male and female ways and who secretly long to return to comfortable stereotypes lately condemned by prudish ideologues. In this vein, Tannen confides that many people are pleasantly surprised to find on meeting her how "nice or so feminine" (*YJDU* 240) she is in spite of her "high level of status." In reporting these compliments, Tannen simultaneously dispels one contemporary female stereotype, the "'aggressive,'" "'cold,'" "'hard,'" "'competitive'" (240) careerist, some variant of Rush Limbaugh's "FemiNazi" that his Dittoheads so loved to loathe, even as she adapts a more traditional female stereotype for the new times—June Cleaver with a Ph.D.?—that some in her audience will doubtless be relieved to find still in play. These same revenants from the battle of the sexes that haunt *YJDU* will later be reincarnated, only to be soundly cudgeled, in *AC*, where we find Tannen sternly warning that "[t]he promise of controversy seems an easy and natural way to rouse interest. But serious consequences are often unintended: Stirring up animosities to get a rise out of people, though easy and provocative, can open old wounds or create new ones that are hard to heal" (7).

While the battle of the sexes' appeal is in some sense timeless, timeliness certainly plays a role in the warm reception accorded *YJDU*'s version of the myth. Tannen, like Peters and Waterman before her, found a ready-made audience for her work, many of them already glued to their television sets watching a particularly sordid, real-life performance of the battle of the sexes that could have been lifted right out of Tannen's pages. The Hill-Thomas encounter, it will be recalled, began playing out on national television shortly after *YJDU* was published, and "You just don't understand" could serve as a perfect one-sentence coda for that drama. In a massively "asymmetrical" relationship of the very sort Tannen says American males are partial to in their discourse, a group of powerful white males badgered and vilified a single African American female, volubly and publicly failing to "get it" for far too long.

In what follows, I will not dispute Tannen's characterization of male and female "styles" of discourse in *YJDU*, though I would argue that she overstates the magnitude of those differences. Neither will I contest the notion that the styles of discourse are unequally valued: "The male is seen as normative, the female as departing from the norm. And it is only a short step— maybe an inevitable one—from 'different' to 'worse'" (15). What will be argued is that Tannen retains the traditional binary and simply reverses the position of the male and female styles, all the while denying that either one is privileged. She writes, in short, from the perspective of the non-gendered, objective "expert" while surreptitiously championing a style she labels feminine. While such championing is arguably justified in the name of redressing sexist imbalances of longstanding, her disingenuousness in adopting the pose of arbiter rather than advocate greatly reduces her burden of proof and allows her to avoid many of the most significant issues associated with her subject. Behind these deficient arguments in *YJDU*, one can see at work a questionable understanding of disciplinarity and the limits of expertise that emerges more fully and explicitly in *AC*.

The above observation is particularly significant in the context of Tannen's promise to release her readers from the bonds of gendered perspectives, allowing them to see things from a non-gendered, expert perspective and to become more acute readers of "metamessages" and more astute analysts of "everyday conversations, and their effects on relationships" (*YJDU* 13). Just as Tannen manages to "make sense of seemingly senseless misunderstandings that haunt our relationships" (13), she promises to help her reader attain a similar level of understanding and to be liberated by that expertise: "Understanding genderlects makes it possible to change—to try speaking differently—when you want to" (297). To suggest that Tannen's analysis is itself gendered damages not just her "expert" ethos but the bold promises underwritten by that ethos.

This mostly tacit equation of expert understanding and the female style of communication is explicitly expressed several times in *YJDU*. At one point, for example, she privileges the female perspective in the very act of championing the transcendence of gender. After attributing an unnamed psychologist's faulty interpretation to his/her failure to consider a male perspective, she notes:

> In a sense, the values of therapy are those more typically associated with women's ways of talking than with men's. This may be why a study showed that among inexperienced therapists, women do better than men. But over time, with experience, this gender difference disappears. Eventually, perhaps, male therapists—and men in therapy—learn to talk like women. (121)

To be sure, Tannen, ever scrupulous to be evenhanded in her discussion of gender-based traits, then goes on to applaud women who take assertiveness training to learn how to talk more like men. But clearly, expertise trumps androgyny, and just as clearly, expertise is more strongly associated with a female, not a male, perspective.[2]

On other occasions, Tannen's overt equation of the expert perspective and the female perspective is managed more subtly. Consider for example her discussion of men's and women's ways of arguing. While men often "try to pursue an argument logically, step by step, until it is settled" (*YJDU* 92), women tend to rely more on anecdotal evidence and less "top-down" constructs. From men's perspective, Tannen reports, women's perspective appears to be illogical. Here she offers an anecdote featuring an argument between a husband and wife over a newspaper claim that contemporary students were less idealistic than were students of the 1960s. The wife in Tannen's anecdote challenged her exasperated husband by citing "her niece and her niece's friends" (92) as examples of idealistic students. Tannen characterizes their conflict as follows:

> The logic this woman was employing was making sense of the world as a more private endeavor—observing and integrating her personal experience and drawing connections to the experiences of others. The logic the husband took for granted was a more public endeavor—more like gathering information, conducting a survey, or devising arguments by rules of formal logic as one might in doing research. (92)

Later, Tannen will suggest that the study of "formal logic" (150) of the sort the husband here advocates is associated with formal debate and a tradition of "oral disputation," which "is inherently adversative. With this in mind, we can see that the inclination of many men to expect discussions and arguments in daily conversation to adhere to rules of logic is a remnant of this tradition" (150; compare *AC* 200–201).

Tannen will spend much of *AC* denouncing this "adversative" mode of argument and laying many current social problems at its feet. And while formal logic may serve some people engaged in "research," it is clearly not the model for Tannen's research, which eschews quantitative methodologies, including surveys, and formal demonstrations of truth in favor of close examination and interpretation of discrete events. What Tannen does in her professional work, in fact, looks very much like what the wife in the above example does by way of "integrating her personal experience and drawing connections to the experiences of others."

Interestingly, Tannen's "fellow researchers" find this mode of argument among the most problematic aspects of her work. She has been criticized for relying on discrete events taken from disparate sources—personal experience, videotaped sessions of experimental subjects, news accounts, works of fiction, and so on—and according them seemingly equal authority as she teases sometimes far-reaching conclusions from them. In effect, by suggesting that her evidence is not always commensurate with her conclusions, her academic colleagues play the role of the exasperated husband in the above example.[3]

While Tannen does address some of these concerns in her footnotes by citing supportive conclusions from quantitative research, not all her critics are persuaded. Thus Shari Michaud and Rebecca Warner, in "Gender Differences in Self-Reported Responses to Troubles Talk," supplement Tannen's qualitative research on "troubles talk" with survey research on the grounds that "the examples reported may not be representative; examples are selected to make a point. . . . Furthermore, qualitative studies do not readily lend themselves to precise estimates of effect size" (529). The authors conclude that in their tendency to give advice and to value or devalue responses, male-female differences are significant along gender lines as predicted by Tannen's work; but the differences are relatively slight, perhaps insignificant, especially in view of the tendency they acknowledge for self-reported data such as theirs to exaggerate effect sizes (538).

In this and other instances, whether Tannen is right or wrong in the conclusions she draws or in the methods she uses is less important than the homology between her model of expertise and her model of female discourse style. The coincidence of the female style of discourse and the expert's privileged position outside the male-female binary inevitably leads to a privileging of the female style, a privileging she repeatedly denies throughout her work. Moreover, it also turns her supposedly tripartite structure, which promises transcendence and makes available the neutral ground of expertise to gendered combatants, into just another dualism—the sort of dualism, not incidentally, that Tannen says hypes ratings and sells books.

Argument Culture: How the Demagogues Trumped the Sages

Argument Culture, Tannen's next foray into the mass market, appears to be responsive to at least some of her critics' earlier concerns about the "atomistic character of [her] analysis" (Briggs 1001) and her tendency to downplay the importance of or deny the existence of "patriarchal culture" (Kramarae 667) in favor of a focus on individual pathologies. In *AC*, she shifts her focus to the larger context and examines ways in which American culture is beset by "a pervasive warlike atmosphere that makes us approach public dialogue, and just about anything we need to accomplish, as if it were a fight" (3).

It is perhaps predictable, given its shift in focus, that *AC* would sell considerably fewer copies than *YJDU*. As any guru knows, readers covet advice that they can put to immediate use. While the reader of *YJDU* could set about repairing a relationship (or a defective partner) by following the book's mantra always to understand the other's statements in the context of the other's gendered view of the world, the reader of *AC*, faced with the call for "getting beyond dualism" (284), might be less sure of how to proceed, especially when the source of the problem is some amorphous institution like "the media," whose self-interests appear to be well served by an emphasis on dualism and conflict. Moreover, the passage of reforms that might make the media more thoughtful would seem to require some understanding of which levers to pull and which constituencies to address, matters to which Tannen gives scant attention.

To help her readers imagine alternatives to America's excessively agonistic ways, Tannen offers throughout *AC* many "examples" from other cultures that demonstrate more creative ways of dealing with conflict. Unfortunately, there is a familiar confusion about the rhetorical function served by her exempla. In a complex, not unmixed metaphor, Tannen attempts to rationalize that function as follows: "We will have to cure the circulatory and digestive problems of our body politic in ways that are consonant with our own cultural heritage. Glimpsing through the corner of our eye how other cultures handle conflict and opposition, we can proceed with our eyes focused on that goal" (236). The more literal-minded among her readers may have difficulty picturing all this: Beset by digestive tract distress, we must somehow manage to keep focused on "our body politic" while watching Japanese talk shows and Tonga court proceedings out of "the corner of our eye" to see how they deal with similar ailments? The figurative difficulties raised by Tannen's metaphor reflect the rhetorical confusion of her argument here. To borrow again from the language of Perelman and Olbrechts-Tyteca, are these cross-cultural references to be understood as "examples" that will eventually make generalization possible, as "illustrations" of an already-established principle, or as "models" we are being encouraged to imitate (350)? What exactly are we supposed to *do* with these references besides "glance" at them?[4]

By claiming that her intercultural examples demonstrate only that debate is not "self-evidently the appropriate or even the only path to insight and knowledge" (258), Tannen reduces an already minimal burden of proof to near zero. One counterexample suffices to put paid whatever claim she opposes. And were these counterexamples understood to be models, we might be considerably more skeptical about some of the costs that go with their promised boon. Thus, while we might join Tannen and Walter Ong in admiring the ancient Chinese for rejecting "disputation" on the grounds that it is "'incompatible with the decorum and harmony cultivated by the true sage'" (*AC* 258), we may not wish to extend that admiration to more recent manifestations of Chinese resistance to disputation, including the brutal silencing of dissent in Tiananmen Square and Chinese leader Deng Xiaoping's pronouncement, cited by Paul Theroux, that "'execution is the one indispensable means of education'" (51).

If in ancient times "Asian rhetoric was devoted not to devising logical arguments but to explicating widely accepted propositions" (*AC* 258), relying less on reason than on intuition, observation, and experience, it bespeaks an extremely conservative culture as readily as it does a tranquil one. Moreover, when argument is rejected in favor of "exposition" and "intuition," the status quo is invested with enormous authority, and dissenters are robbed of their most effective nonviolent tool for promoting change. Indeed, it is not clear that Tannen's "Asian rhetoric" would even qualify as a rhetoric under most standard definitions of the term.

From Aristotle's "finding the available means of persuasion in a given circumstance" to Wayne Booth's "discovering warrantable beliefs and improving those beliefs in shared discourse " (xiii), influential theories of rhetoric stress invention over "exposition."[5] Certainly the case could be made for our adoption of other cultures' creative solutions to conflict. But by limiting her treatment of these cases to the occasional "sidelong glance," Tannen avoids having to deal with the full implications and entailments of her examples.

Within the context of her entire argument and her assumptions about disciplinarity, the example of the Chinese sages is especially telling. The figure of the ancient Chinese sage could stand in for today's "leading scholars" and "experts," not to mention "national leaders," who are depicted throughout *AC* as having their harmony shattered by indecorous attacks launched by members of the media and lesser figures from their fields out to enhance their circulation or status by counting some particularly prestigious coup. From the president on down (the Clintons are cited more than forty times), authorities are rudely disrespected and forced to expend energies better spent elsewhere in fending off attacks. "In innumerable small dramas . . . , our most creative thinkers can waste time and effort responding to critics motivated less by a genuine concern about weaknesses in their work than by a desire to find something to attack" (19).

Elsewhere, Tannen treats this knee-jerk hostility as a form of what Dave Grossman has called "'manufactured contempt'" and says it is exemplified by "how journalism today trains average citizens to adopt an attitude of contempt toward public figures and how some academics learn to adopt an attitude of contempt toward scholars who work in a different theoretical framework" (248).[6] Even, as it turns out, some scholars who share a "theoretical framework" may manufacture contempt for each other. In this regard, she cites "a leading researcher in psychology" (269) who tells Tannen that he was ambushed by "two young colleagues" who earned tenure by publishing attacks on his work, even though one of them later confided to the psychologist that he actually agreed with his work. According to Tannen:

> Attacking an established scholar has particular appeal because it demonstrates originality and independence of thought without requiring true innovation. After all, the domain of the inquiry and the terms of the debate have already been established. The critic has only to say, like the child who wants to pick a fight, "Is not!" Younger

or less prominent scholars can achieve a level of attention otherwise denied or eluding them by stepping into the ring with someone who has already attracted the spotlight. (269–70)

The vehemence of Tannen's critique here reminds us of the starting point of her book. Like the psychologist above, Tannen herself has also, she tells us, been unfairly and arbitrarily disrespected by some of her colleagues. One year after *YJDU* became a bestseller, she reports,

> I began reading attacks on my work that completely misrepresented it. I had been in academia for over fifteen years by then, and had valued my interaction with other researchers as one of the greatest rewards of academic life. Why, I wondered, would someone represent me as having said things I had never said or as having failed to say things I had said? (*AC* 5)

In pursuit of an answer to that question, she corners one of her critics and demands, "'Why do you need to make others wrong for you to be right?'" According to Tannen, her antagonist responded by claiming that because they were having an argument, anything goes. "Aha, I thought, that explains it. When you're having an argument with someone, your goal is not to listen and understand. Instead, you use every tactic you can think of—including distorting what your opponent just said—in order to win the argument" (5).

To the extent that she has been misquoted and misrepresented, Tannen certainly deserves our sympathy. But absent a detailed account of these particular attacks, it is hard to assess the validity of her complaints. And while one can understand how "manufactured contempt" might prevail in popular media, it is harder to understand its appearance in peer-reviewed academic journals. Why might an academic journal publish a faux and baseless onslaught, apparently unchallenged by peer reviewers or editors, by two nonentities against an eminent figure? And what department awarded these two insolent puppies tenure on the basis of their malicious attacks? Without denying that pettiness, envy, and backbiting exist in academe, one can still question the representative nature of her example. Ultimately, her characterization of academic disputes suggests a clash between venerable sages of ancient China, who harmoniously and decorously dispense enlightenment, and less savory "demagogues" of ancient Greece, who rely on "a dangerous power to persuade others by getting them all worked up" (*AC* 259). Tannen's argument culture is a world where sophists ambush sages and truth is grounded to an extraordinary degree in personal authority. And while she claims to find argument, critique, and even "'invective'" (7) occasionally justified, she laments the "ubiquity, the knee-jerk nature of approaching almost any issue, problem, or public person in an adversarial way" (8). But given the anecdotal nature of her evidence, how does one gauge the "ubiquity" of the problem?

Absent any extensive empirical evidence in support of her quantitative claims, Tannen's norm for discourse in American culture appears to be unrealistically high-minded, some variant of Habermas's "ideal community of communication" in which uncoerced, disinterested people engage in transparent discourse that results in mutuality and consensus. It is, to be sure, an appealing ideal—and a much contested one. A number of critics, particularly pragmatists and feminists, complain that the model is not only unrealizable but inefficacious. In asking people to transcend their interests (including gender), their language, and their situatedness, the model may well elide important understandings accessible only by virtue of our willingness to claim our situatedness. Nancy Fraser, for example, offers an especially acute critique of any "ideal public sphere" that fails to acknowledge the usefulness of alternative public spheres, in particular those "'access routes' constructed by women and people of color to public political life" (61). Many of Fraser's complaints appear applicable to Tannen, who seems blandly to assume a monolithic "ideal speech situation" requiring no justification.

To be sure, Tannen herself appears to reject this sort of ideal on several occasions. At one point, for example, she criticizes the media for maintaining a stance of "false objectivity," a practice she likens to "speeding along in a car that has no brakes. Far safer would be acknowledging that objectivity is impossible and finding ways to safeguard against inevitable bias" (*AC* 60). But once again, her explicit claims conflict with the lessons and implications of her countless anecdotes. She repeatedly cites cases in which narrow partisanship interferes with true justice and calls on people within the worlds of sports, entertainment, journalism, academe, and the law to put aside their narrow self-interests and embrace a point of view beyond dualism and desire in the name of the greater good—in short, to repent of those inevitable biases, those modes of "not seeing" that for Kenneth Burke constitute the inevitable concomitant of seeing.

"I Am Not an Essentialist"

According to Tannen, she initially resisted doing "gender research" (*YJDU* 14) out of a fear that her work, because it stressed gender-specific differences, would be unfairly labeled essentialist. While sympathetic with those who wish there were no differences between men and women, Tannen declares that "my research, others' research, and my own and others' experience tell me it simply isn't so" (17). And only by acknowledging these differences "can we begin to realize our opportunities and escape the prison of monolithic conversational style" (18). While these differences on the one hand appear to be pervasive and invariant, they do not, we are repeatedly assured, rise to the level of essential differences. But Tannen also explicitly rejects a notion she attributes to "social constructionists," that "women are no different from men by nature, so any noticeable differences result from how society treats women" (*AC* 275). The constructionist view, she says, "has won ascendancy in academic theory (that's why we have the epithet 'essentialist' to describe those who hold the view that is in disfavor but no commonly used epithet to sneer at the constructionist view)" (275). It has, ironically, led to "rigid dichotomies" that Tannen links, tu quoque, to the essentialization of the opposing positions on essentialism. Citing Gloria Steinem, Tannen suggests that the tendency of constructionists to label their opposition "essentialists" is typical of academics (and journalists) who "have a habit of—and a stake in—manufacturing polarization and the appearance of conflict" (276).

To what extent, if any, might it be fair to charge Tannen with essentialist leanings, and why might it matter? If one sees Tannen as an essentialist of the sort Stephen Jay Gould has in mind when he attacks the argument in Richard J. Herrnstein and Charles Murray's *Bell Curve* that "race and class differences are largely caused by genetic factors and are therefore essentially immutable" (11), the label would be fatal to the conclusions Tannen draws in *YJDU*. If we are hardwired to communicate in "male" and "female" ways, a self-conscious awareness of our tendencies will not go far toward helping us remove the straitjacket of genderlect (*YJDU* 295). So, to what extent does Tannen lean toward a determinist view of things? As usual, it is hard to say, given her aversion to comment on matters of "too much or too little" (*RM* 45) that lie at the heart of rhetoric. Earlier, Tannen has declared that nature and nurture, "biological and cultural factors . . . must, and can only, be understood together" (*AC* 21). But the matter of proportion is, she declares, unimportant. "For our concerns, it hardly matters what percentage of influence is cultural versus biological; what matters is that the patterns exist and we have to understand them and then decide whether we want to encourage or modify them" (206).

While it is easy to agree with Tannen that complex interactions between biology and culture probably account for most human behavior, it is difficult to accept her offhand dismissal of any concern for the proportion of influence each enjoys. While being self-aware may help us resist cultural conditioning, it would seem to be considerably less useful in countering genetic predispositions. Moreover, her failure to explore the interaction of culture and biology in gender formation underscores that for Tannen, as for many traditional commentators on gender and language, "it is *language* that is taken as the phenomenon to be explained, and gender which constitutes the explanation. Gender itself remains untheorized: it is a given, the bottom line" (Cameron 39).[7]

Tannen's refusal to assess the degree to which biology or culture influences us makes it difficult to conclude that she is an essentialist of the ontological sort for whom either culture or biology or both might be destiny. But there is a weaker, rhetorical sense of the term that does appear salient here. For Burke, "'Essence' is an aspect of 'efficiency'" (*ATH* 253), with efficiency being a necessary consequence of our inability to "say everything at once" (248). Unable to say all at once, we necessarily "throw strong light upon something, and in the process cast other things into the shadows" (248). What appears in our "strong light" will by default be the essence, or "gist," of our subject. Like virtually everything else in Burke, an essence may be good or bad. To the extent that an essence "violates 'ecological balance,' stressing some ingredient rather than maintaining all ingredients by the subtler requirements of 'symbiosis'" (250), an essence distorts more than reflects its subject.

Burke's essence is not, in the Scholastic formulation, "That without which the thing would not be what it is" so much as it is the rhetor's "take" on his or her subject. And there is nothing wrong with thinking in terms of such gists or with reducing complex work to gists, provided that one's gist is not simplistic and one does not confuse such gists for the truth of things. The latter tendency is exemplified for Burke by the journalist who starts from the premise that "each article must have one simple theme" (*ATH* 252) and the polemicist who omits contrary arguments from his argument. His concern is with the treatment of the essentialized ingredient in the context of the whole ensemble of ingredients that comprise the subject. Or to borrow language used by Tannen's critics in linguistics, essentialism can be understood as a tendency to get the "direction" of a phenomenon right while overstating "the effect size" of the phenomenon. Thus, to say that "women" say/do X while "men" say/do Y, instead of saying that in a given situation women are slightly more likely to say/do X while men are slightly more likely to say/do Y, is to "violate ecological balance." To the extent that one widens one's focus and eschews "one simple theme" in favor of a more "ecological balance," one moves away from an essentialist treatment of one's subject toward Burke's "substantial" understanding of that subject "in terms of" multiple, sometimes incongruous, perspectives on the subject. By this standard, at least, Tannen appears vulnerable to the charge of essentialism.

Essentialism and the Peaceable Kingdom of Disciplinarity

In defending herself against charges of essentialism, Tannen makes especially clear what the implications of her essentialist views are for her views on disciplinarity. In particular, she views debates about essentialism and other ideological matters as peripheral to the sociolinguistic enterprise and a major distraction from the discipline's real business, which is the creation of new knowledge. More than once she expresses exasperation at having to take time out from expanding the sum of sociolinguistic knowledge in order to rebut critiques—not to be confused with criticism—of her writing. She finds such critiques arbitrary and unnecessary, suspect in their motivation, and unlikely to produce "true innovation" (*AC* 269). Indeed, "true innovation" and critique appear to be mutually exclusive activities in Tannen's view: "Again, limiting critical response to critique means not doing the other kinds of critical thinking that could be helpful: looking for new insights, new perspectives, new ways of thinking, new knowledge. Critiquing relieves you of the responsibility of doing integrative thinking" (273).

The problem with Tannen's claim here is that it is basically and viciously circular. It is an evaluative claim disguised as a definition. What is critique? It is critical thinking absent creative and integrative thinking. Why is critique bad? Because it scants creative and integrative thinking. If it is by definition bad, what is there left to talk about? The one obvious candidate for discussion would be a standard for determining what constitutes "innovation" or "integration" and thereby distinguishes critique from critical thinking. When, if ever, might a critique of a theory or rival claim give rise to an alternative way of thinking about important matters? While Tannen leaves such a possibility theoretically open, it is difficult to find many positive examples of criticism or adversarial thinking in her work. And absent any clear standard for determining when critical thought lapses into critique, estimates about the relative proportions of each are difficult to make. What one is left with are examples, a disproportionate number of which show critique in the hands of vocal minorities, extremists, and academic small fry whose self-serving critiques of established scholars render them "less likely to learn from the author's work" (*AC* 273). Controversy in effect violates the "essence" of sociolinguistic practice.

Nowhere is Tannen's aversion to critique and adversarial models of understanding more evident than in her treatment of the American legal system, where, she says, lawyers are encouraged to "manipulate facts and distort impressions" (*AC* 143) in the name of demonstrating "'zeal in advocacy'" (145). The pressures of advocacy tempt lawyers to violate the spirit of the law and to hide behind its letter, as in the case of the young lawyer who attempts to invoke a procedural rule to exclude potentially damaging evidence. In a rare instance of heroic resistance to the pressures of argument culture, a senior, more scrupulous partner rejects the ploy and declares that "'[w]e don't practice law like that in this office,'" a sentiment Tannen seconds: "If the case cannot be won on its merits, it should not be won on a technicality" (145–46).

But who gets to define "merits" and "technicalities"? Do violations of the Miranda rights fall under the heading "technicality"? What about "exclusionary laws" that throw out evidence gathered by police in a suspect manner? And just how does one assess the "merits" of claimed First Amendment violations? "Since the cry 'free speech' seems to be heard only when someone wants to say something outrageous, we have to suspect that the argument culture is the culprit. The First Amendment becomes a pretext to justify the airing of just those views that make for the most entertaining fights" (*AC* 39).

In search of a more rational system, Tannen casts one of her sidelong glances at the German legal system, where judges do the fact-finding and witness-questioning and attempt "to determine what happened, as nearly as possible," in sharp contrast to our system, where lawyers "manipulate facts to the advantage of their side" (*AC* 132–33). She applauds "a system in which experts could set out to discover what really happened, as nearly as they can" (143). German judges—like sociolinguists—cooly observe *wie es eigentlich ist* and report their findings without bias, while American lawyers view matters "through a glass darkly" and distort what they see.[8]

The view of disciplinarity that emerges from *AC* might with justice be labeled excessively narrow and "essentialist" insofar as it excludes those traits that seem necessary to the healthy functioning of a knowledge community. And in that her notion of a discipline looks like Thomas Kuhn's "normal science" absent "creative science," it would appear to fail Burke's test for "ecological balance." For normal scientists, it will be re-called, the reigning paradigm serves "like an accepted judicial decision in the common law . . . [as] an object for further articulation and speci-fication under new and more stringent circumstances" (Kuhn 23). They conduct "[m]opping-up operations" that do not "aim to invent new theo-ries . . . [and] are often intolerant of those invented by others" (24). New discoveries will on occasion intrude on normal scientists' awareness, forcing them to discard or amend standard beliefs and procedures, and as such they are inevitably "destructive as well as constructive" (66). But the level of "destruction" wrought by new *discoveries* in normal science pales in contrast to the controversy generated by new *theories*, whose pur-suit normal science is subsequently "even less directed to . . . than to that of discoveries" (67). And while normal scientists tend steadfastly to ignore anomaly while articulating and specifying the reigning paradigm, theore-ticians fasten on anomaly as a harbinger and lever of paradigmatic change. Anomaly is to Kuhn's normal scientists what extremist views, technicali-ties, and minority critiques are to Tannen's experts and researchers.

This is not to deny the usefulness of normal science or to imply that by pursuing it, Tannen is doing anything ignoble. To echo one of her favorite arguments, it is only when possibilities akin to Kuhn's "creative science" are ruled completely out of play by her model that it becomes problematic. And in the context of her own argument, it is particularly problematic. How can she hope to reform "argument culture," effecting massive changes to the status quo in the process, without recourse to the tools, particularly the rhetorical tools, of creative science? Normal sci-ence is capable of effecting incremental change at best. In the end, para-digms shift, not as the result of normal scientific appeals to brute facts of nature—Kuhn having famously rejected the notion that neutral ob-servation of nature and a neutral language for reporting those observa-tions are available for use—or the cumulative weight of countless little discoveries, but because of the superior rhetorical powers of creative scientists whose discourse is closer in spirit to Greek demagogues than Oriental sages.

The worlds of the normal scientist and of Tannen's researcher bear a strong resemblance to that of the New Thought theologian, whose world expands incrementally and congenially, becoming every day, in every way, bigger and better with minimal "destruction" or dissent, "a process of accretion" (T. Kuhn 3) guided by facts and axioms, overseen by agents unplagued by "essential tension." For Tannen, new knowledge is brought into the world by "leading scholars" without having to displace old knowledge or those who subscribe to that knowledge. The more agonistic view of knowledge production is rejected as an artifact of zero-sum thinking and the old "all-male" (*AC* 257) educational model that still infects academic thinking. "The standard way of writing an academic paper is to position your work in opposition to someone else's, which you prove wrong. This creates a need to make others wrong which is quite a different matter from reading something with an open mind and discovering that you disagree with it" (268–69). Oppositional thinking dominates academic writing to the point that "[s]ometimes it seems as if there is a maxim driving academic discourse that counsels, 'If you can't find something bad to say, don't say anything.' As a result, any work that gets a lot of attention is immediately opposed" (269).

Anyone who has spent much time in academe will have little trouble coming up with anecdotes that support the above view of scholarship. But that said, one is left with a number of questions having to do with "too much" and "too little." For example, how disagreeable must an argument be before it qualifies as agonistic ego-butting? Or to turn the question, and the burden of proof, around: At what point does a claim become so uncontroversial as to cease being significant, let alone innovative? How does any work "get a lot of attention" in a discipline without saying something controversial or without calling into question any existing ideas dearly held by others? Short of totally ab ovo thought, which no one has ever seen at home, or the most pedestrian sorts of normal scientific "articulation and specification," how does one avoid positioning one's work, even if accidentally or unknowingly, "in opposition to someone else's"? And by virtue of such positioning, does it inevitably follow that one cannot maintain a reasonable, if not a "totally open," mind (which is equally hard to surprise at home)? And if one begins a piece of academic writing by acknowledging and questioning existing views, does it follow that the author's thought processes necessarily followed the same route? Might one have discovered one's disagreement along the way rather than "manufacturing" it first?

Without necessarily having to attack existing views or to besmirch those who hold them, any view that "gets a lot of attention" in a field will have to make room for itself in that field following the protocols and rules of evidence common to the discipline. Indeed, disciplines are distinguished as much by their characteristic modes of justification as they are by their modes of inquiry and choice of subject matter. Burke extends this model to all noetic processes when he articulates his tragic model of knowing, "*poiema, pathema, mathema*" (*GM* 264), a model that assumes opposition and sufferance are necessary conditions for learning, not arbitrary distractions from the tranquil process of "articulation and specification."

The Price of Influence

Late in *AC*, in the midst of a complaint about clamorous debate among researchers, Tannen makes a particularly telling observation: "How are outsiders (or insiders, for that matter) to know which 'side' to believe? As a result, it is extremely difficult for research to influence public policy" (269). If people actually have to assess opposing arguments about global warming, say, how can we ever hope to develop sound environmental policy? One would hope they could manage, just as one might hope that citizens could evaluate arguments based in part on their source and the situatedness of their proponents. Only so long as one believes, as Tannen apparently does, that experts can claim complete objectivity and that their arguments can stand aloof from their situatedness is the matter of controversy so troubling. However antithetical that belief may be to the functioning of knowledge communities, it underwrites for her the unproblematic exportation of expert knowledge to popular markets. In popularizing academic research, she is merely simplifying—and as long as experts do the simplifying, it is legitimate—truths that are universal. In crossing borders, entering new vocabularies, no serious discounting need be done, which brings us back to a recurring question: Is there a definition of disciplinarity that allows one to operate responsibly within one's borders while still licensing one to cross those borders? The first response to that question, from Stanley Fish, takes the form of a resounding "No."

Stanley Fish: Academic Border Guard

If an academic speaks to the masses, is anyone there to hear? "No," the skeptics among us are quick to reply: "When academics speak to the masses, they must either speak as academics, in which case no one would understand them, or as nonacademics in languages they are not particularly adept at using in forums that few of the masses are likely to stumble across or linger around." This roughly represents the position, previewed on several occasions above, of Stanley Fish. Or at least that is the strong version of the Fishian strictures against border crossing, typically directed at liberal legal scholars, whom Fish derides throughout *Doing What Comes Naturally: Change, Rhetoric, and the Practice of Theory in Literary and Legal Studies* for their "(doomed) search for a neutral calculus" (580 n. 3), a terminological euro that would allow them to cross borders without discounting their terms. Conducting a discussion about academic border crossing based solely on the strictures of Fish is a bit like conducting a discussion of immigration laws based solely on the strictures of Pat Buchanan. But neither can one afford to ignore those strictures insofar as they represent the most articulate and strongest available case against border crossing. In what follows, thus, Fish's most strenuous arguments against any sort of transdisciplinary or popular excursions will be reviewed, along with the limits of those arguments as pointed up by his critics, as exemplified by his own practices, as revealed by the difficulties Fish has in reconciling various of his own views, and as seen in certain weaknesses marking his analogy between theory talk and explaining the game of baseball. After "cajoling," as opposed to debunking, Fish's most severe and determinist views on disciplinarity, we will return to the question that began this study: Can/should academics compete with and critique success rhetoricians in the marketplace?

Talking to Ourselves: The Art of Asking Academic Questions

Stanley Fish is arguably the most influential opponent of academic border crossing and our most able theorist of disciplinary limits. In recent years, he has moved nimbly between the fields of literature and the law and has engaged along the way with linguists, philosophers, compositionists, and social theorists, chastising one and all for ill-advised—perhaps impossible—attempts to think outside disciplinary boxes. Those on the right he castigates for believing that objective foundations anchor their perspectives and that transparent, bias-free languages are available to represent those foundations. Those on the left, meanwhile, he castigates for forgetting their anti-foundationalism at crucial junctures in their arguments and retreating to higher ground, presumably free of interest and prejudice, where they stand and pass judgment on the rest of the world's interests and prejudices and select from among them only those that, by their lights, promise to do the greatest good for the greatest number. Along the way, he fends off critics from both camps who mistakenly think he has changed his position or contradicted earlier pronouncements.

Perhaps the most direct statement of the Fishian strictures against transdisciplinarity occurs in the preface to *Doing What Comes Naturally* (*DWCN*), where his title is said to name

> the unreflective actions that follow from being embedded in a context of practice. This kind of action—and in my argument there is no other—is anything but natural in the sense of proceeding independently of historical and social formations; but once those formations are in place (and they always are) what you think to do will not be calculated in relation to a higher law or an overarching theory but will issue from you as naturally as breathing. (ix)

There is not a great deal of slack here for the disciplinary agent looking to deviate or depart from the imperatives that issue from a given "context of practice." Practitioners do what the imperatives ("always already in place") of their practice impel them to do as uncritically as they breathe. If one happens to be a literary critic, this means that one offers accounts one believes to be "true" according to community standards of truth, of texts deemed by one's community to be "literary." "One doesn't 'choose' one's readings," Fish later asserts in *Professional Correctness: Literary Studies and Political Change* (*PC*), "one is persuaded to them . . . by coming up with answers that are constitutive of the present practice of producing readings" (48). "Everywhere you go," says the Zen bumper sticker, "there you are," with the "you" in this case being one whose personal and professional identities are isomorphic.

But one should never take Fish at face value. Whether because he changes his mind, contradicts himself, or stretches his principles a bit further than his readers are prepared to countenance, Fish elsewhere appears to modify or soften the saber-rattling, determinist claims that launch his polemics and reinvigorate his argument at key moments. Elsewhere in *PC*, Fish suggests that deviations from prevailing practice are in fact possible in ways not obviously suggested by the above quote. Defending himself against Alan Sinfield's charge that the "immanent intelligibility" of a discipline constitutes an "unresponsive orthodoxy," Fish avers that

> in fact the process of establishing criteria is ongoing and is sensitive to both internal and external challenges. New members of the profession, looking with fresh eyes and nascent ambitions at the way things are done, propose changes and thereby initiate debates about "the purpose and meaning of the activity." (23)

It is hard to know quite how to square this most reasonable and moderate statement with the less moderate statements that precede it or with other somewhat different accounts of initial entry into a profession offered elsewhere in the same book: "[T]he structure of a fully articulated profession, be it negligence law or literary criticism, is such that those who enter its precincts will find that the basic decisions, about where to look, what to do, and how to do it, have already been made" (44).

If not flat contradictory, the statements are puzzling when juxtaposed in much the way that Fish's restriction of practitioners to "unreflective actions" in *DWCN* looks odd next to his celebration of close reading as "an activity as self-reflexive as I become when I engage in it" in *PC* (110). Fish addresses potential tensions between these sorts of statements by suggesting that rules of a profession may be bent and stretched "in all kinds of ways, but not in any old way, for what constitutes a stretch or even a violation will be a function of the rules, or, as I would prefer to say, senses of appropriateness currently in place" (44). When violations "take," according to Fish, the professional decorums will change, but the profession will remain recognizably different from other professions, still engaged in the particular job of work that defines it. This distinction is important for Fish insofar as it checks a move by many contemporary critics and legal scholars to "transform . . . literary studies into a politically emancipatory activity" (44) aping the activity of other professions and thereby losing its "distinctiveness," which for Fish is, usually, a more crucial determinant of professional legitimacy than mere usefulness.

As Fish represents the process of modifying a discipline, the "appropriateness" of the modifications determines their success. What is begged in Fish's account of the process is the question of who determines what is or is not appropriate and on what grounds. And that problem is rendered even more vexing by Fish's definition of "community," which turns out not to refer to "a collection of independent individuals, who, in a moment of deliberation, *choose* to employ certain interpretive strategies, but rather to a set of *practices* [emphasis added] that are defining of an enterprise and fill the consciousnesses of the enterprise's members" (*PC* 14). In this scheme of things, it would appear that individual members of an interpretive community have little to do with the selection and modification of the defining practices of that community that fill every members' consciousness, leaving little room for heterodoxy, free will, or even uncertainty. More or less accidental human agents instantiate substantial practices without tainting those practices with their idiosyncrasies. The "context of discovery" that brought them into a given field in the first place is irrelevant to the "context of justification" (95) (always already given) that they rely on to persuade peers once they have entered that field.

At this point, one might wonder what sort of "persuasion" could go on within a community whose members act unreflexively in accord with practices that fill their consciousnesses. The answer lies apparently in the irregular distribution among the membership of a variety of practices licensed by the community's singular purpose. Exactly how these differences arose in the first place, how Eden gave way to Babel, is a matter of theodicy better left to Fish's fellow Miltonists than to mere rhetoricians.[9] Earlier, in his essay "Change," Fish suggests that "an interpretive community . . . is at once homogeneous with respect to some general sense of purpose, and purview, and heterogeneous with respect to the variety of practices it can accommodate" (*DWCN* 149). But how heterogeneous those practices are and how far a practice may stray from the "general sense of purpose and purview" of the community before being deemed "inappropriate" remain fuzzy—to which Fish would doubtless respond, "Of course, necessarily so, for no 'general account' of change can be offered." One can reconstruct change after the fact, but one can never offer a "theory of change, complete with criteria and a predictive formula" (153). Moreover, the changes that Fish talks about with any degree of specificity in the essay are less concerned with changes *among* the practices, modifications to and displacements of those practices, and more concerned with the changes wrought *by* whatever set of practices happen to be in place for whatever reason. The sense in which an interpretive community is, in one of Fish's best-known phrases, "an engine of change" (150) has to do thus with the fact that it is ceaselessly engaged in the project of reorganizing the world and "seeing phenomena as already related to the interests and goals that make the community what it is" (150). In turn, the community's sensitivity to "external challenge" is limited to those challenges that the community deems relevant; and relevance, like appropriateness, is determined by the goals and practices already in place, which again severely limits the possibilities for internal reorganization of the community. If all this sounds a bit reactionary, Fish happily concurs, pointing out that it is also totally revolutionary, because, after all, "there is no status quo to protect, for its operations are inseparable from the transformation of both its assumptions and interests" (156).

But of course there is palpably and undeniably a status quo, a profession with all its machinery for selecting and interpreting texts, for ranking and excluding people, for deeming some things "appropriate" and others "inappropriate," "relevant" or "irrelevant," and for enforcing its judgments. And while all members of a community nominally speak for the practices they instantiate, some voices in Fish's community carry considerably more weight than other voices, thanks to their position within the communal hierarchy. (The places are well earned, Fish assures us, his community being a meritocracy.) Fish does indeed pause occasionally to wonder aloud just why *his* voice in particular ought to prevail in the matter of deciding what is or is not an appropriate practice. "Who are you to say," Fish asks himself rhetorically at one point, that one must love the academy or leave it, that one can't concern oneself with "important social issues" while embedded within a discipline (*PC* 2)? Why should others cease to be "anxious about entrapment" (2) within a closed system, just because Fish claims to revel in it?

By way of answering the questions he poses for himself here, Fish promptly embarks on a close reading of *Lycidas. This* is what critics can and must do to be members of the literary studies community. While Fish suggests that his reading is at once true and most responsive "to the purpose of the present study" (*PC* 4), he leaves little room in the end for any other sort of reading. But lest potential border crossers begin to despair, they should take heart in the fact that the ten or so pages Fish spends here closely and eloquently reading Milton are the only pages he devotes in *PC* to what he takes to be the defining activity of his community. The rest of the book is devoted to polemical discourse of the sort that has characterized his work for the past twenty years—which looks remarkably like the discourse of his favorite targets.

Yet the cause pursued by Fish in much of that polemical discourse is the centrality of close reading to the profession of criticism. And so, we find his imaginary critic asking again,

> "Who are you to say" what questions we may and may not ask about a literary work; if a sufficient number of persons succeeds in changing the mode of interrogation thought appropriate to literary studies, then literary studies will have a new shape and your strictures will be heard as the dyspeptic complaints of someone whose day has come and gone. (*PC* 68)

Following a path similar to the one he has previously beaten, Fish retorts that while one might produce literary criticism that was politically effective "(it is done all the time)" (69), the losses incurred as a result of adopting such practices far outweigh the gains. In particular, he worries about the loss of "the skills of close reading that are identified with, and give distinctive identity to, the profession of literary studies" (69). The question of authority ("Who are you to say?") once again yields to a concern for the preservation of the skill of close reading, which appears to be tantamount to our professional "essence," the activity without which literary studies cannot be what it is. Speaking through its medium, Stanley Fish, literary studies declares that a concern for political effect is incompatible with and hence "inappropriate" to essential practice—all of which sounds suspiciously like an essentialist argument.

This is a claim Fish anticipates. "I would not want to be understood as taking an essentialist position here. I am not saying that there is a fixed entity called 'literary studies' and that those who reject its decorums are committing a crime against the category" (*PC* 70). But then, as is so often the case with Fish, his anti-essentialist argument here takes an unexpected turn. Instead of *liberalizing* the notion of "literary studies" by treating it as a matter of convention rather than as an ontic essence, Fish's conventionalist view severely *constrains* that notion. Indeed, according to Fish, the very conventionality of literary studies means that a departure, even a temporary one, from its "decorums" could be fatal to its continued practice. Were the practice "natural," its subject would be ontologically secure and could remain intact, awaiting the return of practitioners who ceased temporarily to ask questions of it. But insofar as the subject of literary studies is conventional, the disappearance of the decorums that comprise the practice means that "the facts [the practice] calls into being will no longer be produced or experienced" (70). Once its practitioners quit asking the questions heretofore deemed appropriate to the practice, questions that compel close reading of the sort practiced by Fish, the practice "will have passed from the earth" (70), and different sets of practices will be performed in its name.

While Fish may reassure us here that he has not lapsed unthinkingly into essentialism of the ontological sort that renders literary studies a "fixed entity," he is less convincing that his definition of professional practice is not essentialist in Burke's sense of the term. In reducing the "gist" of literary studies to "doing full justice to the verbal intricacy of a poem" (*PC* 69) and treating any politically or socially consequential end as mostly accidental, Fish arguably violates the "ecological balance" of his practice. And there is a second sense of essence in Burke that Fish also appears to violate. This second sense derives from Burke's practice of naming one thing "in terms of" another. In such cases, the second term serves as the "gist" or essence of the first. In Fish's case, "close reading" would be the second term, hence the essence of, "literary studies." Essence is thus a functional designation, a provisional role—the terms may be reversed, new terms introduced—played by a term in the act of naming. The only thing Burke does not countenance is an invariant relationship between any two terms. Close reading, thus, may serve as the second term "in terms of which" literary studies is understood, but other terms, such as "emancipatory activities," may also serve that role and thereby open up new possibilities for the first term. Such shifts are not arbitrary but are in response to changing circumstances; one is compelled by the principles of sound "discounting" to alter one's terms.

In his "Dictionary of Pivotal Terms," thus, under "discounting," Burke cites Marx's reversal of the "material/spiritual" pair under dialectical materialism by way of illustrating the above point. Marx is motivated, says Burke, by changed circumstances. Whereas earlier "the church had taken 'spirit' as the essence of the pair" (*ATH* 245), Marx's privileging of the material term gives him access to the changing "social texture" of nineteenth-century life and allows him to understand spirituality "in terms of" material conditions. And Marx's renewed emphasis on materialism does not logically exclude spirituality because "[t]he choice of materialism as the essence is not 'logical,' but 'sociological'" (245). Marx here follows the path of pragmatists who understand doctrines "in terms of" consequences and "get the meaning by observing how the doctrines behaved when released into a social texture" (245).

If one were to discount Fish's "close reading/political activism" pair, so as to see the former "in terms of" the latter, one could potentially understand "close reading" in new ways. All sorts of "close readings" could be understood in terms of their politically emancipatory potential. Frederic Jameson's extended meditation on a Los Angeles hotel might well qualify as a close reading qua political activism. But so long as a ten-page analysis of the opening lines of *Lycidas* is our model of close reading, Jameson's meditation looks distinctly deviant.

Fish's reluctance to open up close reading is of a piece with his reluctance to see texts "in terms of" larger contexts. In this regard, Fish rejects attempts, particularly on the part of cultural studies scholars, to explain particular texts by reference to "larger 'cultural texts'" (*PC* 78). To do so is to turn the larger context itself "into an object which is itself in need of the kind of explanation it supposedly provides" (78–79) and so forth, ad infinitum. Moreover, the "larger" context is really just a "different" one and as such "will not provide a deeper apprehension of the literary text or the legal text; rather it will erase them even in the act of referring to them, for the references will always be produced from *its* angle of interest, not theirs" (79).

Thus in *DWCN*, when legal scholar Mark Kelman is scandalized by what Fish takes to be inevitable—basing legal arguments on an "unacknowledged first step," the choice of an "interpretive construct" that determines our rational-sounding argument without itself being open to scrutiny—Fish is quick to demur on familiar grounds. The particular interpretive construct at issue in Fish's response to Kelman is the

> unthinking assumption of a "narrow time frame" within which the moment of criminal action is seen as coterminous with the physical act of pulling the trigger or snatching the purse; if the time frame were broadened and one understood an action as including many of its antecedents, including those social and economic pressures felt by the actor, than the assignment of responsibility would be rendered more problematical and a space could open up in which the question of determinism could be seriously raised. Kelman's complaint is that we never self-consciously debate the appropriateness of alternative time frames and thus enter upon our deliberations with many of the conceptual possibilities already excluded. (393)

Fish chides Kelman for thinking it strange or deviant that no one self-consciously selects this or any other interpretive construct with an eye toward maximizing justice. In Fish's view, Kelman is committing the classic liberal error in asking that we somehow take a position beyond interpretation from which we will view and select "the best" interpretation according to some principle foreign to the practice of law. For reasons that should by now be clear, Kelman's move is not possible according to Fish's notion of a practice.

Ironically, one of the most salient responses to Fish's argument here is an argument Fish himself makes later in a discussion of the Rodney King trial, an argument that echoes uncannily the argument put forth by his erstwhile target Mark Kelman. In this later essay, Fish appears to be working out a view of truth "in terms of" consequences. What Fish demonstrates in his epilogue to *The Trouble with Principle* (*TTWP*), "How the Right Hijacked the Magic Words," is how the defense team in the King trial used a variant of that same "narrow time frame" Kelman criticizes to bamboozle the jury.

According to Fish, the film depicting the King beating was first

> slowed down so that each frame was isolated and stood by itself. Second, the defense asked questions that treated each frozen frame as if everything in the case hung on it and it alone. Is this blow of excessive force? ... Under the pressure of such questions, the event as a whole disappeared from view and was replaced by a series of discontinuous moments. (*TTWP* 309)

This same sort of logical parsing is also practiced with devastating effect in conservative arguments against affirmative action and environmental protection; liberal advocates for such measures are required by conservative opponents to show that "this" harm was done at "that" moment, thereby assuring that "large questions of ecology and justice are pushed into the background by the same segmenting techniques that made it easy for the jurors in Simi Valley to forget it was a beating they were seeing" (309). According to the conservative argument, only individuals are protected under the Constitution, which allows only individual remedies for particular, demonstrable harms. In every case, history must be forgotten: "[E]ither a particular person at a particular moment did it or no one did it" (311).

The success of the conservative stratagem rests on a "sleight of hand. The eye is deflected away from the whole—history, culture, habitats, society—and the parts, now freed from any stabilizing context, can be described in any way one likes" (*TTWP* 312). All of which sounds like Kelman's critique of the narrow time frame construct, a critique that assumes agents have some volition in the choice of constructs, including the choice of "larger contexts" emphasizing the social impacts and origins of acts, over narrower representations of their immediate causes.

In rejecting conservative arguments because of their unjust consequences and their pernicious tendency to erase historical and contextual constraints on the terms in use, Fish also appears to reverse the priority of a pair of terms that he earlier invoked in *PC*, the "truth"/"impact" pair. In the course of dismissing an attempt by literary critic G. Wilson Knight to use *Paradise Lost* to propagandistic ends during World War II (*PC* 66), Fish argues that academics must never subordinate their obligation to seek truth according to the canons of their discipline to their desire to have a salutary impact on an audience. The result in Knight's case is a hybrid unsatisfactory on both ends: it makes for bad propaganda and for weird criticism, not so much "bad" criticism as a non-starter in the game of criticism. Certainly Fish's assessment of the Knight example seems justified—it is hard to imagine how a Miltonic allegory might spark the popular imagination. But in that one can readily imagine examples that might put Fish's principle to a more strenuous test, it remains vulnerable. When he subsequently deviates from that principle in *TTWP*, the deviation seems more persuasive than the earlier affirmation. That "large questions of ecology and justice" have a rightful role in determinations of truth, that one might reasonably ask, "What would it be like if I believed . . . ?," a particular proposition seems consistent with "neo-pragmatist" thinking to which Fish is often linked. It also licenses border crossers to take popular impact into account in assessing their arguments.

But within the Fish canon, the arguments he presents in *TTWP* are, if not anomalous, unusual. And *PC*, the book that precedes *TTWP*, represents perhaps Fish's strongest anti-consequentialist account of vocation. If any of Fish's work appears to merit the "rhetoric for rhetoric's sake" tag that Bruce Robbins applies to Fish (Robbins 105), *PC* would seem to fill the bill, even though Robbins's charge precedes its publication. To be sure, Fish appears to anticipate this sort of charge earlier when he acknowledges that his notion of interpretive community "seems to make disciplinary and professional activity its own end" (*DWCN* 160). But if one were expecting Fish to rebut the charge, one would be disappointed. He accepts it with a vengeance: "But since that end itself is continually changing, the charge can be cheerfully embraced because it says only that the members of a community will always believe in the ends for which they work, and that therefore their work will never be ended even though it will be ceaselessly transformed" (160). This is probably the sort of sentence that Michael Berube had in mind when he likened Fish's polemical skills to those of "a sushi chef applying his manual talents to three-card monte" (*Employment* 149). One remains a bit unsure just what is being connected to what by the words "since," "because," and "therefore" in Fish's sentence. By foregrounding such logical markers, Fish seems to invite his reader to begin parsing the sentence for validity. And on that score it sounds suspiciously circular: *Because one's definition of end is forever changing, one's work never ends. And because one's work never ends, one's work necessarily is its own end.*

Then again, as Fish will later suggest, justification is "not a chain of inferences, but a circle" (*PC* 113), and no justification can be grounded in anything outside itself. Like soon-to-be-discussed Orioles' pitcher

Dennis Martinez, whose task is said to be throwing strikes and keeping people off base, the members of interpretive communities do what they do because that is what they do. What else can you say? What else can Fish say? If you have to have it explained or justified any further, you mark yourself as an outsider. Like candidates to ride on Ken Kesey's psychedelic bus, potential members of interpretive communities must either place themselves "on the bus" with their consciousnesses full of community decorums and no need to justify their presence on board, or they must leave themselves "off the bus," unable to understand why those on board do what they do, incapable of understanding any justification for those behaviors that would be salient to those on the bus.

Because of their circular nature, says Fish, legitimation accounts "proceed, if that is the word, by telling a story" (*PC* 113), not by constructing syllogisms or chains of inferences, which in turn suggests that such justifications should be adjudged rhetorically according to the adequacy of the story for its audience rather than logically according to conventions of validity. But depending on whom one takes Fish's audience to be, his argument would appear to be no more rhetorically effective than logically sound. However compelling Fish's story may seem to those happily embedded within a community that conforms to Fish's definition of same, it seems unlikely to produce the same effects in outsiders (by Fish's lights)—the only sort likely to question the legitimacy of Fish's enterprise in the first place. What is a skeptic to make of a response saying basically that Fish (and by implication anyone else who has pretensions to being a member of Fish's community) must do what he does—close reading—because that is what literary studies compels him to do and that doing it is inherently satisfying and "like virtue is its own reward" (110)? How likely is it that, say, Bruce Robbins will be persuaded to forsake cultural studies and to embark on a career of close readings that strive to do "full justice to the verbal intricacy of a poem" by Stanley Fish's announcement of his immense satisfaction in doing what he does—"reaping the cognitive and tactile harvest of an activity as self-reflexive as I become when I engage in it" (110)? To be fair, no argument Fish might make is likely to persuade Robbins or any of the other literary scholars who have, in the name of new historicism, queer theory, cultural studies, rhetoric, ecocriticism, feminism, and so on, gone off the reservation in recent years to resume a life of close reading as Fish understands it. But the argument he offers here appears perversely unresponsive to the issues being raised and to the audiences raising them.

And when one considers wider audiences for Fish's justification story here, those not even remotely connected to the profession except insofar as they underwrite our pursuits in state legislatures, boards of overseers, foundations, and the like, bodies that are increasingly prone to question the legitimacy of our enterprises, Fish's argument fares even worse. Why should the state or the larger community support literary studies? Because of the immense satisfaction that Stanley Fish derives from engaging in a practice that achieves distinction by being as remote as it can possibly be from the interests of any audience that might question that practice? Why not simply wink and command them to "Trust us"? To be sure, most people performing any sort of work that rises above the level of Burke's "motion" would agree that their work offers inherent rewards apart from the exchange and use values associated with those tasks. Legislators, regents, and foundation officers listening to Fish's story here might well nod their heads sympathetically; they might even break in to share their own tales about the inherent satisfactions associated with insurance brokerage, foot surgery, or wafer manufacture. But these same folks are also doubtless savvy enough not to trot out their inherency stories when negotiating their salaries, justifying the costs of their products, arguing against the reduction of their forces or elimination of their function, or fending off their profession's critics. There are, in situations like these, many possible true stories one might tell one's audience, but the selection of which true story one might tell is inevitably a function of the anticipated impact such story will have on one's audience, and in that regard, Fish's story seems more than a bit "inappropriate."

The story that Fish tells in *PC*, which was doubtless well received by his immediate audience, the choir of Oxford dons and graduate students to which he was preaching, is the sort of argument cum mystification that went down well for much of the past century with middlebrow audiences in America eager to embrace literature as a surrogate religion in which critics played the role of hierophants elucidating the mysteries of canonical literature with virtuoso close readings. But as a number of commentators have lately suggested, and as recent events have too often confirmed, the audience eager for such stories has dwindled considerably. That category of literature that represented for the bourgeoisie such enormous cultural capital is, according to John Guillory in *Cultural Capital*, virtually "dysfunctional" for today's "'New Class,' or 'professional-managerial class'" (x). And as Guillory goes on to argue, justifications of literary studies addressed to these new audiences must somehow appeal "to the social function of the present educational system" (x) rather than to the sublime "uselessness" of such activity. Somehow Stanley Fish, or more urgently Dean Stanley Fish, must make clear what others besides himself—most notably students—take away from their experience of literary studies and how whatever it is that they take away might relate to the social functions of those institutions that underwrite the practice of literary studies. Which is to say, one cannot stay within the borders of one's discipline or one's institutional niche to justify one's activities so long as the continued existence of that discipline and those institutions rests on choices made by extramural bodies.

This brings us back to the curiously arhetorical nature of Fish's rhetoric. However much Fish's vision of community is a rhetorical vision, however persuasive his argument that "it's rhetoric all the way down," his depiction of interactions between and among individuals and his own rhetorical stance vis-à-vis his readers seems largely monological. While his notion of community may not be "monolithic," as some have charged, it is not remarkably heterogeneous. And within that community, the status of the rhetor appears to be a far more decisive determinant of persuasiveness than the appropriateness of the rhetor's argument for his or her audience. Thus, in "Change," Fish tells of a graduate student who, during the course of Fish's seminar, had been converted to Fish's "conventionalist" views. How could this be, the graduate student wondered, if, according to those very views, a movement from one literary interpretive community to another seems so improbable? Fish turns the question back on the student, asking him what he would do if a student in one of his classes asked the same question. The grad student answers, correctly in Fish's view, that he would explain to the student how she had failed to take account of some distinction or "by demonstrating that[,] properly understood[,] his own position already included hers" (*DWCN* 145). In other words, in either case, the truth is there at the end waiting for the addressee; and the truth that awaits her is identical with the position that the authority holds at the outset of their interchange.

What his graduate student would *not* have done, says Fish, "was consider his student's remarks as the occasion for a thoroughgoing rethinking of everything he believed about literature" (*DWCN* 145). What is lost in this last sweeping denial is the possibility that the graduate student's exchange with the student, or Fish's exchanges with his graduate student, might lead to modifications and clarifications, however modest, of their beliefs about literature. Fish does suggest that the memory of this interchange offers him a key insight into the problem of change; but insofar as the insight in question simply reaffirms what Fish has long argued, it is less of an "Aha!" anecdote than a "'Nuf said" anecdote.

The above anecdote might well illustrate what Bill Readings in *The University in Ruins* has in mind when he criticizes Fish's rhetoric for its excess of "subjective calculation" that "does not display a prudent respect for the pole of the addressee; instead, it seeks to erase the pole of the addressee, to render it identical to the pole of the speaker" (159). In the same vein, Bruce Robbins notes Fish's tendency to first invoke "clients and constituents (so as to gain public credit for the speaker). Then, when these extra-professional figures become inconvenient to his case for monadic professional self-sufficiency, he silently drops them" (105). Fish's assumptions about his audience, like his earlier airy dismissal of a "status quo," reflect the sensibilities of what Readings has called the "*magister*" whose discourse, in contrast to the rhetor's, is acontextual and "self-authorizing" (158). It is the rhetoric of someone so thoroughly embedded in a profession that it is understandably difficult for him to imagine his own activities as anything but the defining and "self-authorizing" activities of his profession. Peering out from the cover of his latest book, his name in block print larger than the title; shuttling bicoastally and transoceanically to conferences built around his presence; standing before large rooms full of people and delivering keynote addresses for handsome fees; walking briskly to his office suite in the admin building; soldiering indefatigably on through the pages of *Changing Places* in the guise of alter ego "Morris Zapp," his friend David Lodge's personification of the American literary studies enterprise—these are the moments in the professional life of Stanley Fish. From where he resides, cultural studies and new historicism would quite naturally look to be little more than quixotic misadventures, border skirmishes, to be dispatched with as little expenditure of energy as possible. Or, as one admiring reviewer quoted on the back cover of *PC* suggests, Fish's "stylish, muscular little book" is just the thing to fend off these latest "enemies" of literary study and to prove that "more professionalism just might save the sinking ship."

Perhaps one cannot fully appreciate the tendency for Fish's rhetoric to "erase" the addressee until one has been, more or less, directly addressed by that rhetoric. In the case of my own field, rhetoric and composition, my colleagues' and my pretensions to professional status were long ago deflated by Fish. The teaching of writing, we were told briskly at a national meeting, could be summed up in a phrase he borrows from

J. Hillis Miller—"'you learn to write by writing'" (*DWCN* 354). Miller, to his credit, finally chooses not to believe this conclusion, Fish admits. But Fish persists in part because he believes (falsely, as it turns out) that there is no evidence showing that different approaches to teaching writing yield different results. In a trice, Fish simultaneously erases any need for people like us who teach, study, and write about composition, even as he simultaneously erases our clientele, our addressees, who, it turns out, have little need for our addresses. Perhaps only if one has been the recipient of such "not-very-helpful-news" (355) can one appreciate the obduracy of that status quo Stanley Fish assures us does not exist.

A Word from Morris Zapp

Near the beginning of David Lodge's *Changing Places*, co-protagonist Morris Zapp, en route to a term-long teaching exchange in England, pauses to reflect on a critical enterprise he is considering in the wake of a string of stunning scholarly successes that leaves him, at a relatively young age, atop a profession with which he is utterly disillusioned. His plan is to write a series of commentaries on the novels of Jane Austen so exhaustive

> that when each commentary was written there would be simply *nothing further to say* about the novel in question [which would thereby] . . . put a definitive stop to the production of any further garbage on the subject. The commentaries would not be designed for the general reader but for the specialist, who, looking up Zapp, would find that the book, article or thesis he had been planning had already been anticipated and, more likely than not, invalidated. After Zapp, the rest would be silence. (44)

Without totally confusing the Lodge-infused musings of Morris Zapp for the thinking of Stanley Fish, there appear to be some instructive parallels here between the rhetorical stance we have just been exploring and the one assumed by Lodge's character. After 1975, the year *Changing Places* was published, one can easily imagine Zapp forsaking the empty, too-easy triumphs of traditional literary criticism to enter the far more challenging and better publicized lists of contemporary theory and taking up positions on things like professional legitimacy, very much like the ones assumed by Stanley Fish. What one might not anticipate someone like Zapp undertaking would be Fish's extensive commentaries on legal and political questions and his service as one of our profession's most articulate, most widely recognized public spokespersons on a variety of social issues. Indeed, while Fish may lack the mass market appeal of a Deborah Tannen, he himself offers an intriguing model for boundary crossing.

So how does Fish manage to editorialize on all sorts of social issues in such popular organs as the *New York Times*, even as he continues to chide others for attempting to seek impact rather than truth and for pursuing "politically emancipatory" ends rather than those less altruistic ones prescribed by their practices? Primarily, it would appear, because of his skepticism about principle and theory, a skepticism that overrides virtually any generalization he might make that appears principled or theoretical. Like Morris Zapp, Fish appears (at least from my perspective) as often as not to do the right thing *in spite of* those flawed (again from my perspective) principles he espouses. Whatever generalizations he may make about the limits of professionalism and the need for literary studies to perform a particular, distinctive job of work in order to legitimate itself, his practices have not been notably constrained by those strictures. What he does, "as naturally as breathing," is not guided or anticipated by any theory (his own included) any more, he says, than the actions of baseball players are guided or anticipated by theories of baseball. And the extent to which he is and is not right about the operation of theory in baseball clarifies, I shall argue, the nature of the theory/practice relationship for potential border-crossers.

Practice *Is* Perfect: Stanley Fish and the Baseball Question

What follows is an extended exploration of an analogy, developed most fully by Fish in "Dennis Martinez and the Uses of Theory" (*DWCN* 372–98), between playing baseball and practicing a profession. Some might object that such an extensive exploration is disproportionate given the place of that analogy in Fish's major argument; others might object that his somewhat fanciful figure is being taken far too literally. In response, I will argue that the points Fish makes through the baseball analogy are perfectly consistent with the points he has been making about the operation of theory in other domains for many years. Moreover, it is by taking his baseball analogy seriously and literally that one can most readily recognize the limits of Fish's arguments in other domains.

Some would, of course, dismiss out of hand Fish's equation of the theory/practice relationship in baseball to the theory/practice relationship in criticism on the grounds that generalizations about physical activities can never rise to the level of theory about cognitive activities. Playing baseball, the argument would go, is as self-evidently a non-theoretical event as reading a complex text is self-evidently a theory-rich event. According to this view, when Fish dismisses claims by baseball players and aficionados that they consult "theories" independent of baseball practice, he is doing little more than touching a match to an analogy made (by him) of straw. Of course, baseball people do not use "theory" in the same way that literary critics use the term. But—so goes the argument that follows—if one can make a brief for the place of theory in baseball, one renders Fish's larger case against theory in realms that have been traditionally theorized considerably more vulnerable.

The reason why it is critical for the larger argument of this book to call into question Fish's reduction of baseball to a pure practice has to do with the consequences of that view, in all its many guises, for professional identity and in turn the legitimacy of academic practitioners taking their wares to the public marketplace. To the extent that disciplines can be reduced to sets of practices always already in place, largely beyond the control of practitioners, the notion of practicing one's discipline in a foreign realm makes no sense. One's professional domain, the disciplinary space replete with decorums and traditions, *is* the discipline. The denizens of that realm, meanwhile, cease to be whatever they are within that realm whenever they leave it. In the context of these assumptions, academic criticism moving to the marketplace makes as little sense as Canada emigrating to Brazil.

Fish's view of theory as it has so far emerged and will continue to emerge in his baseball analogy is at once liberating (theory is, in theory anyway, devoid of a prioris, foundations, or a stodgy status quo) and rigorously determinist (theory can only offer after-the-fact rationalizations for practices that are always already in place, always filling one's consciousness). If one is unlikely to become a narrow ideologue in Fish's world, one is all too likely to become an obsessive-compulsive practitioner. In Burke's terms, Fish's practitioners do not "act" so much as "move" to the tune of their practices. Consequently, their ability to self-reflect is drastically restricted. To borrow the language from Fish's baseball analogy, "[T]here are two distinct activities—playing baseball and explaining playing baseball—and . . . in a strict sense (which I shall soon elaborate), there is no relationship between them whatsoever" (*DWCN* 374). In a latter-day version of the mind-body problem, baseball announcers, newspaper pundits, and fans spend endless hours analyzing, explaining, and understanding the game, while baseball players, standing in here for practitioners of every sort, simply, and unreflectively, play it. And ne'er the twain shall meet.

Or at least, that is the nature of the relationship in the "strict sense." And in the strict sense of theory, as Fish defines it here, one is hard-pressed to dispute his characterization.

> I reserve that word for an abstract or algorithmic formulation that guides or governs practice from a position outside any particular conception of practice. A theory, in short, is something a practitioner consults when he wishes to perform correctly, with the term "correctly" here understood as meaning independently of his pre-conceptions, biases, or personal preferences. (*DWCN* 378)

Any attempt to offer up a less rigorous definition, Fish assures us, will finally serve to make "everything theory, and if one does that there is nothing of a *general* kind to be said about theory" (378). Let us concede at the outset that one would find it difficult to show that theoretical physicists, let alone baseball players, draw upon theory as they would "a blueprint or set of directions according to which the performance is unfolding" (378). But in the course of his analysis, here and elsewhere, Fish offers a number of specific observations about the relationship between practice and theory generally, and between the practices of baseball players and their thinking about those practices specifically, that leave one ample room to depart from his extraordinarily stringent definition of theory. In articulating the terms of his baseball analogy, for example—practice is to playing the game as theory is to explaining the game—Fish would not seem to require players to transcend practice or to follow algorithms to qualify as theorists. Somewhere in the limbo between practice in the strict sense and theory in the strict sense, or in Burke's parlance, between "talking" and "talking about our talk about," there is a realm of praxis or "talk about" that is sufficiently self-conscious and disengaged from the immediate task at hand to qualify as theory, even as it is sufficiently engaged and task-centered to still be implicated in practice. If "explaining the game" qualifies as a theoretical event in the above sense, and if one allows that explanation may be an ongoing, anticipatory activity as well as an after-the-fact justificatory activity, then baseball players may be said to "practice" theory.

The starting point of Fish's baseball analogy involves an encounter between Martinez and his manager, Earl Weaver, witnessed by sportswriter Ira Berkow. Unable to hear what transpired in this pregame strategy session, Berkow asks Martinez just what "'words of wisdom'" the manager had imparted. Martinez's response is, according to Fish, a brilliant "two-stage narrative" that serves as "a wonderfully deadpan rebuke to the outsider [in this case, Berkow] who assumes the posture of analyst" (*DWCN* 372). The "rebuke" lies in the simplicity of Weaver's counsel and of Martinez's response to that counsel. Whereas Fish assumes that Berkow is looking for "some set of directions or an articulated method or formula or rule or piece of instruction which Martinez could first grasp . . . and then consult whenever a situation seemed to call for its application," what he gets is simply "a reminder of something that Martinez must surely already know" (372)—which is to say, "'Throw strikes and keep 'em off the bases.'" And Martinez's rejoinder to that advice—"'What else could I say? What else could he say?'"—is the sort of celebration of necessitarian principles sure to resonate with Fish.

It is a fascinating example on a number of levels. The first level has to do with the relationships among Fish, Berkow, and Berkow's readership; Berkow, Martinez, and Weaver; and Fish, Martinez, and Weaver. As Fish has characterized these relationships, there are two outsiders in the anecdote—Berkow and his readers, whose hunger for inside information, even when it is spurious, follows from their needy outsider status—and three insiders, Martinez, Weaver, and . . . Stanley Fish, who already possesses the very sort of info outsiders so avidly seek. The inside info to which Fish is privy and Berkow is not involves an understanding that requires no special knowledge of baseball. It is the special knowledge of those who think about relationships between theory and practice in a variety of fields including baseball, literary studies, and the judiciary. The kind of knowledge that Fish possesses, in short, looks like the sort of knowledge that Berkow would like to extract from the interchange between Weaver and Martinez: a general rule ("practitioners are not guided in any strict sense by general rules") that proves to be applicable in a variety of situations, including baseball managers' pregame counsel to pitchers.[10]

What Fish has managed to do here is the very sort of thing he has suggested elsewhere it is impossible to do. He has, to use one of his favorite metaphors, pulled himself up by the bootstraps to rise above the outsider status he nominally shares with Berkow and his readership and transformed himself into someone whose general knowledge of systems trumps Berkow's understanding of the game of baseball. What Berkow is chagrined to discover is what Fish has known all along, which leads one to wonder, what does Fish know about the game of baseball other than what he has gleaned from people like Ira Berkow, who, after all, has served a function for baseball fans not unlike the function that Stanley

Fish has served for students of Milton for nearly as many years? What assures Fish that the general rule he invokes here, a rule that basically "erases" the value of Berkow's field-specific wisdom, fully accounts for the situation at hand?

Putting aside for the time being some of the various "perplexities of perspective" implicit in Fish's account, the "truthfulness" of Fish's conclusions deserve some scrutiny—which is not to challenge Martinez's account of what Weaver said to him or Martinez's endorsement of that counsel. Rather, it is to challenge the degree to which this particular anecdote is representative, let alone exemplary, of baseball practice and the relationship of that practice to the theories, rules, and general considerations that guide its practice. Indeed, as advice goes, it is spectacularly unsound for several reasons: (a) it is an impossible ideal, because no pitcher is capable of throwing a strike every time; (b) it is self-contradictory, because if any pitcher *did* throw a strike every time, he would be hit unmercifully and the bases would be chockablock with runners; and (c) it is overly narrow in that it substitutes a partial means (throw strikes) for a larger end (don't allow the opposition to score more runs than we do). And if this response seems excessively literal-minded, that is part of its point. Literally, this advice makes no sense except as a piece of "phatic communication," which Burke describes as "the use of speech as such for the establishing of a social bond between speaker and spoken-to" (*RM* 270).

In this regard, I liken Weaver's counsel to the words "Wait for your pitch!" that a former college coach would obsessively yell at me and my teammates every time we stepped into the batter's box. I never understood that to be meaningful advice, let alone any sort of algorithm insofar as it was far too general to be helpful in the forever-unfolding situation of the game. I certainly never understood it to be exhaustive of all the considerations that one took into account in a given situation. And while I never consulted a "blueprint" between each pitch that would dictate subsequent behaviors, I did adjust my expectations and behaviors in accordance with the changing situation and a set of rules appropriate to each new situation, rules that occasionally included "waiting for my pitch." Knowledge of those rules and expectations generated by that knowledge in turn guided my reading of the "signs," the coded signals sent from the bench to batters and base runners prior to every pitch since the beginning of baseball.

In sum, my understanding of the relationship between theory and practice was, in its attention to the particularities of that situation and the need to adjust to those particularities in a rule-guided way, rhetorical. Or at least today I would understand my thinking as rhetorical. Then, I just thought of them as the adjustments and "paying attention" in a way that was only partly "natural as breathing" and partly conscious and calculated. Because I was less talented than many I played against, I was doubtless considerably more conscious of these processes than others in my never-ending search for an edge. While Fish recognizes that self-evident nostrums like "There's a man on first base" (*DWCN* 373) can serve as verbal cues to remind practitioners about a whole host of variables and options, he seems to believe that every practitioner will respond in the same way to the cue. Indeed, saying there's a runner at first makes some things more likely and other things less likely to happen. Depending on the particulars of the situation—for example, the score, the inning, the speed of the base runner, the strengths and weaknesses of the pitcher and the hitter—all the actors will make predictions, adjustments, and decisions by their best lights. If everyone always responded in totally predictable ways to the description of the situation implied by a nostrum, there would be no advantage to such theorizing. But clearly, having a theory, any theory, is useful insofar as it directs one's attention, limits the variables one takes into account, and allows one to test one's hypotheses; and just as clearly, some practitioners with more thoughtful theories gain a significant advantage over competitors with less thoughtful ones.

Indeed, Fish's exemplar, Dennis Martinez, went from an immensely talented underachiever with a drinking problem at the time of Fish's essay to a not-so-talented, sober overachiever. Martinez managed this transformation not simply by throwing strikes and keeping men off base—those are outcomes, not practices—but by becoming a more thoughtful practitioner. Martinez followed a very Burkean path to wisdom: he acted, suffered, and learned. And one of the biggest things he learned was how to better predict the expectations of his opponents and how to best disappoint those expectations. If one thinks of baseball in Burkean terms, each pitch constitutes an act. One's choice of how to act is guided by one's interpretation of the variables charted by the various nostrums ("Runner at first!" "Two down!"). The nostrum provides the grounds for one's interpretation, but one's theory determines which of the grounds one attends to or ignores, emphasizes or slights. In effect, the baseball equivalent of theorizing begins where the nostrums leave off. And depending on the outcome of one's act, one's theory will undergo constant adjustment. Contrast this interpretive dynamic to the one proposed by Morris Zapp.

Zapp's hypothetical master commentary on Jane Austen's fiction that would correctly anticipate every possible interpretation of her work is futile for the same reasons that baseball nostrums cannot correctly anticipate every possible response to situations they describe or actions they promote. And in literary criticism, as in baseball, practitioners are bountifully rewarded for devising unanticipated responses that will stymie master commentaries and master nostrums alike.

That said, Fish could still respond that baseball theory still does not *generate* baseball practice. All this knowledge is simply knowledge accumulated through a process of trial and error in which the player attempts to replicate a certain model based not on any theory but on the performance of other practitioners/exemplars. Theory talk in this instance serves as "a verbal place-marker" or "mnemonic" (*DWCN* 581) that reminds the player to do what he already knows from practice must be done. The latter analysis in fact summarizes a lengthy footnote to the Martinez essay in which Fish dismisses the claims of theoretical status for the teachings of Charlie Lau, a batting coach credited with changing the hitting approach of many big league players. Again, key to Fish's argument here is the rejection of the possibility that there might be multiple approaches to hitting that are systematically different from one another. Fish assumes that when Lau repeated "pieces of his theory to his students," he was not telling them anything they had not previously learned by experience; he was simply reminding them that "something wasn't being done just right" (581). And the model of "just right" is not theoretical, it is the model of a swing used by successful hitters. In this case, Fish offers up the swing of Ted Williams, the greatest hitter in baseball history, as just such a model.

Whether Fish is simply being puckishly provocative here or if he has in fact stumbled by chance onto the one example most likely to undo his argument is unclear. To suggest that Charlie Lau's theories would culminate in a swing like Ted Williams's is akin to suggesting that the theories of Frederick Jameson would result in commentaries like those of T. S. Eliot. Lau's and Williams's theories of hitting are best understood in contrast to one another. Indeed, Williams's theories and his book on hitting constituted the reigning paradigm that Lau's theories and books set out to topple in the early 1970s, and the crusty Williams took considerable pleasure in denouncing Lau's theories at every opportunity. But because there's heat does not of course mean there's necessarily fire. The differences between Lau and Williams might be manufactured in the same way some scholarly disputes seem contrived. Are there in fact demonstrable differences between hitters belonging to the Williams school of hitting and the Lau school of hitting that are generated by the two practitioners' theories?

In a word, yes. And those differences are visible to the naked eye, both when one observes Lau's and Williams's most ardent pupils at the plate and, less decisively, when one consults their students' lifetime hitting records. They use clearly different, if inevitably overlapping, means to accomplish less clearly differentiated outcomes. As happens in practices of every sort, baseball practitioners tend not to be purists and have in recent years melded the theories, borrowing elements from both. But the theoretical differences are real and specific, if not absolute. Thus, while Lau's pupils exaggerate the weight shift from the back foot to the front foot and try to make contact with the pitch just as their weight has fully shifted to the front foot, releasing the bat with their top hand on impact, Williams's pupils tend to emphasize the weight shift less and place more emphasis on the rotation of the upper body, keeping both hands on the bat beyond impact. Not surprisingly, these differences in approach tend to yield different results. Lau's pupils tend to make contact more often, to strike out less, and to hit more line drives and ground balls to all fields. Williams's pupils tend to swing and miss and to strike out more often but also "pull" more fly balls in the direction of their swing for home runs.

Like all theoretical shifts, the underlying explanation for the emergence of Lau's theory and the eventual movement back toward Williams's requires one to consult the larger context. That is, Lau's theory was in ascendance throughout the 1970s when a number of baseball teams adopted dual purpose (football/baseball) stadiums with synthetic turf and spacious outfields. Players who hit ground balls and line drives were rewarded with singles that previously would have been outs and doubles that would have been singles in the older, smaller parks with slower grass surfaces. Now that "old style" parks are back, there has been a movement back to Williamsist hitting doctrines.

All of which leaves us a bit down the road from a baseball philosophy that rests on "Throw strikes and keep 'em off the bases," a gross oversimplification potentially as mischievous (in interestingly similar ways) for baseball practitioners as "*Cogito, ergo sum*" once was for practitioners in other fields. Let us review then where it leaves us in regard to the question of the theory/practice relationship. According to our understanding, practitioners have more options of what to do in any given situation, are to varying degrees conscious of those options, and select their options by consulting, if not blueprints, something like topoi that offer different models of behavior appropriate to the specifics of their situation. And the audience for one's acts plays a major role in the choices one makes about those acts and introduces a major element of uncertainty into the process. Thoughtful baseball players, like thoughtful writers, create "an appetite in the mind of the auditor" and then strategically frustrate the satisfaction of that appetite so that "in the end these frustrations prove to be simply a more involved kind of satisfaction" (CS 31).

The importance of the Lau v. Williams theoretical divide, meanwhile, is that it offers a clear example of two different theories systematically generating visibly different practices and, less clearly, visibly different consequences. And this latter uncertainty, the imperfect and not wholly predictable relationship between a practitioner's adoption of a particular theory and the consequences of that adoption, should not blind us to the very real impact of theory choice on consequences. The fact that the choice of a particular theory only makes the sought-for outcome more probable rather than inevitable does not justify the conclusion that theories have no consequence beyond persuading others that our practices are efficacious.

Underlying the differences so far adumbrated between Fish's theory/ practice, playing baseball/explaining baseball analogy and the baseball analogy developed here in opposition to his are basic phenomenological differences. Fish's baseball players, like his judges and his literary critics, have little room to hesitate or to doubt their beliefs as they act. Indeed, doubting a belief appears to be oxymoronic for Fish. In Michael Berube's phrase, borrowed from Joyce, people in Fish's world never seem to be of "twosome twiminds" about anything. Or, in the words of Jules David Law, commenting on Fish and his fellow neopragmatists in the context of Wittgenstein's On Certainty:

> [K]nowledge, belief, and action [are] isomorphic. As a picture of an individual at a given fraction of a second, this account may be difficult to refute. But as soon as we widen our focus to consider individuals acting through time and in a community, that isomorphism breaks down. (335)

By the lights of our account of pitching, as opposed to Fish's version of Dennis Martinez, an individual acts through time and adapts to constraints imposed by his community, particularly his primary antagonist, the batter, pitch by pitch and moment by moment. And no mere nostrum suffices to remove uncertainty from the act of pitching, which is in fact a series of discrete but related acts, each of which must be executed in the absence of complete knowledge, the outcome of which changes the considerations in play in each subsequent act. At the moment of decision, to be sure, a pitcher must feel confident that what he is doing is the "right" thing; but that momentary certitude must, like all postlapsarian wisdom, be earned by processes of doubt and self-reflection, not by simply breathing in and out. In this scheme, self-reflection does not, as Fish suggests, involve some impossible act of levitation. It is, as Burke's "tragic" model of learning suggests, an inevitable result of being thrown back upon oneself and needing to regroup after one's actions (for example, hypotheses) have aroused opposition or been met with recalcitrance.

As noted earlier, Fish does make some allowance for such a possibility. Particularly in the case of novices, practitioners might not automatically see things by the lights of the community and hence might be capable of experiencing conflict, even doubt, and expressing their consternation productively. In "The Anti-Formalist Road," which introduces *DWCN*, he expands on that possibility by way of countering charges that his notions of community and practice are "monolithic and unproblematic" (30). Here Fish hastens to assure us that no community member's beliefs, certainly not his own, comprise a "seamless totality" and that by virtue of the fact that all of us are members of "innumerable interpretive communities in relation to which different kinds of belief are operating with different weight and force" (30), our convictions can never be as pure as they might seem in his necessarily broadbrush treatment of the matter.

Fish appears here to allow for all manner of being of "twosome twiminds"; indeed, he goes on at some length to enumerate his own many roles, including those of teacher and parent, that might at a given moment conflict. The problem is that while one can readily find cases in which Fish rejects out of hand the interference of personal beliefs or "emancipatory" doctrines with professional obligations, examples of productive conflict are much harder to find. In this regard, he offers another baseball analogy, this time in support of his point that to view tort law through the lens of ("in terms of") some "foreign ideal" such as "the concern to redistribute wealth as evenly as possible . . . would be a tort decision in name only" (*PC* 23). For Fish,

> [i]t would be as if a batter in a baseball game, aware that the opposing pitcher was in jeopardy of his job and unhappy at the prospect of depriving someone of his livelihood, chose to strike out

rather than advance the runner at first base; the criticism properly directed at him would not be that he was playing the game badly, but that he was not playing the game at all. (23)

Like so many of Fish's hypotheticals, this one is difficult to dispute. Absent the inclusion of any extenuating circumstances, Fish's deviant practitioner appears not to be playing the game. But what happens if we turn our attention to actual cases rather than "purpose built" illustrations? Certainly there have been cases in baseball history, particularly in the final days of a season, when pitchers "let up" on batters needing a hit or two to win a batting championship or served up a "room service" fastball to a hitter in pursuit of a home run record. Conversely, pitchers have been known to walk batters in pursuit of records because they were more concerned to thwart a hated rival than to win a game. Perpetrators of such acts are required by baseball's code of silence never to admit guilt, though they may well proclaim their innocence with a wink. All of which suggests that the process of distinguishing a "foreign ideal" (foreign to whom and on what grounds?) from a professional decorum is considerably more complex than Fish's example might suggest. To understand why this might be so, in baseball and by extension in other realms, we turn to a more challenging example of "foreign ideals" apparently trumping "professional ideals."

The example comes from a scene in *Bull Durham*, written and directed by former minor league baseball player Ron Shelton, in which the protagonist, veteran catcher Crash Davis, tired of having his signs shaken off by the talented but clueless young pitcher "Nuke" Laloosh, tells the hitter what pitch is coming, thereby allowing him to hit a home run. In passing along this information, is Crash "not playing the game at all"? Or has he simply expanded the definition of playing the game to include one of his other professional roles, that of teacher? I would opt for the latter and argue that the conflict depicted in *Bull Durham* is not so much a clash between professional ideals and some "foreign ideal" imported from beyond the borders of the profession as it is a struggle between two or more "decorums" native to the game.

The conflict represented by Crash's betrayal of Nuke originates in the multiple dimensions of decorum that operate simultaneously within the game of baseball and, I would argue, within every profession. Specifically, Crash's punishment of Nuke is licensed by "the code" of baseball, one of at least three guides that govern players' behaviors, the other two being "the rules" and "the book." Tension among these three guides is constant in baseball and, especially when exacerbated by idiosyncratic interpretations and applications by individual practitioners, are the source of most overt conflict in the game.

The rules are the simplest and most straightforward source of practitioner behavior. They are codified and enforced, albeit selectively, by presumably disinterested officials (umpires and league officials), who also claim the right to make all final judgments about rule interpretations. They dictate all manner of things such as the distance between bases, the specifications for regulation equipment and uniforms, the pitcher's movements on the mound, the various reasons for declaring a player "out," and so on. Insofar as practitioners have relatively little control over the application of the rules—other than to violate or circumvent them—they are the least interesting and most rigid source of appropriate practitioner behavior.

The book, meanwhile, determines practitioner behaviors in more subtle ways. It is an uncodified set of strategies presumably based on probability but in fact often grounded in traditions ("always already in place") and, until recently, rarely submitted to scrutiny. The effects of the book are ubiquitous. On any given play, the placement of the fielders, the intentions of the hitter and the pitcher, and the movement of the runners are all influenced by the book, which is consulted both by coaches (continually) and players (variously) to better anticipate the opposition and to set their own behaviors in motion. While there is general consensus about the book's core beliefs, it is the most open to interpretation of the three guides; in fact, hewing too closely to the consensus view renders one's intentions transparent to the opposition, thereby allowing them to "cheat" successfully. Cheating is a risk/reward strategy based on one's reading, not just of the book, but of one's opponents' reading of same. Thus, for example, if a team always bunts with runners at first and second and fewer than two outs, opposing infielders can "cheat" in closer to the batter and thwart the bunt attempt, ignoring the possibility that the batter may hit a life-threatening line drive. The use of the word "cheat," meanwhile, simultaneously acknowledges the force of the book's prescriptions and the license granted to individual agents to take risks based both on their reading of the prescriptions and their opponents' reading of same.

And finally, there is the code. Rarely articulated, never written down, the code in effect straddles the line between professional and extraprofessional concerns. Bearing traces of both a warrior's code and a courtier's book of etiquette, it dictates the manner in which one performs one's tasks. It also licenses outright violations (not to be confused with "cheating") of the rules and the book in the name of individual honor and sacred tradition. It is the code, thus, that demands a pitcher throw at an opposing batter in retaliation (an act specifically outlawed by the rules and frowned on by the book) for some perceived breach of the code by the other side, even if it entails the banishment of the pitcher and negatively affects the outcome of the game.

In refusing to throw the pitches called by his veteran catcher, Nuke is simultaneously violating the code (which requires the young to be guided by their elders) and the book (which guides Crash's selection of pitches). His own behavior, meanwhile, is unwarranted by any set of decorums. It is an act of pure hubris, resulting from his inordinate gifts which have heretofore allowed him to ignore the decorums of the game and simply "bring the heat." Nuke's behavior is symptomatic of one who is neither embedded within a practice nor at all reflective about that practice, which makes him the mirror opposite of Crash, the journeyman of few gifts and no illusions who is thoroughly embedded within a practice and yet thoroughly self-reflective about that practice. Crash's superiority lies not in any talent or understanding that he exercises "as naturally as breathing." His superiority lies in his ability to deal with the tension among the various practical guides and in the wisdom he displays, determining which will guide him at a given moment. By Crash's lights, it is Nuke who is "not playing the game"—by the book *or* the code—and he, by betraying Nuke to the hitter, who is situating him once again within the game.[11]

All of this affirms something Fish already claims, however unpersuasively, to believe in, which is that no community's practices are "monolithic and unproblematic." But beyond affirming Fish's exceptionally modest claim, the present argument would claim that every community's practices are *actively problematic* much of the time, thanks to the existence of multiple, often conflicting, decorums from which practitioners might seek guidance. It would also claim that native ideals may be readily mistaken for "foreign" ones, depending on which of the multiple decorums is being privileged and who is doing the privileging.

The next step to be taken in liberalizing the strictures that define appropriate professional behaviors, thereby further easing traffic across disciplinary boundaries, is to recognize the active role played by extra-professional considerations in professional practices. The more liberal view of profession urged here is, in Bruce Robbins's apt phrase, a considerably more "porous" one than the one advocated by Fish. And it is a view of profession more consistent with rhetoric generally and Kenneth Burke specifically. Burke's representative professional figure, it will be recalled, is the shepherd, whose pastoral care of his flock is forever confounded by the inevitable outcome of that care, the fleecing and slaughter of his sheep. Burke's example is in support of his own rejection of the "inherency" argument for professional legitimacy: "The fact that an activity is capable of reduction to intrinsic, autonomous principles does not argue that it is free from identification with other orders of motivation extrinsic to it" (*RM* 27), which further implies that one ought, like William James, "to maintain the widest notion of vocation, vocation not as a *specialist*, but as a *man*" (*ATH* 14). Consequently, attempts to invoke professional canons to justify violations of one's obligations to "*a wider context of motives*" get short shrift in Burke, for whom "one's morality as a specialist cannot be allowed to do duty for one's morality as a citizen" (*RM* 31). And the tensions between the decorums of one's profession and one's civic obligations are not occasional and anomalous in Burke; they are continuous and crucial. "Profession," like any other term in Burke, is what it is "substantively" and as such derives "from a word designating something that [it] is *not*. That is, though used to designate something *within* the thing, *intrinsic* to it, the word [substance] etymologically refers to something *outside* the thing, *extrinsic* to it" (*GM* 23). For Burke, a "profession" cannot be equated with the particular job of work its practitioners (or subsets of practitioners) claim as their "distinctive" job of work. A profession is also identified, willy-nilly, with interests beyond itself, different from, even antithetical to, those claimed by its practitioners.

While Fish does grant—at least some of the time—the possibility that professional practitioners are not forbidden by the law of contradiction or the functional definition of their profession from performing socially useful work beyond its borders, such excursions are not encouraged. And while Fish does readily acknowledge the possibility that acts of public scholarship, however rare and contingent, are possible, he spends the bulk of his time celebrating the inherent value of staying at home and joyfully doing the distinctive job of work one's vocation impels one to do. From a Burkean perspective, such a view of practice inevitably falls prey to the paradox of purity. Which is to say, fully realized—and given the modesty of the task Fish sets for practice, full realization is unavoidable—its aspirations are self-canceling. Like "perfection," the moment of full realization is the moment at which "rot" sets in. This is why Burke allies himself with the "meliorist" (*ATH* 3) perspective of people like William

James, who set out to improve upon a given situation in the name of ideals (for example, Burke's "good life"), which inevitably straddle personal and professional obligations. As a meliorist, James "resented in Hegelianism a verbalizing device that 'encouraged men to *see* the world good rather than to *make* it good'" (*ATH* 7), the sort of sentiment that will later prompt Richard Rorty to include James among those "edifying" philosophers marked by their "distrust of the notion that man's essence is to be a knower of essences" (*Mirror* 367). Seeing the good and knowing essences are not ignoble pursuits, any more than close reading poems and throwing strikes are ignoble pursuits. It is only when they are substituted for larger ends within one's profession as a philosopher, critic, or baseball player and discourage one from asking how one's professional activities make the world good, or at least better, according to standards not provided by one's profession that they become problematic.

The Perils of Being Consequential: Academics at Large

To the extent that the preceding argument against Fish's vision of "professional correctness" is cogent, academic border crossing would seem permissible, possibly inevitable, even desirable. But licensing academics to bring their professional acumen to bear on social issues, politically emancipatory agendas, and all manner of "transdisciplinary" concerns does not gainsay the practical impediments to such ventures. Here, Fish's arguments are both more straightforward and more difficult to dispute. As he suggests in response to Donald Pease's call to connect "'disciplinary practices and oppositional political movements'" (*PC* 56), such liaisons are theoretically permissible and, at the level of "general truth," already accomplished. But to expect this liaison to be consequential is an altogether different matter, dependent "on the relays of power and influence that are currently in place. It is in relation to those relays or routes and not in relation to the strength of an idea that the impact of one sphere on another will be either immediate or etiolated or something in between" (57). It is the absence of such "relays or routes" between academic critics and political institutions that causes Fish to view Pease's project skeptically.

Indeed, the history of success rhetoric and guru literature over the past century in America should give anyone committed to academic border crossing pause. Particularly in recent years, right-wing academics and former academics who tend to be either insufficiently skeptical of, or cheerleaders for, success rhetoric and its underlying assumptions have enjoyed the greatest success reaching mass audiences. Conservatives, according to Thomas Frank, have appropriated the language of populist thought to sell market capitalism and, according to Stanley Fish, have hijacked the language of 1960s liberalism to serve social conservatism. They have thereby forestalled liberal criticism and created a fertile ground for a rhetoric of success stressing individualism, instrumentalism, and exceptionalism while privatizing virtue and demonizing community obligations beyond those owed the corporation or family. The ineffectuality of the left, within and beyond academe, at capturing the hearts and minds of those targeted by these arguments has been remarkable.

In this regard, Michael Berube offers an interesting observation about the ironies inherent in right-wing complaints about the "unreadable" theories foisted off on academe by leftist adventurers and their associated complaints about the larger "literacy crisis" that these theories have fomented. The irony of these complaints, Berube points out in the context of the political correctness debate, lies in the fact that those who make them and those who report them appear to lack the very rigorous critical reading skills required by the theories they critique:

> In fact, the crisis of PC and the universities is itself partly a crisis of reading: the PC scandals swept through the press so easily because so few of our "traditional" intellectuals and mainstream journalists are capable of reading interpretively, reading intelligently, or (in some cases) reading at all. . . . To put this impasse another way: while we academic readers have been devising more and more exacting ways of reading our texts, our worlds and our critics, the reading skills and reasoning facilities of the *Partisan Review* regulars . . . have become a cause for national alarm. (*Public* 264–65)

Given these formidable material constraints, including the limited ability of many in the popular press to understand, let alone endorse, some of the most important ideas emerging within academe and the absence of readily accessible and supportive "relays and routes," how might academic scholars render their work more consequential in the nonacademic world and mitigate the inordinate influence of success rhetoric on the everyday lives of American citizens?

In response to this question, one might cite both promising new routes that have emerged in the last decade and hopeful changes in the more traditional routes. The current depressing state of the publishing industry, for example, has been heralded by some as the last gasp of corporate control and "massification" of the written word, where every player was depressingly the same and the profit margins of every one of them were tied to the fortunes of a dwindling number of fiction "giants" like John Grisham and a handful of nonfiction gurus like Stephen Covey who subsidized the failures of countless Grisham and Covey wannabes. Requiring ever larger sales to justify the publication of ever fewer books, publishers severely limited their lists in ways that especially disadvantaged serious authors of trade books. But of late, big fish media conglomerates, discouraged by the publishing industry's modest profit margins, have been spitting back minnow-sized independent publishers as rapidly as they once swallowed them.

Eventually, as former Random House editor Jason Epstein, among others, has argued, these changes and the systemic changes underlying them may end up working to the advantage of serious authors. In the case of those who command large audiences, Epstein argues, current technology allows them to bypass the publishing industry even today. As the extraordinary response to Stephen King's "publication" of his story *Riding the Bullet* over the Internet suggests (400,000 readers downloaded the story for $2.50 each on its first day of availability), the relationship between "publisher," who controls the sale of the book, and author, who takes a royalty on sale, may eventually be reversed. To be sure, as King's ultimate withdrawal from his experiment suggests, authors may choose not to rely on open Web sites and voluntary purchase of their product. They may ultimately choose to allow some version of an electronic "publisher" to relieve them of commercial hassles and worries. Epstein foresees the day when a successful author may offer a 15 percent royalty to her publisher for taking the trouble to edit and publicize her work, for the association of her book with a "venerable name," and perhaps for maintaining a state-of-the-art Web site on her behalf (58).

The new reality underlying both the preceding examples is that the formerly prohibitive costs of capitalization in the publishing industry, costs that made it difficult to enter the field and compete against established media giants, are declining significantly, ultimately allowing small concerns and even individuals to establish a niche in the market. Books can be transmitted digitally to handheld computers and read on-screen at virtually no cost; or, for those readers still wedded to the book, those same digital transmissions can be printed on site, in a bookstore, library, copy shop, or university, in the form of a book that is virtually indistinguishable from books printed by more traditional means. Clearly, the economic efficiencies of these delivery systems promise to reduce costs dramatically.

Because of their already low, rapidly deflating costs, Internet portals, Web sites, Web logs, and the like seem destined to eventually supplement, if not supplant, university presses and journals and academic libraries as the primary access points for "serious" ideas. (Indeed, many proprietary and academic journals have already been forced by their subscribers and authors to place articles on the Internet for free review within six months of publication. And Google recently announced that it will place online the contents of several world-class libraries, offering free access to literally millions of important texts.) But the role for academics may well be intensified rather than diminished by this movement. As information gets ever cheaper to distribute, not to mention ever more plentiful, the importance of filters to ensure the quality and salience of information will grow exponentially. By virtue of our training and our relative independence from profit motives, academics can assess the value and significance of ideas and texts by a much wider variety of metrics than can most for-profit vendors.

All of which speaks to leveling the playing field in terms of audience access, not necessarily securing a wide audience for one's ideas. Once access is established, scholars, whether they operate within academe or outside it, need to become more intentional about the tailoring of their message for broader audiences. Certainly there are some promising models for such activity. Christopher Newfield's strategy of extending the logic of management gurus' arguments from the private to the public sphere offers one such model. And Michael Berube offers a number of suggestions about how to extend the range of academic prose for popular audiences.[12] As for the very real dangers inherent in the "popularization" of academic ideas, it is important to recall the benefits as well as the costs attending such a move. Every approach to understanding, Burke reminds us, including even his own "perspective by incongruity," must, if it is widely used, be routinized and "bureaucratized" such that one achieves "the 'mass production' of perspectives ... [and thereby] 'democratizes' a resource once confined to a choice few of our most 'royal' thinkers. *It makes perspectives cheap and easy*" (*ATH* 228–29). But while the process of bureaucratization runs the risk of eventually rendering any perspective too cheap and easy, Burke continues to resist limiting access to "our most 'royal' thinkers".

Beyond discovering new accesses for their ideas and new ways of exploiting those accesses, academics will need to take a hard look at reforming institutions that support their work. As has been argued throughout this study, academic models of disciplinarity and profession and the assumptions about success that attend those models can interfere with, even enjoin, reasoned critique of the success ethic that prevails in the wider sphere. The vexed issue within the academy of "public scholarship" and how to assess and reward it reflects a deep divide within the academy that must be clarified, if not resolved. On the one hand, growing numbers of academics have accepted calls like John Guillory's to rethink the ways in which they justify their work in light of new constituencies and new economic realities; on the other hand, one finds a large number of academics recoiling in horror from such calls to which they ascribe "instrumentalist" or, worse yet, "vocational" motivations.

Which is not to say that one or the other side must prevail in this matter. While Stanley Fish is right to suggest that there is not room—or need—for *everyone* to engage in public scholarship, that is not an argument for *anyone* to refrain from doing it. There is now and always will be important work for academics to perform that will be of little interest to the general populace. Not now nor in the foreseeable future will it be necessary to dragoon traditional academics into the service of public scholarship. Neither is it necessary to belittle and debunk traditional scholarship to make room for more public scholarship. Indeed, the two would appear to require each other, in much the way that "basic" and "applied" researches are generally seen as necessary complements in the physical sciences. As Pierre Bourdieu concludes in *On Television*, his extended meditation on many of this chapter's concerns, academics operating in "autonomous" fields are obligated to use the popular media to make "cutting edge research" intelligible through their teaching and to "universalize the conditions of access to the universal" (66). Bourdieu supports this cause even after spending a bulk of his time denouncing those forces within the media that distort and corrupt the messages they mediate. In the name of using these media without capitulating to them, Bourdieu argues, we must work either to

> firmly delimit the field and endeavor to restore the borders threatened by the intrusion of journalistic modes of thought and action ... [or to] quit the ivory tower ... to impose the values nurtured in that tower and to use all available means within one's specialized field and without, and also within the journalistic field itself, to try to impose on the outside the achievements and victories that autonomy made possible. (73)

In order to promote and encourage the wide dissemination of scholarship "that autonomy made possible," we need to rethink the methods we use to reward various professional behaviors insofar as those methods now heavily favor the "job of work" performed by traditional academic scholars.

Finally, though Fish seems to find the connection a remote one, our greatest potential for impact lies in our capacity to educate students such that they might form audiences for serious work on public issues. This is not to say that it is either possible or desirable to educate students to think like us. As Michael Berube notes, we must accept at the outset that educating students to be more critical readers and thinkers does not ensure that they will use those critical faculties to arrive at the same conclusions, let alone the same professional stations, we may have arrived at. In particular, Berube cites what he calls "the 'reversibility' of the knowledge we circulate in the humanities," a phenomenon that is sure to thwart our propagandistic ends insofar as it prescribes that "as a major in English can teach you to see through corporate capitalism while working for IBM, so too, somehow, can the study of Shakespeare serve revolutionary and conservative social forces at the same time" (*Employment* 145). So, let there be no misunderstanding that a renewed commitment to the teaching of critical thought and expression in the humanities will ensure politically emancipated audiences or even widespread acceptance of our own definitions of "politically emancipated." We can only hope to make them less credulous readers of the most spurious flapdoodle served up by gurus and more discerning, demanding readers of views we endorse, doubt, or despise. And perhaps a few of them, instead of becoming reproductions of us, will spend their lives in the public sphere making arguments that carry the day in the wider world.

Such are the not particularly outsized hopes of an academic boundary crosser in the age of the gurus. There is too much cunning and too little scope in their rhetorical appeals for gurus to render us better people, and there is far too little useful information in their books to make us any more effective ones. But unless we critically entertain these texts, gain public forums for our critique of these texts, educate others to form a more critical audience for these texts, and offer this audience alternative visions to ones offered in these texts, they will remain, like our political representatives, the ones we deserve.

Notes
Works Cited
Index

Notes

1. Kenneth Burke and the Paradoxes of American Success

1. In his insistence on understanding any given entity "in terms of" that which the entity is not, an insistence that will be returned to throughout this study, Burke aligns himself with the pragmatist tradition of Richard Rorty. At the heart of that philosophic tradition, as seen particularly in Dewey, is the notion of a self very much at odds with the excessively "inward" notions of selfhood assumed by success rhetoric, notions that themselves are an inheritance of a philosophic tradition running from Plato through Descartes and Locke. Pragmatists find fault with the latter model of self insofar as it is too narrow, suggesting a

> cold, self-interested, calculating psychopath. . . . If we really were such selves, the question "Why should we be moral?" would be forever unanswerable. . . . But if we follow the pragmatists' advice to see everything as constituted by its relations to everything else, it is easy to detect the fallacy which Dewey described as "transforming the (truistic) fact of acting *as* a self into a fiction of acting always *for* the self." (Rorty, *Social Hope* 77, emphasis Dewey's)

So long as the starting point of identity formation is the atomistic, fixed self, acting "for" others will remain an inconsistent or incoherent notion.

2. MacIntyre anticipates, and rejects, calls for "creative dissensus," which he would surely see as a "eulogistic" cover for the "dyslogistic" reality, namely "pluralism": "In the domain of fact there are procedures for eliminating disagreement; in that of morals the ultimacy of disagreement is dignified by the title 'pluralism'" (32). But one can be cognizant of the inevitability of disagreement without championing the "ultimacy" of disagreement. To champion its ultimacy is to encourage its spread and accept an "I'm OK, you're OK" outcome to all disputes. In acknowledging the limits of my ability to persuade those whose views are grounded in different principles, I do not forego allegiance to my own views or quit proselytizing on their behalf. I simply accept that there is no universally

acknowledged truth, equally binding on all parties to a dispute, to which I might appeal, thereby putting paid to all other arguments.

3. My own view of Taylor is closer to that of Alan Ryan than to that of Smith. Ryan calls Taylor "for the most part a Deweyan without knowing it" (361).

4. Richard Harvey Brown also acknowledges Locke's concept of self as being optimally "suitable" for modern bureaucratic society. According to Brown:

> Locke and after him Rawls posited a self that occupies an "original position" and retains whatever is necessary freely to enter into a "social contract" with similar others. Yet the very abstractions that create such transcendental subjects deprive them of any *principium individuationis*. Such selves are noumenal ghosts thought to exist prior to the very communities of interest and value that in fact create them. (58)

5. Nothing much appears to have changed over the past century. One can find ample evidence that twentieth-century America shares nineteenth-century America's "general failure to recognize the political import of economic power" and the tendency of Americans to distinguish "between political and economic power; to fear and restrict political power, to regard economic power as essentially benevolent" (Cawelti 44). A quick perusal of most American newspapers would suggest that our dark suspicions about government's desire to thwart and control us is tempered only by our cynical faith in government's inability to achieve any end, devious or otherwise, thanks to monumental incompetence.

Given the overwhelming evidence of the past two decades that American business is anything but benevolent—the $600 billion savings and loan crisis; the use of junk bonds to mount hostile takeovers of companies, strip mine their assets, and sell them off for a pittance; the mass layoffs ordered by CEOs with nicknames like "Chainsaw" and "Darth" in the name of downsizing or rightsizing but which served mainly to inflate CEO stock options without significantly benefiting the company; the cover-ups, the phony science, and the cynical appeal to young people by the tobacco industry; the tenfold increases in energy prices managed by companies like Enron, which used phony accounting practices to inflate its worth and then, after company executives sold off their stock, announced their peccadilloes, and declared bankruptcy, financially ruining thousands of Enron employees they had barred from selling stock in the process—our continued capacity to compartmentalize our ethics and our view of business is, to say the least, impressive.

2. Bruce Barton, Advertising Man

1. Stephen Fox in *The Mirror Makers* notes that Edward Bok of *Ladies' Home Journal* established an annual set of prizes for advertising in 1923. Barton had to withdraw from the jury of prize selectors because so many of his own agency's ads were nominated. Indeed, according to Fox, "Barton's agency won more [prizes] than any two other agencies combined" (106) during the life of the competition.

2. In response to Ruth's signing, one writer asked if he really thought he ought

to be paid so much more than the president of the United States. "Sure," answered the Bambino with his customary humility. "I had a better year than the president." Ruth's response constitutes one of the wittier notices on record that money had become the unifying ground, the "god term" of disparate motives, in the new century, a theme Burke elaborates on extensively (*GM* 92–117).

3. Latter-day gurus tend to finesse this particular problem by shifting the focus from the business leader to the corporation. As Thomas Frank suggests, the legitimation project of American management theorists in the 1990s turned on their pronouncement that "the corporation, as a creature called into existence by the market, was of special and even superhuman nature. In fact, the corporation was democratic in a way that transcended our limited understanding of the term. The correct attitude when in its presence was childlike awe" (220–21). Insofar as the market expresses our collective will, the market *is* us, which makes the corporation our creature, our "culmination," and the purest embodiment of our hierarchy's "ruling principle."

3. The Profession of Success

1. Donald Meyer, author of *The Positive Thinkers* (1965), traces this process in Peale, who, while he aimed to increase people's power,

> hardly imagined himself addressing people afflicted with Promethean urges, Faustian drives, people with limitless desires. It is simple to think that the "winning" to which he referred was simply success—success in the simple meaning of more money and higher status, the "material" rewards that good and persevering men deserved. As in the gospel of success and mind cure, Peale's gospel of positive thinking did indeed embrace this equation. "There was a time," Peale said, repeating Fillmore and the preachers of success, "when I acquiesced in the silly idea that there is no relationship between faith and prosperity." (264)

What was problematic in Barton—the need to spiritualize the material—is axiomatic in Peale, for whom the spiritual *is* the material.

2. Getting in tune with the infinite, it turns out, may involve little more than synchronizing your movements to the hum of mechanical devices around you. In a vision that unwittingly evokes scenes from Charlie Chaplin's *Modern Times*, Peale tells of "[a] friend of mine, an industrialist in a large plant in Ohio, [who] told me that the best workmen in his plant are those who get into harmony with the rhythm of the machine on which they are working. . . . He points out that the machine is an assembling of parts according to the law of God" (33). Peale here offers a eulogistic version of Burke's dyslogistic notion that "under industrial capitalism," vocations are reduced to "sheer motion" when "certain near-automatic tasks [are] performed to the timing of the conveyor belt" (*GM* 14).

3. According to Mary Douglas and Aaron Wildavsky in *Risk and Culture*, abundance theology, in the form of "an expanding sum view of wealth" (88) as opposed to a "zero-sum view," is a hardy perennial in American culture, an

orientation that greatly influences our view of risk. In the expanding sum view, "the most gloomy theorems" (88) are trumped by the prospect of expansion. Consequently, those holding a zero-sum view of the universe are more likely to be concerned with social justice in the here and now, while those holding an expanding sum view rationalize current inequities in the name of future bounty awaiting all residents of the universe.

4. Nixon's 1968 presidential nomination acceptance speech, reprinted at the front of the 1968 edition of the book, is rife with such deflating allusions. In one particularly tortuous instance, Nixon plods through his own version of Martin Luther King's "I Have a Dream" speech. "I see the face of a child," Nixon proclaims (xv), a child whose dreams have been reduced to despair by a damaged American system. Then, says Nixon, "I see another child" who manages to live out the American dream, thanks to helpful individuals who reach out to him along the way. The second child turns out to be . . . Richard Nixon. King's vision of social justice becomes in Nixon's version a self-aggrandizing account of personal triumph, "by the numbers," an account of a largely discredited myth in no small part responsible for the very injustices King decries.

5. As it turns out, Nixon himself offers perhaps the most astute gloss on this dicey business of planned sincerity. In a 1968 TV interview, he assures his questioner, "I'm not an actor. I'm just going to be myself; and I'll continue to play that role" (Charnes 75). I am thankful to my colleague Curtis Perry for calling this citation to my attention.

6. Coover skillfully captures the staginess of Nixon's manner of presentation simply by inserting long quotations from *Six Crises* into dramatic situations where the portentousness of the prose overburdens the slightness of the circumstances. What Coover says of the *New York Times*—"this monument . . . [this] effort to reconstruct with words and iconography each fleeting day in hope of discovering some pattern, some coherence, some meaningful dialogue with time" (191)—applies equally to Nixon's sometimes desperate searches after significance for each of his "crises." Thus Nixon's comments on mob violence (Coover 207–8) are taken directly from Nixon's mob encounters in South America (Nixon 213, 228–29, 235). Coover simply compresses Nixon's most overheated observations—"A mob is bloodthirsty. A taste of blood will whet its appetite for more violence and for more blood" (Coover 207; Nixon 229)—and presses on until the climactic moment when one of the youngsters in the mob who Nixon imagines is out to get him asks him for his autograph, and he turns out to be a Boy Scout who avidly supports the Rosenberg execution.

4. The Business-Religion Anoints Its Own

1. Walter Fisher argues in *Human Communication as Narration* that Reagan's individualism is what Robert Bellah et al., authors of *Habits of the Heart*, called "ontological individualism" as opposed to a more salutary "sacred individualism." That is, rather than stressing the "inherent dignity" of all people, Reagan's individualism stresses the primacy of the individual over the communal, the

former being natural, the latter artificial: "Any organization is in actuality only the lengthened shadow of its members" (Reagan 201). Or, in the words of Reagan's British doppelgänger, Margaret Thatcher, "'There is no such thing as society, only individuals and their families'" (qtd. in Slater 10). Mikhail Bakhtin alerts us to the self-deluding character of such notions in his analysis of individualism as a form of "self-experience." The very confidence one has in one's sovereignty is itself an artifact of

> the objective security and tenability provided by the whole social order, of one's individual livelihood. The structure of the conscious, individual personality is just as social a structure as is the collective type of experience. It is a particular kind of interpretation, projected into the individual soul, of a complex and sustained socioeconomic situation. (89)

The more thoroughly embedded one is in "bourgeois" socioeconomic orders, the more likely one is to experience oneself as the heroic loner sustained by a faith that "a man's gotta be what a man's gotta be" (Fisher 146), and the more appealing one is likely to find messages and messengers that reaffirm that illusion.

2. Richard Harvey Brown—himself a former public sector manager—notes that modernist organizations often use organizational plans to serve the rhetorical function that Peters and Waterman assign to managers. Such plans "define the limits of responsible opinion and in general . . . impose the planners' or managers' definition of reality upon discourse and conduct within and around the organization" (76). Brown is considerably less sanguine than the authors of *ISOE* about such practices.

3. "Attitude" is of course an incipient act for Burke, though the gap between the bending of an attitude and an act motivated by that attitude may be considerable. According to Hans Blumenberg, the recognition that one is "compelled to act" despite "the lack of norms in a finite situation" (437) is at the heart of rhetoric. And what distinguishes science—which could stand in here for academic research—from civic discourse for Blumenberg is that the latter "cannot in fact afford . . . the endlessness (in principle) of rationality in the form that it takes in science" (437).

4. In *After Virtue*, Alasdair MacIntyre derides all pretensions by "sciences" of human affairs (especially business management) to predict the future (93–108). Indeed, organizational predictability is seen as fatal to organizational survival insofar as, to be effective, any organization must "tolerate a high degree of unpredictability within itself" (106). MacIntyre is particularly useful in dealing with the guru propensity to be at once unfailingly self-deprecating and humble about their power to predict and relentlessly opportunistic in proclaiming and charging for that power. Commenting in 1987 on the growing tendency to fetishize "bureaucratic skills" (107), MacIntyre argues that absent these elaborate predictive claims, managers "could never legitimate the possession or the uses of power either within or by bureaucratic corporations in anything like the way or on anything like the scale on which that power is wielded" (108).

5. The offer was made on August 28, 1999. The payoff for Peters is doubtless understated here. By 1999 he was, according to his Web site, up to seventy-five seminars per year. Moreover, he now has his own eponymous consultancy, The Tom Peters Group, which comprises "three training and communication companies ... [that] produce videos, churn out a regular newsletter, and generally help to stretch his brand" (Micklethwait and Wooldridge 47). In addition to his Web site, he produces audiotapes and CDs, writes newspaper and magazine columns, and recently devised "The Tom Peters Business School in a Box."

In stressing the great wealth that Peters's reaps from his ventures, one does not wish to seem merely to debunk his professed motives. In fact, great wealth is not just a *result* of his rhetorical skill but a *part* of his rhetorical appeal. As Burke reminds us a half-century before the explosion of CEO salaries and guru fees, there is "a 'magical' need for the higher officials in the typical business corporation to receive an income 'awesomely' greater than that of any ordinary worker. It comes to seem dubious whether 'authority' could be preserved by any other means" (*RM* 260).

6. The transformation of Covey from a modestly successful consultant, obscure academic, and Mormon author to guru was surely aided by his signing on with Tony Robbins's agent, Jan Miller, who "maintains a stable of ghostwriters" (Stewart 47) to render her clients' prose readable. Miller is particularly attracted to "ambitious," "genuine," and "media savvy" types for whom she creates "mind maps" (49), laying out the necessary steps for leveraging books into profitable spinoffs.

7. The growing importance of obedience as a virtue within the Mormon church at the time Covey was writing—in the wake of extensive domestic unrest—is shown by a survey of BYU students conducted in 1935 and again in 1973. When asked, "Do you place obedience to authority above your own personal preferences?," the response is striking. "In 1935 the positive response was 41 percent; by 1973 this figure had risen to a resounding 88 percent" (Ostling and Ostling 224).

8. In his profile of church leadership, Armand Mauss laments the diminution over the past fifty years in the numbers "of men with demonstrated scholarly credentials and accomplishments in the world's terms" (82) and "a corresponding diminution with that leadership of their capacity to accommodate diversity, relativity, or ambiguity in church policies or programs, to say nothing of doctrines" (84–85).

All of which is doubtless fine with the indefatigable Dr. Hugh Nibley, whose multivolume exegesis of Mormonism had, as of 2000, reached fourteen volumes and who devotes an entire chapter to the perfidies of intellectuals in his *Approach to the Book of Mormon*. The publishing history of Nibley's book illustrates some of the perplexities facing anyone attempting to identify reliable sources of information about Mormonism. The book was originally published in 1957 by "the Council of the Twelve Apostles" to be used as part of "a course of study for the Melchizedek Priesthood Quorums of The Church of Latter-day Saints" (Nibley copyright page). Then, in 1964, its publisher is listed as the Deseret Book Company, an LDS company that, in 1976, reprinted the book as part of its "Classics in Mormon Literature series." The book's third edition, published in 1988, lists only Nibley as the copyright holder with Deseret as the publisher. While the book clearly reflected church doctrine in 1957, the extent to which it may or may not reflect church doctrine since 1988 is a trickier matter to determine.

5. Academic Border Crossers and Border Guards

1. Tannen's work has been widely reviewed and discussed in academic and nonacademic sources alike. A representative sampling of academic commentators includes Briggs; Elizabeth Kuhn; Rose; Michaud and Warner; Kramarae; Crawford; Bucholz; Cameron; and Romaine. While Tannen comes in for tough criticism, especially on the score of her adherence to the "two culture" model of discourse, "which posits that women and men belong to two different cultures" (E. Kuhn 119) and assigns responsibility for redressing gender inequalities to individuals, and for her highly selective qualitative methods, the criticisms tend to be respectful and finally supportive of her attempts to make sociolinguistics relevant to people's everyday lives.

2. While Tannen appears to charge both sexes with the responsibility of understanding the opposite sex from the other's gendered perspective, her equation of female and expert perspectives tacitly shifts that burden. Deborah Cameron in "Rethinking Language and Gender Studies" protests this tendency in Tannen and others to make women responsible for "avoiding or resolving cross-sex misunderstandings" (36).

3. Thus, for example, Briggs's review (1991) of Tannen's academic work *Talking Voices* (1989) sees as a "major limitation" of the book

> the atomistic character of the analysis. The discussion proceeds by designating one global category (e.g., repetition), presenting a loose typology of forms and/or functions, and illustrating each with short textual excerpts. The reader gains little insight into the way these elements are connected either in analytical terms or as instantiated in particular texts. (1001)

Briggs generally finds Tannen's tendency to treat each conversation as a discrete or "bounded unit" (1001) to represent a "step backwards" from a more Bakhtinian understanding of conversation as a reciprocal event linked to preexisting understandings inherent in language itself.

4. Tannen's tendency to obfuscate relations between parts and wholes is most readily apparent in *AC* when she proposes to "cite some examples of abuses that lawyers have given, not to suggest that the abuses are typical but to show that these things have gotten worse and, perhaps more important, to claim that those who commit abuses are falling into traps laid by the adversary [*sic*] nature of the system" (151). Which leads one to wonder: how can "legal abuses" be said to "worsen" absent a standard for abuse or quantitative evidence about the state of such

abuses then and now? These examples may be atypical, she cheerfully grants, but she is confident that they prove things are worse than they used to be.

5. If one wanted evidence that "argument culture" is a chronic, or at least regularly recurring, feature of American culture, Booth's book, written a quarter-century earlier in the midst of campus upheaval and war protest, provides it. Beset by "irrationalists" on one side and "scientismists" on the other, Booth finds "degradation of the rhetoric on all sides" (8) and gamely sets to work finding a middle ground where ordinary people might follow the model of "experts" who "still argue together effectively" (xi) in the midst of chaos. While Booth's argument suffers from some of the same weaknesses that I find in Tannen's, his analysis of the causes seems far more astute.

6. Thomas Frank has rejected arguments like Tannen's, suggesting that "[t]he problem with the press . . . was that it's too darn divisive. The media are too interested in finding fault, in tearing down rather than building up" (313). To the contrary, he argues, the media's biggest shortcoming is the "across-the-board consensus that its sound and fury served to obscure" (313). And, he continues, "[c]onsensus sometimes deserves to be just as rudely debunked as conflict" (314).

7. Appearances to the contrary notwithstanding, the present argument is not inconsistent with the argument against an overreliance on numbers in chapter 4. While the assumption that quantitative evidence is always decisive in arguments about human affairs was earlier critiqued, the suasive force of data was not dismissed. Indeed, to the extent that one's conclusions are, like Tannen's, quantitative and probabilistic, one's evidence should be commensurate with one's findings. Further, the earlier critique "cajoled" the assumption that quantitative arguments could discredit claims resting on plausibility. That is, while Peters and Waterman's anecdotes are serviceable in establishing the plausibility of their various "motherhoods," Tannen's anecdotes are less serviceable in establishing the magnitude of the problem she analyzes, calculating differences between past and present magnitudes of the problem, determining the contribution of gender-based differences in communication style to the problem, and proving that significant gender-based differences in communication style actually exist.

8. One can't help wondering, given Tannen's liberal loyalties, what her response might have been to the 2000 Supreme Court ruling that stopped the presidential vote recount in Florida. The Republican lawyers in the case argued against "hypertechnicalities" invoked by the Democratic lawyers and rejected manual recounts on the grounds of their subjectivity; given her aversion to both subjectivity and technicalities, one would expect these arguments to resonate with Tannen. The majority ruling, meanwhile, relied heavily on precedent from the same Supreme Court that gave us *Plessy v. Ferguson*. Perhaps, after all, U.S. Supreme Court justices were not what Tannen had in mind when she argued for taking power out of lawyers' hands and putting it in the hands of judges.

9. Fish's failure to account for the origins of difference in his community is not insignificant. Indeed, John Guillory sees a similar failure as a fatal weakness

in Barbara Herrnstein Smith's account of community. By substituting "coincidence of contingencies" for "consensus" as the basis of community, Smith in effect renders all dissent involuntary according to Guillory.

> What we are not capable of describing in the terms of this theory is the effect of a value judgment which deliberately [as opposed to "incorrectly"] disputes the normative judgment of one's own community, unless we can posit at the same time some "limited population" which would affirm that disputative judgment. In other words, there is no place in Smith's formulation for describing the effects of a dissenting judgment *on the community whose judgment is disputed*. Within this theory we have no way of describing the effects of struggle in general. (285)

10. Without making any strenuous claims for insider status on my own behalf, I should note that I am drawn to Fish's baseball analogy and am particularly sensitive to its implications in part because of a lifelong love for the game of baseball, a game I spent half my life playing. Rather than establishing any sort of privileged position vis-à-vis Fish on the subject of baseball, however, I prefer to think of my experience as an illustration of "occupational psychosis" with all the vexing ambiguities that attend that state.

Further, recent developments in major league baseball would seem to support my view that the importance of insider/outsider status is exaggerated by Fish and that the borders between professions and the general populace can be more porous than he suggests. As a number of commentators, most notably Michael Lewis in *Moneyball*, have suggested, baseball orthodoxy and hierarchy have been profoundly shaken in recent years by the adoption of "Sabremetric Principles" of the game put forth originally by Bill James, the erstwhile statistical geek outsider who is currently a member of Boston Red Sox management. As demonstrated by a handful of youthful baseball executives with no playing experience but a sure grasp of and belief in statistical analysis, traditional baseball wisdom was deeply flawed and vulnerable to outsiders with fresh views.

11. Extending the baseball analogy to the field of composition, teachers face a dilemma similar to the one faced by Crash most often in the context of grading. One's grading may be guided by official rubrics, by policy statements from on high warning against "grade inflation," by official adoption of institution-wide grading curves, and so forth. But every teacher makes decisions about grades that are responsive to all sorts of other concerns, including their reading of their students. And in the case of, say, the Vietnam draft, many teachers made grading decisions almost entirely based on "foreign ideals."

12. See especially Berube's "Cultural Criticism and the Politics of Selling Out" in *The Employment of English*.

Works Cited

Agger, Ben. *Fast Capitalism: A Critical Theory of Significance*. Urbana: U of Illinois P, 1989.

Aristotle. *The Rhetoric and The Poetics of Aristotle*. Trans. Rhys Roberts and Ingram Bywater. New York: Modern Library, 1954.

Bakhtin, M. M. [V. N. Volosinov]. *Marxism and the Philosophy of Language*. 1929. Trans. Ladislav Matejka and I. R. Titunik. Cambridge: Harvard UP, 1986.

Banta, Martha. *Failure and Success in America: A Literary Debate*. Princeton: Princeton UP, 1978.

———. *Taylored Lives: Narrative Production in the Age of Taylor, Veblen and Ford*. Chicago: U of Chicago P, 1993.

Barlow, Philip. *Mormons and the Bible: The Place of the Latter-day Saints in American Religion*. New York: Oxford, 1991.

Barthes, Roland. *Mythologies*. Trans. Annette Lavers. New York: Hill, 1972.

Barton, Bruce. "Human Appeals in Copy." *Masters of Advertising Copy: Principles and Practice of Copy Writing According to Its Leading Practitioners*. New York: Frank-Maurice, 1925. 65–77.

———. *The Man Nobody Knows: A Discovery of the Real Jesus*. Indianapolis: Bobbs, 1925.

———. *More Power to You: 50 Editorials from Every Week*. New York: Grosset, 1917.

Becker, Ernest. *The Denial of Death*. 1973. New York: Free, 1997.

Bellah, Robert, et al. *Habits of the Heart: Individualism and Commitment in American Life*. Berkeley: U of California P, 1985.

Bercovitch, Sacvan. *The Rites of Assent: Transformations in the Symbolic Construction of America*. New York: Routledge, 1993.

Berube, Michael. *The Employment of English: Theory, Jobs, and the Future of Literary Studies*. New York: NYU P, 1998.

———. *Public Access: Literary Theory and American Cultural Politics*. New York: Verso, 1994.

Bledstein, Burton. *The Culture of Professionalism: The Middle Class and the Development of Higher Education in America.* New York: Norton, 1976.

Bloom, Harold. *The American Religion: The Emergence of the Post-Christian Nation.* New York: Simon, 1992.

Blumenberg, Hans. "An Anthropological Approach to the Contemporary Significance of Rhetoric." *After Philosophy: End or Transformation?* Ed. Kenneth Baynes, James Bohman, and Thomas McCarthy. Cambridge: MIT P, 1987. 429–59.

Boorstin, Daniel. *The Image: A Guide to Pseudo-Events in America.* 1961. New York: Vintage, 1992.

Booth, Wayne C. *Modern Dogma and the Rhetoric of Assent.* Chicago: U of Chicago P, 1974.

Borges, Jorge Luis. "Pierre Menard, Author of *Quixote.*" *Collected Fictions.* Trans. Andrew Hurley. New York: Penguin, 1998. 88–95.

Bourdieu, Pierre. *On Television.* Trans. Priscilla Parkhurst Ferguson. New York: New, 1996.

Boyett, Joseph, and Jimmie Boyett. *The Guru Guide: The Best Ideas of the Top Management Thinkers.* New York: Wiley, 1998.

Bradbury, Malcolm. Introduction. *Catch-22.* By Joseph Heller. 1961. New York: Knopf, 1994. vii–xxvi.

Briggs, Charles I. Rev. of *Talking Voices,* by Deborah Tannen. *American Anthropologist* (December 1991): 1001.

Brown, Richard Harvey. *Society as Text.* Chicago: U of Chicago P, 1987.

Brummett, Barry. "Rhetorical Theory as Heuristic and Moral: A Pedagogical Justification." Rpt. in *Rhetoric: Concepts, Definitions and Boundaries.* Ed. William Covino and David Jolliffe. New York: Allyn, 1997. 651–64.

Bucholz, Mary. "Bad Examples: Transgression and Progress in Langauge and Gender Studies." *Reinventing Identities: The Gendered Self in Discourse.* Ed. Mary Bucholz, A. C. Liang, and Laurel A. Sutton. New York: Oxford, 1999. 3–24.

Burke, Kenneth. *Attitudes Toward History.* 3rd ed. Berkeley: U of California P, 1984.

———. *Counter-Statement.* 2d ed. Chicago: U of Chicago P, 1957.

———. *A Grammar of Motives.* Berkeley: U of California P, 1969.

———. *Language as Symbolic Action.* Berkeley: U of California P, 1966.

———. *Permanence and Change: An Anatomy of Purpose.* 3rd ed. Berkeley: U of California P, 1984.

———. *The Philosophy of Literary Form: Studies in Symbolic Action.* 1941. New York: Vintage, 1957.

———. *A Rhetoric of Motives.* Berkeley: U of California P, 1969.

———. *The Rhetoric of Religion: Studies in Logology.* Berkeley: U of California P, 1970.

Burns, Rex. *Success in America: The Yeoman Dream and the Industrial Revolution.* Amherst: U of Massachusetts P, 1976.

Cady, H. Emilie. *Lessons in Truth*. Lee's Summit, MO: Unity School of Christianity, 1955.

Calkins, Ernest Elmo. *Business the Civilizer*. Boston: Little, 1928.

Cameron, Deborah. "Rethinking Language and Gender Studies: Some Issues for the 1990s." *Language and Gender: Interdisciplinary Perspectives*. Ed. S Mills. New York: Longman, 1995. 31–44.

Capon, Noel, John U. Farley, James M. Hulbert, and David Lie. "*In Search of Excellence* Ten Years Later: Strategy and Organization Do Matter." *Management Decision* 29 (1991): 12–21.

Carey, Lewis J. *Franklin's Economic Views*. New York: Doubleday, 1928.

Carnegie, Andrew. *The Empire of Business*. 1902. New York: Doubleday, 1933.

Carnegie, Dale. *How to Win Friends and Influence People*. 1936. New York: Pocket, 1975.

Cawelti, John. *Apostles of the Self-Made Man*. Chicago: U of Chicago P, 1965.

Cervantes, Miguel. *Don Quixote*. 1906. Trans. P. A. Matteaux. New York: Dutton, 1954.

Charnes, Linda. *Notorious Identity: Materializing the Subject in Shakespeare*. Cambridge: Harvard UP, 1993.

Coover, Robert. *The Public Burning*. New York: Viking, 1977.

Covey, Stephen. "Effects of Human Relations Training on the Social, Emotional, and Moral Development of Students, with Emphasis on Human Relations Training Based on Religious Principles." Diss. Brigham Young U, 1976.

———. *The 7 Habits of Highly Effective People: Powerful Lessons in Personal Change*. New York: Fireside, 1989.

Crawford, Mary. "Analyzing Female and Male Conversation." *Psychology of Women Quarterly* 19.1 (1995): 156–58.

Crosswhite, James. *The Rhetoric of Reason: Writing and the Attractions of Argument*. Madison: U of Wisconsin P, 1996.

Crusius, Timothy. *Kenneth Burke and the Conversation after Philosophy*. Carbondale: Southern Illinois UP, 1999.

Curti, Merle. "The Changing Concept of 'Human Nature' in the Literature of American Advertising." *Business History Review* 45.4 (Winter 1967): 335–57.

Douglas, Mary, and Aaron Wildavsky. *Risk and Culture*. Berkeley: U of California P, 1983.

Duncan, Hugh Dalziel. *Communication and Social Order*. New York: Oxford, 1968.

———. Introduction. *Permanence and Change: An Anatomy of Purpose*. By Kenneth Burke. 3rd ed. Berkeley: U of California P, 1984.

Epstein, Jason. "The Rattle of Pebbles." *New York Review of Books*, Apr. 27, 2000: 55–59.

Ewen, Stuart. *Captains of Consciousness: Advertising and the Roots of Consumer Culture*. New York: McGraw, 1976.

Feyerabend, Paul. *Against Method*. London: Verso, 1978.

Fish, Stanley. *Doing What Comes Naturally: Change, Rhetoric, and the Practice of Theory in Literary and Legal Studies*. Durham, NC: Duke UP, 1989.

———. *Professional Correctness: Literary Studies and Political Change.* Cambridge: Harvard UP, 1995.

———. *The Trouble with Principle.* Cambridge: Harvard UP, 1999.

Fisher, Walter R. *Human Communication as Narration: Toward a Philosophy of Reason, Value and Action.* Columbia: U of South Carolina P, 1989.

Fox, Richard Wightman, and T. J. Jackson Lears, eds. *Culture of Consumption: Critical Essays in American History, 1880–1980.* New York: Pantheon, 1983.

Fox, Stephen. *The Mirror Makers: A History of American Advertising and Its Creators.* New York: Vintage, 1984.

Frank, Thomas. *One Market under God: Extreme Capitalism, Market Populism and the End of Economic Democracy.* New York: Doubleday, 2000.

Franklin, Benjamin. *Autobiography.* Ed. Leonard Larabee. New Haven: Yale UP, 1964.

Fraser, Nancy. "Rethinking the Public Sphere: A Contribution to the Critique of Actually Existing Democracy." *Habermas and the Public Sphere.* Ed. Craig Calhoun. Cambridge: MIT P, 1992. 109–42.

Frederick, J. George, ed. *Masters of Advertising Copy: Principles and Practice of Copy Writing According to Its Leading Practitioners.* New York: Frank-Maurice, 1925.

Frus, Phyllis. *The Politics and Poetics of Journalistic Narrative: The Timely and the Timeless.* New York: Cambridge UP, 1994.

Gallagher, Catherine, and Stephen Greenblatt. *Practicing New Historicism.* Chicago: U of Chicago P, 2001.

Geertz, Clifford. "Thick Description: Toward an Interpretive Theory of Culture." *The Interpretation of Cultures.* New York: Basic, 1983. 1–21.

Gelley, Alexander. *Unruly Examples: On the Rhetoric of Exemplarity.* Stanford: Stanford UP, 1995.

Gellner, Ernest. *The Psychoanalytic Movement: The Cunning of Unreason.* Evanston, IL: Northwestern UP, 1993. Rev. of *Gender and Conversational Interaction,* ed. Deborah Tannen. *Economist,* Dec. 3, 1994: 86.

Gerrig, Richard. *Experiencing Narrative Worlds: On the Psychological Activities of Reading.* New Haven: Yale UP, 1993.

Gillespie, Richard. *Manufacturing Knowledge: A History of the Hawthorne Experiments.* Cambridge: Cambridge UP, 1991.

Gould, Stephen Jay. "Curveball." *The Bell Curve Wars: Race, Intelligence and the Future of America.* Ed. Steven Fraser. New York: Basic, 1995. 11–23.

Greenblatt, Stephen. *Learning to Curse.* London: Routledge, 1990.

Greene, Theodore P. *America's Heroes: The Changing Models of Success in American Magazines.* New York: Oxford UP, 1970.

Guillory, John. *Cultural Capital: The Problem of Literary Canon Formation.* Chicago: U of Chicago P, 1993.

Gusfield, Joseph. "Bridge over Separated Lands: Kenneth Burke's Significance for the Study of Social Action." *The Legacy of Kenneth Burke.* Ed. Herbert W. Simons and Trevor Melia. Madison: U of Wisconsin P, 1989. 28–55.

Hacking, Ian. *The Taming of Chance*. Cambridge: Cambridge UP, 1990.

Hall, G. Stanley. *Morale: The Supreme Standard of Life and Conduct*. New York: Appleton, 1920.

Heller, Joseph. *Catch-22*. New York: Simon, 1961.

Hilkey, Judy. *Character Is Capital: Success Manuals and Manhood in Gilded Age America*. Chapel Hill: U of North Carolina P, 1997.

Hoffman, Daniel. *Form and Fable in American Fiction*. New York: Oxford, 1961.

Hofsteader, Richard. *Anti-intellectualism in American Life*. New York: Random, 1963.

Hopkins, Claude. *Scientific Advertising*. 1923. New York: Crown, 1966.

Huber, Richard. *The American Idea of Success*. 1971. New York: Pushcart, 1987.

Huczynski, Andrzej. *Management Gurus: What Makes Them and How to Become One*. London: Routledge, 1993.

Jameson, Frederic. "Postmodernism, or the Cultural Logic of Late Capitalism." *New Left Review* 146 (July-August 1984): 53–92.

Johnson, Spencer. *Who Moved My Cheese?* New York: Putnam, 1998.

Kaminer, Wendy. *I'm Dysfunctional, You're Dysfunctional: The Recovery Movement and Other Self-Help Fashions*. Reading, MA: Addison, 1992.

Kramarae, Cheris. Rev. of *You Just Don't Understand*, by Deborah Tannen. *Signs* (Spring 1992): 666–71.

Kuhn, Elizabeth. "Gender and Language." *National Women's Studies Association Journal* 8 (Summer 1996): 117–26.

Kuhn, Thomas. *The Structures of Scientific Revolution*. 2d ed. Chicago: U of Chicago P, 1970.

Larson, Magali Sarfatti. *The Rise of Professionalism: A Sociological Analysis*. Berkeley: U of California P, 1977.

Law, Jules David. "Uncertain Grounds: Wittgenstein's *On Certainty* and the New Literary Pragmatism." *New Literary History* 19.2 (1988): 319–36.

Lawrence, D. H. *Studies in Classic American Literature*. 1923. New York: Viking, 1961.

Lears, T. J. Jackson. *Fables of Abundance: A Cultural History of Advertising in America*. New York: Basic, 1984.

———. *No Place of Grace: Antimodernism and the Transformation of American Culture, 1880–1920*. New York: Pantheon, 1981.

Lebergott, Stanley. *Pursuing Happiness: Economic Well-Being*. Princeton: Princeton UP, 1993.

Lentricchia, Frank. *Criticism and Social Change*. Chicago: U of Chicago P, 1983.

———. "Reading History with Kenneth Burke." *Representing Kenneth Burke*. Ed Hayden White and Margaret Brose. Baltimore: Johns Hopkins UP, 1982. 119–49.

Leone, Mark. *Roots of Modern Mormonism*. Cambridge: Harvard UP, 1979.

Lewis, Michael. *Moneyball: The Art of Winning an Unfair Game*. New York: Norton, 2003.

Lodge, David. *Changing Places*. London: Penguin, 1975.

Lorimer, George Horace. *Letters from a Self-Made Merchant to His Son*. Boston: Small, 1902.

MacIntyre, Alasdair. *After Virtue*. 2d ed. Notre Dame, IN: Notre Dame UP, 1984.

Marchand, Roland. *Advertising the American Dream: Making Way for Modernity, 1920–1940*. Berkeley: U of California P, 1985.

Marden, Orison Swett. *Pushing to the Front, or Success under Difficulties*. New York: Crowell, 1894.

———. *Rising in the World: Or, Architects of Fate*. New York: Success, 1897.

Marty, Martin. "Two Integrities: An Address to the Crisis in Mormon Historiography." *Faithful History: Essays on Writing Mormon History*. Ed. George D. Smith. Salt Lake City: Signature, 1992. 169–88.

Mather, Cotton. *Bonifacius: An Essay to Do Good*. 1710. Gainesville, FL: Scholars' Facsimiles, 1967.

Mauss, Armand L. *The Angel and the Beehive: The Mormon Struggle with Assimilation*. Champaign-Urbana: U of Illinois P, 1994.

McCloskey, Donald. *The Rhetoric of Economics*. Madison: U of Wisconsin P, 1985.

Meyer, Donald B. *The Positive Thinkers: A Study of the American Quest for Health, Wealth and Personal Power from Mary Baker Eddy to Norman Vincent Peale*. Garden City, NY: Doubleday, 1965.

Michaud, Shari L., and Rebecca M. Warner. "Gender Differences in Self-Reported Responses to Troubles Talk." *Sex Roles* 37 (1997): 527–40.

Micklethwait, John, and Adrian Wooldridge. *The Witch Doctors: Making Sense of the Management Gurus*. New York: Random, 1996.

Mintzberg, Henry. "The Manager's Job: Folklore and Fact." *Harvard Business Review* 53.1 (1975): 49–61.

Newfield, Christopher. "Corporate Pleasures for a Corporate Planet." *Social Text* 44 (Fall/Winter 1995): 31–44.

———. "Recapturing Academic Business." *Social Text* 51 (Summer 1997): 39–66.

Nibley, Hugh. *An Approach to the Book of Mormon*. 3rd ed. Salt Lake City: Deseret, 1988.

Nixon, Richard. *Six Crises*. 1962. New York: Pyramid, 1968.

O'Dea, Thomas. *The Mormons*. Chicago: U of Chicago P, 1957.

Ohmann, Richard. *Selling Culture: Magazines, Markets and Class at the Turn of the Century*. New York: Verso, 1996.

Ostling, Richard N., and Joan K. Ostling. *Mormon America: The Power and the Promise*. San Francisco: HarperCollins, 1999.

Peale, Norman Vincent. *The Power of Positive Thinking*. New York: Ballantine Books, 1956.

Perelman, Chaim, and L. Olbrechts-Tyteca. *The New Rhetoric: A Treatise on Argumentation*. Trans. John Wilkinson and Purcell Weaver. Notre Dame, IN: U of Notre Dame P, 1969.

Perry, Lewis. *Intellectual Life in America*. New York: Franklin Watts, 1984.

Peters, Thomas J., and Rob Waterman. *In Search of Excellence: Lessons from America's Best-Run Companies*. New York: Warner, 1982.

Peters, Tom. Interview with Virginia Postrel. *Reason* (October 1997): 42–49.

Readings, Bill. *The University in Ruins.* Cambridge: Harvard UP, 1996.

Reagan, Ronald. *A Time for Choosing: The Speeches of Ronald Reagan, 1961–1982.* Chicago: Regenery Gateway, 1983.

Robbins, Bruce. *Secular Vocations: Intellectuals, Professionalism, Culture.* New York: Verso, 1993.

Romaine, Suzanne. *Communicating Gender.* Mahwah, NJ: Erlbaum, 1999.

Rorty, Richard. *Achieving Our Country.* Cambridge: Harvard UP, 1997.

———. *Philosophy and Social Hope.* London: Penguin, 1999.

———. *Philosophy and the Mirror of Nature.* Princeton: Princeton UP, 1979.

Rose, Ruth. Rev. of *You Just Don't Understand,* by Deborah Tannen. *Sex Roles* 24 (1991): 785–87.

Ross, Lee. "The Intuitive Psychologist and His Shortcomings." *Advances in Experimental Social Psychology,* vol. 10. Ed. Leonard Berkowitz. New York: Academic, 1977. 173–220.

Ruland, Richard, and Malcolm Bradbury. *From Puritanism to Postmodernism.* New York: Viking, 1991.

Ryan, Alan. *John Dewey and the High Tide of American Liberalism.* New York: Norton, 1995.

Schumacher, E. F. *Small Is Beautiful: Economics as if People Mattered.* New York: Harper, 1973.

Sennett, Richard. *The Fall of Public Man.* 1976. New York: Norton, 1992.

Sheard, Cynthia Miecznikowski. "*Kairos* and Kenneth Burke's Psychology of Political and Social Communication." *College English* 55 (March 1993): 291–309.

Slater, Don. *Consumer Culture and Modern Identity.* Cambridge: Polity, 1997.

Smith, Barbara Herrnstein. *Contingencies of Value: Alternative Perspectives for Critical Theory.* Cambridge: Harvard UP, 1988.

Smith, Walter Bedell. *Eisenhower's Six Great Decisions: Europe 1944–1945.* New York: Longman, 1957.

Spitzer, Leo. "American Advertising Explained as Popular Art." *Representative Essays.* Ed. Alban K. Forcione, Herbert Lindenberger, and Madeline Sutherland. Stanford: Stanford UP, 1988. 327–56.

Steinbrun, John. *The Cybernetic Theory of Decision: New Dimensions of Political Analysis.* Princeton: Princeton UP, 1974.

Stewart, James B. "Best Seller: The Agent from Texas That New York Can't Ignore." *New Yorker,* Sept. 9, 1997: 44–49.

Suleiman, Susan Rubin. *Authoritarian Fictions: The Ideological Novel as a Literary Genre.* New York: Columbia UP, 1983.

Tannen, Deborah. *Argument Culture: Moving from Debate to Dialogue.* New York: Random, 1998.

———. *You Just Don't Understand: Women and Men in Conversation.* New York: Ballantine, 1990.

Taylor, Charles. *Sources of the Self: The Making of the Modern Identity.* Cambridge: Harvard UP, 1989.

Theroux, Paul. *Fresh Air Fiend: Travel Writings, 1985–2000*. Boston: Houghton, 2000.

Trachtenberg, Alan. *The Incorporation of America: Culture and Society in the Gilded Age*. New York: Hill, 1982.

Twain, Mark. "The Story of a Good Little Boy." *The Complete Short Stories of Mark Twain*. Ed. Charles Neider. New York: Doubleday, 1957. 67–70.

Twitchell, James. *Adcult USA: The Triumph of Advertising in American Culture*. New York: Columbia UP, 1996.

Weber, Max. *Protestantism and the Spirit of Capitalism*. Trans. Talcott Parsons. Gloucester, MA: Smith, 1988.

Weiss, Richard. *The American Myth of Success: From Horatio Alger to Norman Vincent Peale*. New York: Basic, 1969.

White, Hayden. *Tropics of Discourse: Essays in Cultural Criticism*. Baltimore: Johns Hopkins UP, 1978.

Widstoe, John. *Rational Theology*. Salt Lake City: n.p., 1915.

Williams, Raymond. *Keywords: A Vocabulary of Culture and Society*. Rev. ed. New York: Oxford UP, 1983.

———. *Marxism and Literature*. Oxford: Oxford UP, 1977.

Williamson, Judith. *Decoding Advertisements: Ideology and Meaning in Advertising*. London: Boyars, 1978.

Wills, Gary. *Nixon Agonistes: The Crisis of the Self-Made Man*. Boston: Houghton, 1970.

Wolfe, Alan. "White Magic in America." *New Republic*, Feb. 23, 1998: 26–35.

Wolfe, Tom, and Thomas Johnson, eds. *New Journalism*. New York: Harper, 1973.

Wyllie, Irvin G. *The Self-Made Man in America: The Myth of Rags to Riches*. New Brunswick, NJ: Rutgers UP, 1954.

Index

abundance theology, 113–14, 116, 130, 225–26n. 3

academia, 129; audience and, 134, 136, 218; community, 7–8; conservative academics, 167–68, 215–16; critique of management literature, 132–39; divide between administration and faculty, 5–7; instrumentalism of, 28–29; lack of studies on Mormonism, 156–57; neglect of success rhetoric, 4–5, 10, 25–32, 26, 167; popularization of academic thinking, 167, 185, 218–20; professions and, 29–31; reform of institutions, 218–19; rhetoric of excellence and, 26–29, 30; university of excellence, 27, 31

academic border crossing: limitations of, 185, 187, 215; by right-wing academics, 215–16; routes to, 216–17. *See also* Fish, Stanley; Tannen, Deborah

accounting industry, 138

acquisitiveness, 46, 47–48

"Acres of Diamonds" (Conwell), 77

advertising, 63; linked with religion, 65–66; mass market magazines and, 52–53; parables, 77–82; reliance on consumer, 88–89; self-referential, 69–70, 85; significance and, 85–86; soft-sell vs. reason-why, 82–85, 93–94. *See also Man Nobody Knows, The*

After Virtue (MacIntyre), 227n. 4

agent/act relationship, 18–19, 20

American Idea of Success (Huber), 149

anecdotes, 22–23, 103; deflection of reality and, 15, 23–25; "George," 107–8, 109, 110; mustard seed, 103–5; representative, 18–25

appearance, 114

Approach to the Book of Mormon (Nibley), 228–29n. 8

Argument Culture: Moving from Debate to Dialogue (Tannen), 10, 170, 173, 174–78; Chinese sage example in, 175–76, 177; criticism of manufactured contempt in, 176–78, 181–82; disciplinarity in, 10, 181–85

arguments, 173, 230n. 5; academic vs. business, 135–36; battle of the sexes myth, 170–71; gender and, 172–73

Aristotle, 35, 37, 46, 79, 176

Asian rhetoric, 175–76

attitude, 135–36, 227n. 3

audience, 8, 50, 53, 77, 79; for academic ideas, 134, 136, 218; of management literature, 39–40, 129–30, 133–34; role of, 43–44

authenticity, 8–10, 20

authority, 190, 191

Autobiography (Franklin), 45

Bacon, Francis, 95

Barlow, Philip, 160

Barnum, P. T., 56

John Ramage has been a teacher and an administrator at Montana State University and Arizona State University, where he is presently an associate professor of English. He has coauthored, with John Bean, *Form and Surprise, Writing Arguments,* and *The Allyn and Bacon Guide to Writing.* He is currently completing a book on teaching argument in composition classes. In recent years, he has written articles on writing program administration, curricular issues, and teaching assistant training.